Booktalking
the Award Winners

Children's
Retrospective Volume

Edited by
Joni Richards Bodart

The H.W. Wilson Company
New York   Dublin
1997

Some of the booktalks are reprinted or adapted from *Booktalk! 2* (Wilson 1985) copyright © 1985 by Joni Bodart; *Booktalk! 3* (Wilson 1988) copyright © 1988 by Joni Bodart-Talbot; *Booktalk! 4* (Wilson 1992) copyright © 1992 by Joni Richards Bodart; *Booktalk! 5* (Wilson 1993) copyright © 1993 by Joni Richards Bodart; *The New Booktalker I* (Libraries Unlimited 1992) copyright © 1992 by Joni Richards Bodart; *The New Booktalker II* (Libraries Unlimited 1993) copyright © 1993 by Joni Richards Bodart; *100 World-Class Thin Books* (Libraries Unlimited) copyright © 1993 by Joni Richards Bodart; *Booktalking the Award Winners: Young Adult Retrospective Volume* (Wilson 1996) copyright © 1996 by Joni Richards Bodart.

International Standard Book Number 0-8242-0901-X

Library of Congress Cataloging-in-Publication Data

Booktalking the award winners. Children's retrospective volume / edited by Joni Richards Bodart.
    p. cm.
    Retrospective supplement to Booktalking the award winners series covering award-winning titles prior to 1992.
    Includes bibliographical references (p.   ) and index.
    ISBN 0-8242-0901-X
    1. Children—United States—Books and reading. 2. Teenagers—United States—Books and reading. 3. Book talks—United States. 4. Literary prizes. 5. Literary prizes—United States. 6. Children's stories, American—Book reviews. 7. Young adult fiction, American—Book reviews. 8. Children's stories, English—Book reviews. 9. Young adult fiction, English—Book reviews. I. Bodart, Joni Richards. II. Booktalking the award winners. Z1037.A2B66Suppl.
028.5'5—dc21
                                    97-8202
                                        CIP

Printed in the United States of America

TABLE OF CONTENTS

DEDICATION

For Patty, Cathi, Patty, and Martha,
the best friends anyone could ever have—am I lucky, or what?

ACKNOWLEDGMENTS

First of all, I'd like to thank the booktalkers whose names appear on the following pages, both the new contributors and the veterans of this series. Without their creative enthusiasm, this collection couldn't exist.

I'm also grateful (as always!) for the support system of family and friends who help me get going and keep going. The staff at the Hampden Branch of the Denver Public Library have been wonderful too, willing to locate stacks and stacks of books and staying cheerful despite the extra work. Jeff, Tom, Margie, Lisa, and Betty—you've all been great!

Thanks are also due to the people at the Wilson company who help me put these books together, especially Norris Smith, Frank McGuckin, and Rhonda Bell.

And finally, thanks to all of you, readers and booktalkers, who believe that reading is important and that books will never go out of style. It's because of your efforts that kids are still discovering the magical adventures that can take place between the covers of a book. Keep up the good work!

—*J. R. B.*

INTRODUCTION

Welcome to the Children's Retrospective Volume of the Booktalking the Award Winners series. Here's a chance to browse through the award winners of the past, check out those you may have missed, and renew your acquaintance with some old friends. The field of children's literature is an old and well-established one, in which the best books tend to endure. Some that were written ten, twenty, or even fifty years ago are very much alive today—not dated, not stuffy, but still as entertaining and absorbing as they were when they were first published. The problem is that, while good stories don't wear out, their bindings do, and children tend to prefer books with attractive covers to those that have seen more than their share of wear and tear. Librarians often tell me they find it hard to "sell" the older volumes in their collection—once the dust jackets have perished, the books just don't look as appealing as the latest titles. But these are stories that have gripped generations of readers (have, in fact, *created* generations of readers) and they won't disappoint kids today—if only you can persuade them to open those battered covers and start reading.

That's where booktalking comes in, and that's why we decided to supplement the annual BAWS volumes with retrospective collections, that would cover some of the older titles in the library. For this volume, we tried to choose titles that won awards before 1992, when the annual series began, that have not become dated, and that are still in print today. We leaned heavily on two long annual lists: Notable Children's Books, chosen by ALA's Association of Librarians in Service to Children, and *School Library Journal*'s Best of the Year, chosen by the magazine's staff. We also considered not only the winners of awards like the Newbery and the Golden Kite, but the runners-up as well. (All the awards represented here are listed and described in the section starting on page 231. Since the word "children" means different things in different awards, we have also included an index by age level, starting on page 251—not all the award-winning titles are suitable for grade-schoolers.)

We ended up with an enormous list of books, and of course we couldn't include them all. Several filters had to be applied to reduce the original list to a manageable size. We eliminated a lot of attractive picture books because they really weren't suitable for booktalking—they were meant for a preschool audience. Then we tried to identify titles that for some reason wouldn't appeal to kids today. This involved some tricky judgment calls. The best children's books are closely attuned to the developmental needs of young readers, which change little from generation to generation; the elements that date are often the social settings of the stories and the underlying assumptions about roles and situations. It can be a sobering experience to revisit an old favorite and discover, in the dialogue or in the background, inaccuracies, unquestioned prejudices, or moralistic agendas. A more common problem for children today, however, may be the number of references to unfamiliar events and obsolete technologies—the everyday world has changed. Not surprisingly, some of the most enduring books for children have been works of fantasy or of historical fiction, divorced by design from any contemporary reality. (A few books that were originally contemporaneous have simply *become* historical fiction.)

However, the single criterion that eliminated the largest number of titles was the mundane requirement that they be in print. Some titles have stayed in print in hardback editions, some have gotten a second chance at life as paperbacks, but many older titles (and, sadly, a few newers ones as well) have simply disappeared from publishers' backlists forever. Availability was a practical consideration we couldn't ignore, so we had to drop out-of-print titles. A second practical consideration was finding a booktalker who wanted to tackle the title in question, and there we were fortunate—I have rarely worked with such an enthusiastic and versatile group of contributors.

If any of you are booktalkers and would like to become contributors yourselves, to the annual volumes in this series, please get in touch with me through Wilson or at the e-mail address or box number below. I'm always glad to welcome new volunteers (there's plenty of booktalking to be done!) and would like to work not only with library and education professionals but also with students who have produced booktalks for class assignments (instead of those tedious book reports). So if you're a booktalker already or interested in becoming one, please send me a note and a couple of sample talks—if you've got e-mail, that's probably the most efficient way to do it. And don't assume that your talks won't be good enough, just because you've never been published before. At my booktalking workshops, I've frequently encountered beginnners with real talent, people who seem to have an instinctive sense of what makes a booktalk work. Remember, there's always a first time for publication—and maybe your time is now! We had fun (most of the time) putting this collection together, and we hope you'll have fun using it. Be sure to let me know what you think—if there's a favorite of yours that we left out, drop me a note. Who knows? Perhaps there'll be another volume of golden oldies some day! Happy Booktalking!

e-mail: JoniRB@aol.com   —Joni Richards Bodart
post office: Box 370688   February 1997
Denver, CO 80127-0688

CONTRIBUTORS OF BOOKTALKS

Mark Anderson
Fairfax County Public Library
Falls Church, VA

Jo Berkman
Dodd Junior High School Library
Freeport, NY

Jeff Blair
Olathe South High School Library
Olathe, KS

Marvia Boettcher
Bismarck Public Library
Bismarck, ND

Susan Bogart

Julie Bray
Jasper County Public Library
Rensselaer, IN

Suzanne Bruney
Storyteller
Lancaster, OH

Nancy L. Chu
Western Illinois University
Macomb, IL

Mary Cosper
Terrebonne Parish Library
Houma, LA

Bernice D. Crouse
Fulton County Library
McConnellsburg, PA

Dorothy Davidson
Ward Elementary School LRC
Abilene, TX

Diane L. Deuel
Central Rappahannock Regional
Library
Fredericksburg, VA

Judy Druse
Washburn University CRC
Topeka, KS

Susan Dunn
Salem Public Library
Salem, OR

Sister M. Anna Falbo, CSSF
Villa Maria College Library
Buffalo, NY

Lesley S. J. Farmer
Redwood High School Library
Larkspur, CA

Patricia Farr
Central Rappahannock Regional
Library
Fredericksburg, VA

Mary Fellows
Weston Public Library
Weston, OH

Dara Finkelstein
Elmhurst Public Library
Elmhurst, IL

Barbara Flottmeier
La Crosse Public Library
La Crosse, WI

Sarah Flowers
Morgan Hill Public Library
Morgan Hill, CA

Barbara K. Foster

Eileen Gieswein
Lincoln Elementary School
Concordia, KS

Nancy Bardole Hanaman
Barron Library
Barron, WI

Mary Hedge
La Porte County Public Library
La Porte, IN

Linda Henderson

Carol Kappelmann
Dover Grade and Junior High
School Library
Dover, KS

Deb Kelly
Park County Library
Meeteetse Branch
Meeteetse, WY

Abbie V. Landry
  Watson Library
  Northwestern State University
  Natchitoches, LA

Anne Liebst
  Baker University Library
  Baldwin City, KS

Janet Loebel

Cynthia L. Lopuszynski
  Crystal Lake Public Library
  Crystal Lake, IL

Colleen Macklin
  Henderson County Schools
  Henderson County, NC

Cathi Dunn MacRae
  VOYA Editor
  Scarecrow Press
  Lanham, MD

Rene Mandel
  Framington, MA

Katherine Mattson

Diantha G. McCauley
  Augusta County Library
  Fishersville, VA

Judy McElwain
  Durango, CO

Kaite Mediatore
  Emporia Public Library
  Emporia, KS

Kathy Ann Miller
  Ottawa Public Library
  Ottawa, KS

Beverly Montgomery
  Junction City Junior High School
    Library
  Junction City, KS

Claranell Murray

C. Allen Nichols
  Rocky River Public Library
  Rocky River, OH

Linda Olson
  Superior Public Library
  Superior, WI

Elizabeth Overmyer
  Berkeley Public Library
  Berkeley, CA

Sue Padilla
  Ida Long Goodman Memorial
    Library
  St. John, KS

Evette Pearson
  Northwestern State University
  Natchitoches, LA

Susan Perdaris

E. Lynn Porter
  North Harris County College
  Houston, TX

Marianne Tait Pridemore
  San Jose Public Library
  San Jose, CA

Margie Reitsma
  St. Mary's-St. Catherine's School
  Remsen, IA

Vicki Reutter
  Casenovia High School Library
  Casenovia, NY

Tracy Chesonis Revel
  Sussex Central Junior High School
    Library
  Millsboro, DE

JoEllen Rice
  Niles Library
  Fremont, CA

Paul H. Rockwell
  Alameda County Library
  San Lorenzo, CA

Donna L. Scanlon
  Lancaster County Library
  Lancaster, PA

Helen Schlichting
  Sac Community School Library
  Sac City, IA

Lynda Smith

Suzi Smith
  Maxwell Park Library
  Tulsa City-County Library System
  Tulsa, OK

Pam Spencer

Colleen Stinson
  Town of Haldimand Public Libraries
  Caledonia, Ontario, Canada

Ru Story-Huffman
  Pine Forest Regional Library
  Richton, MS

Anne Sushko
  Jefferson Junior High
  Dubuque, IA

Pam Swafford
  Teachers College Resource Center
  Emporia State University
  Emporia, KS

Cecilia Swanson
  Bainbridge Library
  Geauga County Public Library
  Geauga County, OH

Pamela A. Todd
  Carbondale Public Library
  Carbondale, IL

Susan Trimby
  Fossil Ridge Public Library
  Braidwood, IL

Cara A. Waits
  Tempe Public Library
  Tempe, AZ

Melinda Waugh
  Topeka Public Library
  Topeda, KS

Maureen Whalen
  Rochester Public Library
  Rochester, NY

Melanie L. Witulski
  Toledo—Lucas County Public
  Library
  Toledo, OH

BOOKTALKS

The Abduction
By Mette Newth
(SLJ/C 1989)

Osuqo knew that at last she was a woman. Today she would help row the women's boat on the walrus hunt. And soon, she knew, the great hunter Poq would choose her to be his wife.

When the women's boat rounded the headland she saw it: the foreigners' ship—huge, dark, and threatening. Osuqo was frightened, even though she knew her people often traded with the foreigners. As the women brought out things to trade, Osuqo's father beckoned to her. "The foreigners have invited us to visit their ship," he said. Osuqo was still frightened, but she could not refuse the invitation—that would be discourteous. Poq went with them. Once they were on board the horrors began. Osuqo's father was attacked and killed. She and Poq were made prisoners and tightly bound—at the mercy of the foreigners. They had no way of knowing that they were headed for Norway, where they would be exhibited like zoo animals, gawked at, humiliated, and blamed for all the troubles of the town. Was there any hope for a future after the abduction?

—*Helen Schlichting*

Across Five Aprils
By Irene Hunt
(Newbery Honor 1965)

Early one evening in February, 1863, the representatives of the Federal Registrars arrived at the Creightons' home looking for Ebenezer Carron, deserter from the Army of Tennessee—for Eb, the cousin who had lived with them for as long as Jethro could remember. Not Eb! He wouldn't be a deserter!

1

But the men insisted he was and proceeded to search the house and outbuildings. When they didn't find anybody, they warned the family that there would be dire consequences if Eb showed up and they didn't report it.

A few days later, Jethro was working in the fields when he heard what sounded like a wild turkey. When he investigated, he found Eb, a very changed Eb, starving, dirty, and frightened half to death. Eb told him that he was sorry he'd left the army and wished he could go back, but he was afraid he'd be arrested. Jethro agonized about what to do now, about how much of a risk to take. In the end, he decided to go straight to the top—he wrote to President Lincoln.

The war had affected everyone, tearing families apart, making children grow up too fast. As Jethro had been told, "The beginnin's of this war has been fanned by the hate till it's a blaze now; and a blaze kin destroy him that makes it and him that the fire was set to hurt."

—*Carol Kappelmann*

An Actor's Life for Me!
Lillian Gish
(Notables 1987)

Lillian Gish was born about 95 years ago, and she made *The Whales of August* when she was ninety-two! Because she started acting when she was just six, she's been working as an actress for 86 years!

When Lillian started her career, there were no TVs, movies, or airplanes. There were a few cars, but most people used horses or trains to get around. Lillian, her sister Dorothy, and their mother rode the train to get from job to job. They were part of a group of traveling actors who stayed in each town just long enough to give one performance of their show, and then on to the next town. For the people in those little towns, a play was a big event, because they got to see only two or three a year.

There were lots of things about the actor's life that Lillian enjoyed: no school, dressing up and acting every night—and getting paid for it! But some things really weren't fun at all, like staying in dirty hotel rooms, with none of the conveniences that we have today, or trying to sleep on a cold, bumpy train, knowing that she had to be rested for the performance the next day—no yawning on stage! And some of the parts Lillian had to play were difficult, or dangerous, or both. In one, Lillian was supposed to "fly" across the stage, but her support wire snapped and she fell. In another play, she was accidentally sprayed with buckshot while she was on stage—but she finished the play anyway. One of her least favorite memories is of the play where she was thrown into a lion's cage—with a live lion in it!

But Lillian loved the actor's life in spite of it all. As she got older, she got better at it, and when "flickers" were invented, Lillian became a movie star!

Would you love an actor's life the way Lillian did?

—*Julie Bray*

Adam of the Road
By Elizabeth Janet Gray
(Newbery 1943)

For the past five months, Adam Quartermayne has had three things to comfort him while father is away: his harp, his dog Nick, and his best friend Perkin. Perkin is his constant companion at the Abbey school where they're both staying. The small harp was a gift from his father, and now Adam plays it for company as well as to keep in practice while he waits for his father's return. And Nick has been there from the beginning, when he was just a bundle of red fluff—now he's the smartest, friendliest dog in England.

But much as Adam loves Nick and Perkin, he loves his father more. Roger Quartermayne is a minstrel, who travels from manor to castle playing his musical instruments and singing French romances for the lords and ladies. While Roger's away in France, learning more songs and stories, Adam must stay at the Abbey school, wishing he could be with his father.

As soon as Roger returns, he and Adam set out on the road. They perform at the wedding feast of a great lord's daughter, and sing for their supper at an inn. Adam loves the life of the road—until he wakes up one morning to find Nick gone, stolen in the night by another minstrel. Adam and Roger start out after the thief but are separated on the road, and now Adam, alone, must find not only his dog but the way back to his father.

—*Evette Pearson*

After the Dancing Days
By Margaret I. Rostkowski
(Golden Kite 1987, Notables 1986)

The man with the melted face haunted her dreams. She'd seen him just once, when the troop train that brought her father home from the Great War was unloading. Even among the most severely wounded and crippled soldiers, the melted man stood out, his face a shapeless mass of bluish skin, with a hole where a mouth should be.

The war had come at great cost to Annie's family. Her beloved uncle was buried somewhere on the battlefields of France, and her father, an Army doctor, had been away for years. Now that he was home again and working at the veterans' hospital outside town, Annie hoped the war could be put behind them.

But war scars run deep, almost as deep as those of the men at the hospital. Against her mother's wishes, Annie found herself drawn there, volunteering to spend time with the patients. She uncovered the humanity that still lived beneath the melted flesh of the man she'd seen unloaded from the train, and she also uncovered some truths about herself.

—Jeff Blair

After the Rain
By Norma Fox Mazer
(SLJ/C 1987)

Rachel doesn't want to go and see her grandfather. But Mom and Dad insist, so off she goes to Grandpa's apartment with her parents. Mom flits around, fussing over him: Is he eating enough? Is he warm enough? Is he sleeping? Is he keeping busy? Dad sits with Grandpa and makes awkward conversation. Rachel leans against the wall and waits to go home. Visiting her grandfather is always such an ordeal. He's a stubborn, opinionated old man, but now that he's sick he needs someone to keep an eye on him. Rachel's parents are both busy—she's the one who'll have to stop by and check on him. Grandpa wants to walk, but Mom doesn't want him to go out by himself, so Rachel has to go with him. It's difficult at first; Grandpa doesn't talk much, and what he does say isn't usually very pleasant, but as the days go by, Rachel learns more about the grandfather she's never known. She learns about the work he did when he was younger, about his wife, about his ideas.

But Grandpa is growing weaker. His sickness is taking its toll. How can Rachel lose her grandfather now, just as she is getting to know him?

—Colleen Stinson

Afternoon of the Elves
By Janet Taylor Lisle
(Notables 1989, SLJ/C 1989)

Elves! There was an entire village of them living in Sara-Kate's junky, jungle-like backyard. Teeny-tiny houses, teeny-tiny wells, teeny-tiny walls, teeny-tiny everything.

Sara-Kate Connolly and Hillary Lenox were neighbors—not friends, neighbors. Sara-Kate was older and different. She wore men's work boots and ill-fitting rumpled clothes, and she had no friends. Nobody ever saw her family. Hillary, on the other hand, lived in a nice house, with a loving family and had lots of friends. One day Sarah Kate, who never spoke to anyone, asked Hillary over to see the elf village in her backyard.

As the elf village grew, a friendship developed between Sara-Kate and Hillary. Both of them wanted to see the elves, but, as Sara-Kate said, an elf has to trust you, and it takes time and patience for an elf to show his trust—just like Sara-Kate as she slowly let Hillary into her life.

Sara-Kate lived with her mother, but instead of her mother caring for her Sara-Kate took care of her mother. It wasn't a normal life, but it seemed to work for Sara-Kate, or at least that was what Hillary thought. Hillary half believed that Sara-Kate was a magical being herself, just like the elves. But was she or wasn't she?

—*Cynthia L. Lopuszynski*

Agnes Cecilia
By Maria Gripe
(SLJ/C 1990)

It seemed to happen only when Nora was home alone. Strange phone calls that kept her from walking into danger. Books that fell off shelves and opened themselves to significant passages. Mysterious footsteps that paced through the house, only to stop at the open door of Nora's bedroom.

Then one day her cousin Dag was there when the phone rang, and this time he answered it. The mysterious voice on the other end gave him a message for Nora—"Go to the Old Town in Stockholm, and ask for Agnes Cecilia." Nora didn't know anyone by that name, and she was afraid to go into Stockholm. But Dag volunteered to go with her, and now the two of them are standing outside a toy shop in the Old Town, waiting to meet Agnes Cecilia, whoever—or whatever—she is.

—*Kaite Mediatore*

The Agony of Alice
By Phyllis Reynolds Naylor
(Notables 1985)

Alice McKinley is entering sixth grade and she's very excited about being an upperclassman. No more older boys to tease her on the playground. No more older girls to harass her in the bathroom. Sixth-graders *are* the older students: they're always asked to help in the office and the halls, and they get to be on the safety patrol. Oh, this is going to be a great year for Alice!

Alice's family has just moved, and the school she is going to enter is a new one, which is great because now she can leave all her embarrassing moments behind. She can make a fresh start: no one at her new school will know that she ate crayons when she was little; no one at her new school will know about the love poem she wrote to the milkman; no one at her new school will know how her dad walked in when she was trying to kiss Donald Sheavers. No one at the new school will know about any of those embarrassing moments. But even before Alice starts her new classes, she begins to create *new* embarrassing moments for herself, starting when she puts her foot in her mouth in front of Elizabeth's mother.

Alice's own mother died when she was much younger, and now she decides that a mother-like person in her life might help her avoid these embarrassing moments. When school begins she meets the sixth-grade teachers for the first time and picks out the perfect mother substitute— or so she thinks. But it isn't long before she realizes that looks aren't everything—it's what inside that really matters. Find out what Alice learns, and who ends up teaching her.

—*Cynthia L. Lopuszynski*

Alice in Rapture, Sort of
By Phyllis Reynolds Naylor
(SLJ/C 1989)

It's the summer between sixth grade and seventh grade for Alice McKinley, "the Summer of the First Boyfriend," her dad says. Alice lives with her dad and her older brother. Her mother died when she was much younger. This creates problems for Alice because she doesn't have anyone to answer the serious questions that girls have—you know, questions about boys and growing up and all.

This summer Alice has a boyfriend, Patrick. In sixth grade they were just good friends, but this summer he becomes a boyfriend. And that's important. As one of Alice's classmates says, "If you don't have a boyfriend when you enter seventh grade, you will have *no* social life!"

This is a summer of ups and downs, new experiences, and questions, lots of questions—like, what to wear to a special dinner, how to chew in front of your boyfriend, how old should you be to kiss? The answers aren't always easy, or what you'd expect, especially where you have no mother to help!

—*Cynthia L. Lopuszynski*

All Together Now
By Sue Ellen Bridgers
(BGHB 1979, Christopher 1980)

She didn't want to be there. With her father fighting in Korea and her mother working two jobs, Casey's world had changed enough. She wanted to spend the summer in familiar surroundings, with friends, not in a small Southern town with relatives she barely knew. But at twelve, decisions get made for you, "for your own good," so there she was.

It turned out to be a wonderful summer. Casey came to love them all: her father's parents, solid, loving, and kind; her Uncle Taylor, who was crazy about stockcar racing; Hazard and Pansy, the friends of her grandparents who finally got married that summer; and most of all, Dwayne Pickens, the boy across the street.

Like any other twelve-year-old boy, Dwayne loved baseball and of course he hated girls. But Dwayne was also special. Although he was really thirty-three years old, mentally he was still twelve. He had lived in the town all his life, except for a short time years before, when he'd been sent to a "special school," and ever since he'd been afraid of being sent away again.

When Dwayne first met Casey, with her jeans and short hair, he assumed she was a boy. Because she was lonely, she let him believe it, and the lonely pair became friends. They played baseball and cheered Uncle Taylor at the races. They went to the arcade, to the movies, and to the five-and-ten for candy. Taylor took them fishing and taught them both to drive. But then Dwayne's brother, Alva, tried to send Dwayne away again, and Casey and her whole family were drawn into the struggle to save Dwayne.

—*Evette Pearson*

Along the Tracks
By Tamar Bergman
(Notables 1991)

They called them "the abandoned ones"—children without parents or families, wandering across war-torn Europe, struggling to survive. They had not been abandoned deliberately; they were casualties of war. Often their fathers had been killed fighting Hitler, their homes destroyed, and their families separated. Sometimes their mothers and their brothers and sisters had already died of disease, starvation, or the freezing cold of winter. The children themselves were in danger of death. They had no money, no food, no warm clothes or safe shelter. To survive they had to steal, and they roamed the marketplace in packs—one or two of them to distract the merchant while the others sneaked in and grabbed what they could. Later the loaf of bread or the raw potatoes would be shared, but no one got more than a few bites. "The abandoned ones" were always filthy—especially in winter, because the best place to sleep was in the pile of used coal at the railway station. If they burrowed down too deep, they'd be burned by the embers, but just under the surface they'd be comfortably warm—and they didn't care if they got covered with black, gritty coal dust. There was no place to bathe, so the children were also crawling with lice. When the itching got too bad, the local blacksmith shaved their heads for free.

Yasha was eight years old when he was separated from his mother and sister. His father had joined the army, and the rest of the family, along with other Jewish refugees, had fled from the invading Germans into the Soviet Union. Yasha's mother had managed to find space for herself and her children on a train going across the country, but during this war, even passenger trains were at risk. Every time German planes appeared in the sky, the train would stop and all the people on board would jump off and run for cover under the trees, in case the planes were there to bomb the train. When the planes had gone, the people would come out of hiding and climb back on the train, which would move off as quickly as it could. But one day, when the train stopped, Yasha ran too far into the woods. It took him a little too long to run back, and when he reached the spot, the train wasn't there. It had gone on without him, carrying away his frantic mother and sister. He was alone, one of "the abandoned ones," and for the next four years he would wander from town to town, following the railroad tracks, his only chance to find his family again.

—Susan Dunn

Amy's Eyes
By Richard Kennedy
(Notables 1985)

When Amy was just a baby, her mother died, and her father, a poor tailor, couldn't take care of the baby by himself. With much regret, he put her in a basket and left her outside an orphanage. Tucked into the basket with Amy was a doll that her father had made for her—a doll that looked just like a sea captain. Amy loved that doll and treated it like a living, breathing person, and the power of her love made it come true—the Captain became a real, live person! When he had to flee for his life, he promised to come back for Amy. But alas, the messages he sent were kept from her, and, believing he was dead, she pined away. When the Captain finally made his way back to the orphanage, he discovered that Amy had turned into a lifeless doll. But he kept his word; he took the Amy-doll with him as he set out for further adventures. Years ago, Amy's love had brought him to life. Can his love do the same for her?

—*Maureen Whalen*

Anastasia Again!
By Lois Lowry
(Notables 1981)

"Hello there, Anastasia Again." That's what Gertrustein says. Anastasia Again isn't really my name, and Gertrustein isn't really hers. I'm Anastasia Krupnik, and she is Gertrude Stein, but my little brother can't say that, so he calls her Gertrustein, and it's caught on. Gertrustein lives next door to us, next door to our new house, that is.

We used to live in an apartment in the city. I loved it there, and I didn't want to move, but Mom and Dad said we had to, because we were outgrowing our apartment. I guess we were, but I still didn't want to move. Mom and Dad said my brother and I could help pick the new house. So I said I wanted a bedroom in a tower. I figured they would *never* find a house with a tower. But they did, and now we live in it right next door to Gertrustein's house. I met Gertrustein the very first day we moved in, when I went over to borrow a pitcher for lemonade. She was mean, way back then, and not very nice-looking, either. But I fixed that. Just the way I try to fix a lot of things. Too bad I can't fix everything, but I do try!

—*Colleen Stinson*

And One for All
By Theresa Nelson
(Notables 1989, SLJ/C 1989)

Wing Brennan and Sam Daily were like magnets—opposites attracting each other, lifelong best friends. Sam was smart, athletic, and the pride of the class of '67. Wing was a walking time-bomb, ready to explode (and about once a month he did). Wing's twelve-year-old sister, Geraldine, had tagged along with them all her life. Together they were like the Three Musketeers—in 1960 they'd even pledged their friendship for all eternity by carving their initials in a sacred copper beech tree. In 1967, though, when Sam and Wing were seniors, life began to change for all of them. Geraldine was falling in love with Sam, and Wing was getting into more and more trouble.

In 1967, young men all across America were scrambling to get into college to avoid the draft. Not Wing. He joined the Marines to go to Vietnam. Sam, on the other hand, went to Washington and joined a peace march. As they went their separate ways, following their own hearts, their friendship cracked and broke. Geraldine and Sam worked together to mend it, to bring Wing safely home, and to renew their eternal oath—"All for one, and one for all."

—Sue Padilla

The Animal, the Vegetable, and John D. Jones
By Betsy Byars
(SLJ/C 1982)

Two weeks with Dad at the beach sounded wonderful to Deanie and Clara. Time to work on their tans, rest, relax, and enjoy the sun and water. But before they had even reached the house, Dad informed them that he'd invited a friend, Delores, and her son, John D., to spend the vacation with them—living in the same house, eating at the same table, sharing *their father* for two whole weeks! How could he do this to them? They *never* had enough time with their father!

As it turned out, John D. didn't like the idea any more than the girls did. He had already decided to be as uncooperative, aloof, and unpleasant as possible. What a start for a summer vacation!

Is there any way it can be saved?

—Carol Kappelmann

Annie and the Old One
By Miska Miles
(Newbery Honor 1972)

Annie lives in a Navajo village. She helps her family with their work every day and she rides the big yellow bus to school. But the best times for Annie are the times she spends with her grandmother. They laugh as they work together, and Grandmother tells wonderful stories. That's why Annie is so worried when Grandmother tells her that, when the new rug is taken from the loom, Grandmother herself will go to Mother Earth. Grandmother can't be leaving! Annie has to stop this from happening. So every day Annie plans something to keep the new rug from being completed. She won't let that rug be finished, because once it is finished, Grandmother will be gone.

—Colleen Stinson

Anthony Burns: The Defeat and Triumph of a Fugitive Slave
By Virginia Hamilton
(Addams 1989)

Anthony tried to stay calm when he heard the harsh voice shout, "Hold on, boy!" There'd been a robbery at a jewelry store, the man said, and Anthony looked like the robber. Anthony swore he'd never stolen anything, but the man insisted that he come to the courthouse; if he was really innocent, he'd be able to prove it there. Anthony panicked and tried to run, but men moved out of the shadows to surround him and carry him to the courthouse, where he was closed in a jury room, with the doors and windows barred. Anthony was certain he could prove his innocence—until Charles Suttle and his agent walked into the room. For the first time, Anthony understood what had really happened.

Anthony was a runaway slave, and Mr. Suttle was the man who'd been his master. Escape to Boston had once meant freedom for a runaway, but things had changed—four years earlier, in 1850, the Fugitive Slave Act had decreed that a runaway could be recaptured, even in a free state, and returned to his master. Anthony's future looked grim, but he had the support of his friends in Boston. Could they win his freedom in a court of law or through a bargain with Master Suttle? Or should they try to steal Anthony away from his captors? Follow a battle for freedom, in the true story of Anthony Burns.

—Helen Schlichting

Are You in the House Alone?
By Richard Peck
(Poe 1977)

When Gail wakes up in the hospital examination room with her parents and doctors hovering over her, she knows what's happened. She also knows no one will believe her when she tells them she's been raped by the son of one of the town's most influential families.

—*J. R. B.*

As the Waltz Was Ending
By Emma M. Butterworth
(Notables 1982)

Emma loved to dance. She really didn't know much about dancing, but when she heard music, she almost had to move in time. Still, she was surprised when their neighbor, Frau Fischer, told her that she had talent and offered to send Emma to the ballet school at the Vienna Opera. Emma knew that the competition for entrance to the ballet school was fierce, and she could hardly believe she had a chance. But Frau Fischer was right.

When Emma was accepted into the school, the first thing she learned was that dancing could be hard work. But Emma wanted a career as a ballerina more that anything else in the world. Busy at school, she paid little attention as the world around her began to change. When the Depression hit Austria, her father lost his job, and her family had to give up their comfortable apartment and lifestyle. Many other people were in the same boat, and some began to speak in favor of Adolf Hitler and to support a union with Germany. Emma's parents were opposed to Nazism, but she met its supporters everywhere. Emma just wanted to dance at the opera, but Vienna was no longer a simple, or even a safe, place. Everything was different now. Would her family, her friends, and her dreams survive, as the waltz was ending?

—*Helen Schlichting*

Athletic Shorts
By Chris Crutcher
(SLJ/C 1991)

Meet Angus Bethune, who has, to say the least, an unusual family. Four parents—which isn't all that odd, except that Angus's mothers are married to each other, and so are his dads. But that's not Angus's problem. No, Angus's problem is that he is *huge*. And, of course, his name is Angus, which is a name for a cow, not a kid. All in all, Angus has more than his share of problems.

But today the real problem is that Angus was elected Senior Winter Ball King (a joke), and tonight he has to dance with his dream girl, Melissa Lefevre, Senior Winter Ball Queen. And Angus can't dance. Not to mention what he looks like in his extra-extra-large burgundy tuxedo!

But you never know about life, and this night turns into a magic night, like nothing Angus or anyone else has ever dreamed of.

Now meet Johnny Rivers, who's about to wrestle the match of his life—against his father. And Petey Shropshire, who's about to wrestle the match of *his* life—against a girl.

Those are just three of the stories about love and death and family and friendship and pride and honor that you will find in Chris Crutcher's *Athletic Shorts.*

—Sarah Flowers

Bad Boy
By Diana Wieler
(Canadian Governor General's 1990)

People talk more freely about being gay today. You read about it in the newspaper, you hear about it on TV. It's cool! Live and let live! That's what *I* thought. . . .

Until I found out that my best friend is gay. Tully's his name. We've always been close, always been able to talk about anything. But we can't talk about this. In fact, we're not talking about much at all these days.

Somebody saw Tully with a hockey player everyone knows is gay, and now the guys on our team are starting to talk. And they're starting to wonder about me, because Tully and I are friends.

It makes me so mad! And I can't do anything to stop it—I can't talk to Tully *or* to the guys on the team. The anger keeps building inside me. And the only way I can get rid of it is on the ice. Pound the other guys, slam into the board, slap the puck right through the net. But as soon as I'm off the ice, the anger starts building again. What am I going to do when I can't control it anymore?

—*Colleen Stinson*

The Battle Horse
By Harry Kullman
(Batchelder 1982, Notables 1981, SLJ/C 1981)

My name's Roland and I live in an apartment complex in Ostermalm. In my town, there are two groups of kids: the preppies who go to rich schools and the rest of us whose fathers are laborers. One of the kids nicknamed Buffalo Bill got the idea of having jousts after we had all seen the movie *Ivanhoe.* The preppies would be the knights and the poor kids the horses.

Then one day the Black Knight arrived. No one knew who he was or where he came from, but he could beat any knight who challenged him. The main preppie in my building, Henning, was finally forced to challenge the Black Knight. I was the only boy available to be his horse, but Henning decided I was too small. Instead, he chose Kossan, a large, strong girl who loved to play with the small children in the building and was flattered to be asked to be a horse. Henning practiced riding Kossan and thought he was ready for the Black Knight. But when Henning rode into the arena, his fellow preppies made fun of him because he was riding a girl. Kossan was so embarrassed she could not move, and the Black Knight easily knocked Henning to the ground. Henning was furious and challenged the Black Knight to fight again, this time without cork tips on their lances.

Henning dressed Kossan up as a horse in a costume complete with a horsehead mask and even a bit with reins. As they trained, I noticed that Henning was starting to treat Kossan like a horse, and she was beginning to act like one.

The day of the return match arrived. The biggest crowd ever assembled at Buffalo Bill's arena. The Black Knight came out with his horse dressed in a costume like Kossan's. Henning was furious. The fight began. Who *was* the Black Knight? Would Henning really do anything to win? Was Kossan going to be able to survive the fight? Would anyone care if she didn't?

—*Abbie V. Landry*

Becoming Gershona
By Nava Semel
(National Jewish 1991)

Gershona is a twelve-year-old girl who likes to see things grow. Her grandfather has just come from America to join her family, and her love for him is growing. The town where she lives is growing—this is Tel Aviv in the 1950s, an important time for the new country called Israel. New buildings are going up all over the place, and new people are moving in. And Gershona's friendship with one of them, a boy called Nimrod, is growing too.

Why, then, does Gershona feel she must destroy it all? Because feelings of hurt and distrust are also growing, inside Gershona's heart. Too many people around her are keeping secrets. She has no secrets at all. She was born right here, but everyone else seems to come from somewhere else, and they all have stories they don't want to share. Why won't her grandfather tell her more about America? Why won't Nimrod tell her about the letters he gets from Poland? Who's the boy in the photograph her mother has? Even the plants in her garden seem to be turning against her!

Gershona lashes out. She rips up the beautiful plants in a neighbor's garden. She tells Nimrod to get out of her life. And she runs to the edge of the river and falls asleep in humiliation and disgust.

Her mother is frantic—where is she? And Nimrod wants to show her the first green shoots in her garden. Her father even wants to take her for a ride in his car called Plymouth—the biggest car in town.

There's more, and it's beautiful. Gershona learns a few answers. She learns about patience, and about other people's dreams. And she learns that everybody wants to include her in the future of their world.

—Mark Anderson

Behind the Attic Wall
By Sylvia Cassedy
(Notables 1983, SLJ/C 1983)

"Impossible to handle." That's what they said about Maggie, all of them—the headmistresses at the various boarding schools (one after another) and now even her relatives. "Impossible to handle." Which could be translated as "mean, nasty, disgusting, willful, disobedient, and a downright thief!" No wonder no school would keep her. No wonder there was no one left to take her in but her two great-aunts. And they obviously weren't happy about it. Well, Maggie wasn't exactly thrilled to be living with them, either! All alone with two old women who corrected her all day long. All alone in this huge grey building that used to be a boarding school. All alone—or was she? Because Maggie hadn't been there very long before she began to hear voices. Voices that no one else seemed to hear. Voices that came from nowhere and everywhere. Voices that said ordinary things, like "Water the roses" or "Be careful" or "Time for tea." Was she going crazy, living isolated in this spooky old house? Or was someone else living here too—someone (or something) absolutely mysterious, waiting to be discovered by a newcomer like Maggie, waiting in secret, behind the attic wall.

—*Sister M. Anna Falbo, CSSF*

The Bells of Christmas
By Virginia Hamilton
(Notables 1989)

An Ohio Christmas in 1890. The excitement of the days of preparation, the eager anticipation of the family gathering, the gifts, the joyful service at church, the feast at home.

Will it snow? It's not supposed to, but if it does, can we go out with the horses and the sleigh?

Christmas is for families, no matter what century it is.

—*Carol Kappelmann*

The Best Bad Thing
By Yoshiko Uchida
(Notables 1983, SLJ/C 1983)

Summer is a great time—no school, whole days to play and do whatever you want. At home Rinko doesn't even mind helping out with the laundry that Mama takes in. But going to the country for a month to help Mrs. Hata and her two sons on their cucumber farm is another story.

Rinko knows it would be a good thing to do, a Christian thing to do. Mrs. Hata needs all the help she can get, now that her husband has died. But Mrs. Hata is crazy, in Rinko's opinion, and her boys are the worst little pests you can imagine. Besides, it's summer vacation.

Rinko knows that Mama and Papa will make her go. But they'll come out to visit in two weeks' time. That should be long enough. Maybe then, if Rinko tells them all the terrible things that have happened, they'll take her back home right away.

The two weeks are almost over. But the terrible things don't seem to be happening quite the way Rinko expected.

—*Colleen Stinson*

The Big Book for Peace
By Lloyd Alexander, edited by Ann Durell and Marilyn Sachs
(Addams 1991, Notables 1990)

It's not easy to learn about peace in our world. So much surrounds us that is just the opposite. Friends quarrel, strangers fight, countries war with each other. It's no wonder we long for peace—we never seem to have it.

Seth Laughlin knows about peace. Seth, a Quaker, fights quietly against the evil of slavery in pre-Civil War Virginia, and later against the evil of war itself. Jimbo Kurasaki knows about peace too. A young Japanese-American, he writes from a concentration camp where he is to spend who knows how many years, because America is at war with Japan and Jimbo looks like the enemy. Even animals, though they sometimes fight savagely, instinctively seek peace. Kristy sees that as she watches the song sparrows nesting in the nearby meadow while she awaits her father's return from war.

Peace. What a beautiful word when it is spoken quietly. What a strong rallying-cry when it is shouted fearlessly. And what a magnificent goal toward which to strive.

—*Nancy L. Chu*

Bill Peet: An Autobiography
By Bill Peet
(Notables 1989, SLJ/C 1989)

Do any of you remember reading these books when you were younger? [Hold up a few of Bill Peet's books.] Bill Peet isn't just an author and illustrator, though. He used to work for Walt Disney. Have you seen *Cinderella*? Bill Peet did the mice in that movie. What about *Alice in Wonderland* or *Peter Pan*? Bill Peet worked on both of them. And have you seen *101 Dalmatians* or *The Sword in the Stone*? Bill Peet created both of them, from start to finish!

Of course, Bill didn't start off working on those big projects, or even working for Walt Disney. He started out in Indiana, and grew up in Indianapolis. He started drawing as soon as he could hold a pencil or a crayon, and he got in trouble at school because he drew too much of the time. He liked to draw animals, locomotives, and especially weird critters. [Show page 6.] One day Bill tried to catch a large frog so he could draw it—and this is what happened. [Show pages 11-14.]

As he got older, Bill's drawing got better, and he won some money with a few paintings. But then there was the Depression of the 1930s, when lots of people were out of work. There were too many people and not enough jobs, and Bill had to figure out how to make money. Work for Walt Disney, maybe? So Bill left Indiana for California and a career in the movies.

By the way, who's seen *The Little Mermaid?* Bill's son worked on that movie.

—*Julie Bray*

Bingo Brown and the Language of Love
By Betsy Byars
(SLJ/C 1989)

Bingo Brown is your typical sixth-grade boy. He's concerned about growing a moustache, becoming a teenager, and learning the language of love. Melissa, the love of his life, has moved to the ends of the earth (better known as Bixby, Oklahoma). And after opening a bill for $55, Bingo's mom has cut off his phone privileges. Writing letters to Melissa just isn't the same as talking to her on the phone.

It's hard to speak the language of love with pencil and paper.

And what about CiCi? (That's with two i's, C-i-C-i.). She's Melissa's best friend, but now she seems to be entering Bingo's life. And there's always Billy Wentworth, everybody's favorite neighbor—oh riiight!

Poor Bingo! How will he learn the language of love? Who can he speak it with?

—*Ru Story-Huffman*

Bingo Brown, Gypsy Lover
By Betsy Byars
(Notables 1990, SLJ/C 1990)

Gypsy lover is the role he'd like to play, but Bingo Brown keeps getting sidetracked into other walks of life—big brother, advisor to the lovelorn, confidant, and even love object.

Can he really court Melissa from afar, now that his mom has limited his long-distance phone calls? And why, all of a sudden, does ex-brat Billy Wentworth need all this advice about love? And why, oh why, must a girl named Boots pick Bingo as her leading man? (Aren't boots something you wear on your feet?)

If anyone can sort this out, Bingo can—but it won't be easy!

—*Ru Story-Huffman*

Black and White
By David Macaulay
(Caldecott 1991, Notables 1990)

A boy rides alone on a train. Sometime in the early morning hours, the train stops because a herd of Holstein cows is blocking the track. A mysterious woman joins the boy in his compartment. Later during the trip, the boy sees newspaper scraps blowing through the sky like leaves.

People wait at a commuter station for a train that is way overdue. At first the people read newspapers, but as the wait goes on and on, they start decorating themselves and the station with sheets of newspaper, and singing.

Two children have problem parents, who come home from work acting like little kids, dressed in newspaper costumes and singing.

A burglar who has escaped from jail lets a herd of Holstein cows out of their pasture, and, as any farmer can tell you, once Holstein cows get out of the field they are almost impossible to find.

Are these four stories, or four chapters of one story? In these pages, just as in life, nothing is as simple as "black and white."

—*Maureen Whalen*

Blackberries in the Dark
By Mavis Jukes
(Notables 1985, SLJ/C 1985)

Sometimes it's hard to go back to where you've visited before, especially if things have changed there. That's how Austin feels. He's all set for his annual visit to his grandparents' home this summer, but his grandfather has died, and Austin doesn't quite know how things will be. Will he still go fishing? Will he ride the tractor this year and mow the lawn? Will he have all of the great times he always had before?

Austin meets Grandma at the airport and refuses an invitation to go fly-fishing with the neighbors on Saturday. Grandpa was supposed to teach him how to fly-cast this summer, not the neighbors. Things just seem wrong. Is there any way to make it all right again?

—Susan Trimby

Blossom Culp and the Sleep of Death
By Richard Peck
(Notables 1986)

Blossom Culp likes to think of herself as the Ghostbuster of Bluff City, Missouri. Of course, living where she does and when she does, in 1914, Blossom has never seen a moving picture show, but she certainly has experienced her share of ghostly manifestations.

Things supernatural come naturally to Blossom, who is descended from a long line of gypsies, fortune-tellers, wart-healers, and the like. She has the gift of Second Sight, which allows her to connect with Forces Unknown and contact the Spirit World; she can sometimes enter history, past or future. Unfortunately for her, Blossom's powers tend to come and go at whim. She's never quite sure what she can count on.

She definitely didn't count on the spirit of an Egyptian princess choosing her—Blossom Culp!—as the earthly agent to restore the princess's mummified remains to their former glory. Nor did she count on finding those 3,000-year-old remains right here in Bluff City.

Blosssom knows that the Ancient Egyptians were famous for their highly effective curses. If she fails to pacify the princess, the consequences may be grave. Can Blossom's powers, and her ever-present horse sense, put this irate spirit to rest?

—Jeff Blair

The Blue Sword
By Robin McKinley
(Newbery Honor 1983, Notables 1982)

I always knew that I was different from the people around me. Some whispered that I took after my great-grandmother, who had also been "different," though they would never say how. But I felt myself separate even from my own family, even before my parents were gone. After their deaths, my older brother Richard, who was a professional soldier, arranged for me to stay with Sir Charles and Lady Amelia at their house in Istan, near the border separating us Homelanders from the Hillfolk. As soon as I arrived, I felt drawn to the mountains that loomed up ahead. And that was the basis of my friendship with Colonel Jack Dedham, the only other person in our set who seemed to share my fascination with the hills.

Lady Amelia and Sir Charles treated me with every kindness, and I even had partners at the dances, thanks to my soldier-brother. I had other young ladies for company during the day, but I was restless. The mountains called to me.

Late one night a messenger arrived, announcing that Corlath, king of the Hillfolk, was coming in person to speak with Sir Charles and Colonel Dedham. The king's visit set off a swirl of activity. Corlath had come to ask for our help against a huge army of Northerners who were poised to invade his lands (and ultimately ours as well). Sir Charles didn't believe it; Colonel Dedham did, but there was nothing he could do.

I didn't really understand what was happening, although I saw that Colonel Dedham was worried. I went on with my daily routine. But that night I couldn't go to bed. I dozed off in my chair by the window. When I woke up I realized that I was in motion, slung across the withers of a horse. I raised my head and the horse stopped. The rider carrying me was Corlath himself. What did he want with a Homelander girl like me? Where was he taking me, and why?

—Abbie V. Landry

A Blue-Eyed Daisy
By Cynthia Rylant
(Notables 1985)

Ellie was a pretty girl, and her wishes were simple: she wanted her own room, one not crowded with older sisters. Ellie was tired of teenage sisters. She had four of them. That was too many, in Ellie's opinion, especially since not one of them would share much with her any more.

Maybe that was why she gravitated toward her father. Okey was a drinking man, like many of the miners. When he was drunk (which was often), he would yell at Ellie's mother and sometimes even hit her. His excuse was that he couldn't work. He'd been injured in a slate fall and would never completely recover.

One day Elllie was surprised to see him come back from town with a beagle. Bullet was a quiet dog, a great family pet. Ellie was impressed. But she couldn't imagine why Okey would bring home a hunting dog, when he couldn't go out hunting himself. Okey got a surprise of his own when Ellie announced that she wanted to learn how to hunt. He laughed so hard he almost choked on the whiskey in his throat.

But Ellie, his blue-eyed daisy, learned to hunt, and a whole lot more besides.

—Bernice D. Crouse

The Borning Room
By Paul Fleischman
(Notables 1991, SLJ/C 1991)

The borning room—a room set aside for births and deaths, a place where people enter life or leave it. It's seldom occupied, but when it is, everyone in the house is changed forever. In Georgina's home, the borning room is a small room behind the kitchen, with a bed, a table, a lamp, and two chairs. Georgina was born there, her children were born there, and it's where each of them will go to die. It's the room where she learned about freedom by helping Southern slaves travel north to find it, discovered the power of a vase full of violets, and began her courtship with the man she later married.

Listen as Georgina tells her stories of the borning room.

—Dara Finkelstein, Nancy Bardole Hanaman, and J. R. B.

Borrowed Children
By George Ella Lyon
(Golden Kite 1989, SLJ/C 1988)

Amanda Perritt is twelve. Most twelve-year-olds go to school, make friends, and have fun. But not Amanda. She's too busy. When Baby Willie was born, something went wrong and Mama almost died. She's still very weak and must stay in bed, and that leaves Amanda to take care of the house, cook the meals, and tend the baby. There just isn't enough time to do all that and go to school as well, so Mama and Daddy decide that Amanda will have to quit school for the time being.

Now Amanda's life is very different and very difficult, too: her work never seems to end. She doesn't have time to study or even to read, and she's afraid she'll never get the chance to go back to school. She'll probably have to look after her family for the rest of her life! She'll never leave Goose Rock, Kentucky, to explore New York or Boston or the West Coast.

That's why it's such a wonderful surprise when Mama and Daddy tell her they're going to send her to Memphis to spend Christmas with her grandparents. The excitements of the city, interesting new people, museums, concerts, shops, and shows—everything she's ever dreamed of! And freedom from all the demands of home—what a treat it will be! Amanda can't wait for her adventure to begin.

—*Colleen Stinson*

The Borrowers Avenged
By Mary Norton
(Notables 1982, SLJ/C 1982)

Borrowers' lives depend on never being seen by a human being. These little people live in our houses secretly, "borrowing" corks, spools, pins, stamps, and other small everyday objects to use in their own way—a cigar box becomes a bed, and a thimble makes a good cooking pot.

Pod, Homily, and young Arietty Clock are Borrowers who have just escaped from the wicked Platters, human beings who captured them to put on public display. Right now the Clocks need a new home quickly, where no human will be able to find them.

With the help of their friend Spiller, the Clocks decide to move into the Old Rectory, a huge building that has seen better days. Only two human beings, Mr. and Mrs. Whitlace, live there now, and they live in the kitchen annex; most of the other rooms are closed off and empty. Of all the Borrowers who once inhabited the Old Rectory in bygone times, only one is left: Mr. Peagreen Overmantle, and he's delighted to have some company. He welcomes the Clocks and shows them a comfortable place to live near the library fireplace, and secret ways to get around the house without being seen. At last the Clocks can breathe a sigh of relief. They feel safe and secure in the Old Rectory, and settle in happily.

But the Platters are still searching for them, and in spite of all their precautions, the Borrowers are still in danger. Are they really safe from discovery in their new home?

—*Evette Pearson*

The Boy Who Reversed Himself
By William Sleator
(SLJ/C 1986)

It started the day Laura found a note in her locker. In the first place, it shouldn't even have been there: the lock wasn't broken; the door looked fine; and no one else had her combination. In the second place, the note was written backward—in mirror-writing. When she figured it out, it said, "Study Chapter 10 in the biology book tonight; there will be a surprise quiz tomorrow." And there was. This was weird!

Then one day she left a lab report at home, but when she got to school, there it was in her locker—only now the entire report was backward—everything reversed. Totally weird! It got even weirder, though, later that day, when she couldn't get her locker open and Omar, her new next-door neighbor, showed up and offered to retrieve the report for her. And he did, too, handing it to her just before she went to biology class. Only this time the report was the right way around and *Omar* was reversed. It took Laura a minute to be sure. But his hair was certainly parted on the other side, and everything about him was like looking in a mirror.

Something strange was happening here, and Laura was determined to find out what. And obviously, the first step would be to find out more about Omar, the boy who reversed himself.

—Sarah Flowers

The Boys' War:
Confederate and Union Soldiers Talk About the Civil War
By Jim Murphy
(Carnegie 1991, Golden Kite 1991, SLJ/C 1991)

"We will return as honored soldiers or fill a soldier's grave," promised a Confederate captain. Many did fill those graves, and some of them were boys. The Union and Confederate armies had a rule that soldiers must be at least eighteen, but it was easy to lie about your age back then. Some of those soldiers were fifteen or sixteen years old, younger sometimes, if they were big. At first they didn't have uniforms, so you couldn't always tell friend from enemy. As the war went on, there wasn't enough food. And you never knew when the shooting might start.

Fifteen-year-old Thomas Galway wrote home from the battlefield: "Lieutenant Delaney is shot. Lieutenant Lantry, poor fellow, is annihilated instantly, near me. The top of his head is taken off by a shell. There is but a small group of us left. Fairchild is bleeding; Campion falls, mortally wounded; Jim Gallagher's head is badly grazed and he rolls, coiled in a lump, down into a ditch."

See the Civil War through the eyes of the boys who fought it.

—Cecilia Swanson

Bridge to Terabithia
By Katherine Paterson
(Newbery 1978)

Jess Aarons is the fastest runner at Lark Creek Elementary School—the fastest, that is, until he's challenged by Leslie Burke, a girl! So begins the friendship of two young people who do not conform to the values of rural Virginia life. Jess wants to be an artist, Leslie is immersed in books. The creation of Terabithia, a secret kingdom in the woods, is Leslie's idea. "It could be a magic country like Narnia, and the only way you can get in is by swinging across on the enchanted rope." As they grab the rope, swing across the creek, and enter their beautiful kingdom filled with streams of light, fears and enemies do not exist, and anything they want is possible. Nothing will defeat them. Their lives are changed forever by Terabithia, and the strength of their friendship enables Jess to cope with tragedy.

—Deb Kelly, Anne Liebst, and J. R. B.

The Broccoli Tapes
By Jan Slepian
(Notables 1989, SLJ/C 1989)

Testing . . . one . . . two . . . three . . . is anybody out there?

This is Sara Davidson, reporting to you live from Hawaii. I know you guys think I'm having a great time swimming and sunbathing, but I'd rather be back on the mainland with you. Everything here is strange. The kids at school are nothing like you. And the noises outside my window at night drive me crazy.

Not a friend to be had—unless you count an antisocial cat with bald spots, a torn ear, and a bloody leg. Or maybe that disagreeable boy with the immense chip on his shoulder.

My brother Sam and I met the weird-looking cat on the beach. The poor animal was trapped between a couple of lava rocks with breakers rolling in right to his feet. You never heard such yowling and screeching! When we pulled him to safety, we found that he was practically skin and bones. We were hooked. We wanted to adopt him, even though our dad is allergic to cats and that crazy cat acted as if he were allergic to people. We couldn't begin to tame him until we discovered that he adored cooked broccoli—he really is one strange cat!

Eddie Nutt, the disagreeable boy, is pretty strange too. He seems to be angry at the whole world. When we met him, he was standing on the beach throwing stones, and looking kind of mean. Not very promising friend-material, but when you're as lonely as I am, you can't afford to be choosy. Maybe good friends come in strange packages—people do say they're worth working for.

I'll let you know what happens next. This is Sara Davidson in Hawaii, signing off.

—Bernice D. Crouse

The Bronze Bow
By Elizabeth George Speare
(Newbery 1962)

Daniel is an angry young man. He hates the Romans because they conquered his country. He hates the Romans because they caused the deaths of his father and mother. He hates the Romans because they made his beloved sister, Leah, a captive in her own house. He also hates the brutal master he's apprenticed to, who's cruel to Daniel and the other apprentices. When he can't stand it any longer, Daniel runs away and seeks refuge with Rosh, a mountain outlaw. Daniel worships Rosh, who has proclaimed himself the one who will force the Romans out of Israel.

Daniel has two friends: Joel and Thacia, his twin sister. Joel is studying to be a rabbi, but he too hates the Romans. Thacia is a beautiful girl who resents the rules and restrictions she has to live under just because she's a girl. The three friends swear an oath to do whatever they can to drive the Romans out.

But Daniel's life gradually changes when his grandmother dies and he must go home and look after Leah. He becomes disillusioned with Rosh, who seems to be more of a thief than a liberator. Daniel also discovers that any trouble he causes the Romans will be revenged on his own people.

Daniel is troubled by the words of a carpenter from Nazareth. This rabbi seems to promise the restoration of the Kingdom of Israel but rejects violence and hate. Daniel can neither dismiss nor accept these teachings until his life takes a sudden and dramatic turn: Joel is caught spying by the Romans and Leah becomes deathly ill. Daniel is forced to look at his life, his beliefs, and all his hates before he loses everything. Will the words of the carpenter bring him the answers he seeks?

—Abbie V. Landry

Buffalo Brenda
By Jill Pinkwater
(Notables 1989)

My first day of junior high school had a grim beginning. I missed the bus! When I finally got to school, I had to wander around the halls until I found Room 212. There I met a sour-looking, thoroughly disagreeable teacher named Mr. Osgood.

It was there, before Mr. Osgood and my peers, that I first laid eyes on one Brenda Tuna, who is now my best friend and co-conspirator. I, India Ink Teidlebaum, should have known that my life would never be the same!

Brenda decided that we should go out for an extracurricular activity in order to make our mark in school. Little did I know that the *Florence Weekly Crier* (sometimes referred to as the *Florence Weekly Flounder*) was to be our target! Little did I know that our extracurricular activities would involve a riot, horseburgers, Mr. Osgood, and finally our forced resignation!

However, that was long before Brenda's *really* big idea! If you'd like to know what to do when facing an enraged adult buffalo or how to survive really wild and unbelievable adventures, read *Buffalo Brenda*, by Jill Pinkwater.

—Suzi Smith

Building Blocks
By Cynthia Voigt
(SLJ/C 1984)

Brann lies on the fold-out bed in the TV room and listens to his parents fight. It's the first day of summer vacation, but he should've known better than to expect them to remember that. Ever since they got that letter from the lawyer, a big fight has been brewing—the mother of all their quarrels—and here it is. The letter said that Brann's father had inherited some property—specifically, an old farm out in Pennsylvania. Brann's mother was thrilled, excited to think that once they had sold the farm there would finally be enough money for her to go to law school, something she's been hoping to do for years. But Brann's father doesn't want to sell, and for once he's not giving in. Usually, Brann thinks, his father's a passive wimp, going along with anything his wife says, apologizing for whatever she's mad about. But apparently not this time. In the end, though, Brann thinks gloomily, his dad will put the farm on the market, only by the time he does it the divorce papers will already have been filed and it won't matter any more. Why does his father have to be such a loser?

Tired of listening, Brann throws on some clothes and slips downstairs to the cellar, where he won't be able to hear the angry voices. There, in a corner, he finds a castle his father once built out of some old wooden blocks that were made for him when he was a boy—blocks of oak, cut in all shapes and sizes, golden-smooth from long handling. To keep from thinking, Brann begins to rebuild the fortress to his own design, reinforcing each corner with a tower where look-outs could be stationed. When he finishes, the fortress is big enough for him to crawl inside, and there, curled up on the cellar floor, he falls asleep.

When he wakes up, it's night, and he's in an unfamiliar room. On the other side of the room a scared-looking boy is sitting straight up in bed staring at him. Brann has gone back nearly forty years in time, and the startled boy is his own father!

—*Mary Fellows*

Bully for You, Teddy Roosevelt!
By Jean Fritz
(Notables 1991, SLJ/C 1991)

Theodore Roosevelt wanted to do everything—and all at once, if possible. He studied birds, shot lions, roped steer, fought a war, wrote books, discovered the source of a mystery river in South America (nearly getting killed in the process), and, in his free time, managed to become governor of New York, vice-president of the United States, and finally President. Theodore Roosevelt bounded through his life with amazing energy, and people who knew him found interesting ways to describe him.

Buffalo Bill (who was pretty energetic himself) called Teddy Roosevelt a "cyclone." Mark Twain called him "an earthquake." Others said he was " an eruption," "an express locomotive," "a buzz saw." But Teddy was just enthusiastic. If he liked something, it was "bully," or "DEE-lightful!"

But if you had known Teddy when he was a little boy, you would never have guessed he was going to grow up to be like that. In fact, you might have wondered whether he was going to grow up at all. He was a sickly child. He had very bad asthma, and his parents tried every asthma remedy they knew about, from propping him high up on pillows to help him sleep, to giving him very fast carriage rides in the middle of the night to force the cool night air into his lungs, to, believe it or not, having him puff on his father's cigars!

But he survived all that and grew up to love animals and nature. You never knew what might show up in the Roosevelt house: his brothers and sisters learned to watch for snakes and frogs in the water pitchers, and once his mother had to throw out a litter of dead field mice she found in the icebox. When he grew up and became President, he still loved all wildlife. In addition to his travels around the world and his work to preserve endangered wildlife, he encouraged his own children to keep pets in the White House. At one time, they had two dogs, a macaw, a rat, a flying squirrel, two kangaroo rats, and a pony—which was actually inside the White House once, when one of Teddy's sons was sick and needed cheering up.

Teddy Roosevelt cared about everything he ever did. He worked hard and he played hard. He fought corruption, he worked for change, he fought in one war and won the Nobel Peace Prize for stopping another. Discover one of our most fascinating presidents, and find your own words to describe him.

—Sarah Flowers

The Burning Questions of Bingo Brown
By Betsy Byars
(SLJ/C 1988)

Welcome to Bingo's world. A world of questions—questions with no answers. Such as, "Is my life ever going to be calm?" "Has a principal ever expelled an entire school?" "Will Billy Wentworth have bunk beds?" and "Will I end up without even the desire for burning questions?"

Yes, Bingo has questions. Questions about Billy Wentworth, the class Rambo, and about conversations with girls. What about Mr. Markham, Bingo's English teacher? Has he gone over the edge? Will Bingo go with him? If your name were Bingo, wouldn't you have questions too?

All Bingo really wants is some answers. But all he can come up with are more questions. Everyone has questions, but will Bingo ever find the answers?

—*Ru Story-Huffman*

Buster's World
By Bjarne Reuter
(Batchelder 1990, Notables 1989)

The whole mess started in the locker room, after gym. Someone discovered that Buster had brought a dish towel to school instead of a regular towel. Next thing he knew, the other guys had bundled up his clothes and refused to give them back until he agreed to do his gorilla act. He didn't really want to, but it was better than going to class naked. So Buster obligingly hunched his back, bent his legs, brushed back his hair, and stuffed two erasers into his mouth. The transformation was complete. Suddenly Buster was no longer his usual crazy self, but a live growling gorilla. First he just walked around; then he started to chase the other kids. But just as he began to yell, "Me King Kong, just like old Olsen," who should come into the locker room but Mr. Olsen himself. Only, Buster had his back to the door, so he went right on: "Me hairy ape, me got big hairy chest, me Great Ape Olsen, me . . . me . . . ," and suddenly Buster was face to face with the great ape himself!

So much for his gorilla act. But don't worry about Buster. He'll still be around to drive his friends wild and his enemies crazy. Right here, in *Buster's World.*

—*Sister M. Anna Falbo, CSSF*

By the Shores of Silver Lake
By Laura Ingalls Wilder
(Newbery Honor 1940)

Laura Ingalls and her family, Ma, Pa, Mary, Carrie, and Baby Grace, have left Plum Creek and moved west again, to the prairies of Dakota Territory. Pa is working for the railroad, and the Ingalls family lives in a railroad shanty. Pa works on the railroad all summer so settlers can move west. When construction on the railroad stops for the winter, they all move to the surveyor's house, a grand two-story house with enough supplies to last through the winter.

When spring comes, wagon after wagon of settlers passes through the Ingalls's house, with Ma feeding them and giving them a place to sleep. But all these settlers may be very bad luck for the family, because Pa may lose his homesteading claim if he doesn't get to Brookins, several days away, and file the papers. Will the family have to leave the new home they've found and move on again?

—*Colleen Stinson*

Caddie Woodlawn
By Carol Ryrie Brink
(Newbery 1936)

Caddie Woodlawn is a tomboy. Her mother and sister despair of her ever becoming the proper young lady that a girl in 1865 should be. Becoming a proper young lady is about the last thing Caddie has in mind—there are too many adventures to be had out here in Wisconsin, and too many pranks to be played on her friends and rivals. Hunting, gathering berries, visiting an Indian camp, fighting the school bully, running into a rattlesnake—Caddie Woodlawn really knows how to make her life exciting!

—*Melanie L. Witulski and Mary Cosper*

Call It Courage
By Armstrong Sperry
(Newbery 1941)

We don't think about courage every day. It's something we hope we'll have if we need it, in desperate times. But for Mafatu, every day calls for courage. Mafatu is the son of the great chief of Hibueru. When he was only three years old, he and his mother were out on the sea when a hurricane struck. Mafatu's mother was killed, and ever since then he's been deathly afraid of the sea. The sea gods are still angry at him, he believes, angry that he escaped from their wrath before.

This might not be a problem for most boys, but the sea is the main source of food for Mafatu's tribe—they are fisher people, and he, as a son of the chief, should help lead them out on the water. Because he just can't face the sea, Mafatu is branded a coward. One day, when the name-calling becomes unbearable, Mafatu goes off in a canoe with his pet dog and pet albatross. The challenges he faces are beyond his wildest imaginings—he must confront a storm, sharks, eaters-of-man, and all the anger of his gods before he can hope to return.

—*Mary Cosper*

The Callender Papers
By Cynthia Voigt
(Poe 1984)

When Jean agreed to take the job sorting the Callender papers for the summer, she had no idea what she was getting into.

Jean was a respectable young lady who attended a girls' school in Cambridge in 1894. Her aunt Constance, the only parent she had ever known, was the school's headmistress. When Mr. Thiel, a benefactor of the school, needed someone to sort and catalogue several boxes of his late wife's family papers, Aunt Constance thought of Jean and asked her to consider the job. Jean considered it carefully. She would have to stay at Mr. Thiel's mansion in Marlborough, some distance away, for the entire summer, with only him and his housekeeper for company. But the work would not be difficult (even Aunt Constance was certain she could handle it) and the experience might prove useful. As soon as school closed for the summer, then, Jean boarded the train for Marlborough.

The papers she had to sort involved a family named Callender—Mr. Thiel's in-laws. Jean learned a lot about the Callenders from the old documents, and even more from people who remembered them. She discovered, for instance, that Irene Callender, Mr. Thiel's late wife, had been a friend of Aunt Constance's; and that Irene's brother still lived nearby but no longer spoke to Mr. Thiel. There were strange stories, too, about munitions factories and "hiders," things Jean didn't quite understand.

But let's hope she never understands the significance of the papers in the last box, or recognizes what she has found, or makes the connection to the present. Because if she does, she will expose the secrets of the Callenders—and that can never be allowed!

—*Bernice D. Crouse*

The Canada Geese Quilt
By Natalie Kinsey-Warnock
(Notables 1989)

Her grandmother's stroke, Mama having a new baby—so many things were changing for Ariel, things she wanted to stay the same. She was used to being the only child and was afraid her parents would pay her even less attention when the new baby came.

Grandma had always had time for her when everyone else was too busy. She used to be able to talk to Grandma when no one else seemed to understand. Now she didn't know what to say or how to act. After her stroke, Grandma was different.

Ariel had hoped that Grandma could help her decide on a special gift for the new baby. She didn't know how to make anything, and she was counting on Grandma to help her. Grandma had always made quilts for her loved ones—she had been so good with her hands. But now Grandma was too ill to do anything but stay in her room, alone. Ariel was afraid that Grandma would die, and she remembered all her grandma had done for her and all she had taught her. And then, one day in the fall, watching the geese fly north for the winter, she thought of something special she could do for her grandma, before it was too late.

—Judy McElwain

Carry On, Mr. Bowditch
By Jean Lee Latham
(Newbery 1956)

I was born in Salem, Massachusetts, to a family plagued by misfortune. My father was a ship's captain, but after his ship ran aground and was wrecked in the waves, he went back to his old trade of barrel-making. He seemed a broken man, even more so after my mother died. I think he felt he had lost everything he cared for.

Determined that I should have a settled, landsman's trade, he indentured me for nine years to Ropes and Hodges, ships' chandlers, as a bookkeeper. This nearly broke my heart, for it meant that I had to leave school and give up any hope of going to Harvard.

But I decided to continue my studies on my own, and I added navigation and astronomy to the mathematics I was already learning, as well as two foreign languages. I kept notebooks, and even wrote an almanac. And I counted the days until I would be free of the indenture.

Finally the great day came. Now I could live my own life, but what was I going to do? I was too old to enter the university. I tried surveying and business, but I kept thinking of my studies, and wondering how I could best make use of them. Then I got a chance to go to sea myself, as a clerk and second mate. Would I have better luck than the rest of my family, who had all been broken, killed, or widowed by the sea? I am staking my whole future on my abilities as a mathematician, and my knowledge of the stars and of navigation. Will the bad luck that has stalked my family come to haunt me as well?

—Abbie V. Landry

Castle in the Air
By Diana Wynne Jones
(Notables 1991)

Abdullah doesn't like being a carpet merchant, but he's not a fool. He insists on a demonstration before he buys the flying carpet. Too bad he didn't think to ask about the magic command to get the carpet started. But one night, quite by accident, he utters the command word in his sleep, and from then on his life is much more interesting.

During his nighttime flights he meets and falls in love with a sultan's daughter. Luckily, when she is kidnapped by an evil genie, Abdullah finds a genie for himself. Unluckily, Abdullah's genie is not only temperamental, but hopeless at finding lost princesses. At the moment Abdullah is chained to a tree. And he still doesn't know the magic word that will get his carpet off the ground.

—Cecilia Swanson

Cat Poems
Selected by Myra Cohn Livingston
(Notables 1987)

Have you ever felt a cat's tongue? It's rough, like sandpaper. Have you ever watched a cat's tongue? Fast pink flicks, over and over. Have you ever watched a cat bathe? Lick, lick, lick. Paws, whiskers, tail.

Have you ever watched a cat sleep? Soft and purring, all rolled up on a lap.

Have you ever watched a cat?

—Colleen Stinson

Charley Skedaddle
By Patricia Beatty
(O'Dell 1988)

He didn't stop for anything. Not for the bullets whizzing by him, not for the bodies that littered his path, not for the cries of wounded comrades or the looks they gave him as he went past, not for the boom of the artillery. He just ran—ran like a fear-crazed beast, until he tripped over a root and fell to the ground in the suddenly quiet Virginia forest.

Was this what war was like? It was nothing like what Charley Quinn had expected. What had happened to the glory and grandeur of the military parades that had inspired him to run away from home and join up as a drummer boy for the 140th New York Volunteers? Charley knew people died in war, but coming face to face with the realities of combat had been terrifying. It had meant coming face to face with the body of his friend, and face to face with the man Charley had shot himself. It was more than Charley could take. And so he ran.

How could he stop? He couldn't go back to his unit; he'd seen their faces as he raced past. The Rebs were bound to capture him if he wasn't careful. Charley knew he had to keep moving, keep running, or else he'd come face to face with the last person he wanted to see: himself, and the coward he'd become.

—*Jeff Blair*

Charlotte's Web
By E. B. White
(Newbery Honor 1953)

Papa was going to kill the runt of the litter of pigs, but Fern wouldn't hear of it. And since she didn't let her father kill him, now Fern has to take care of Wilbur herself.

When he grows too big, her parents tell her she must sell him. So her uncle buys Wilbur, so that Fern can still go visit him. At his new home, Wilbur meets the geese, the sheep, the cows, and the horses who share the barn. He also makes friends with Templeton the rat and Charlotte, a large grey spider.

Several months after Wilbur arrives, one of the sheep tells him that *he* is going to be Christmas dinner. "I don't want to die!" screams Wilbur, throwing himself to the ground. "You shall *not* die," says Charlotte briskly. "What?" cries Wilbur, "Who's going to save me?" "I am," says Charlotte.

How can an old grey spider save a frightened pig? Don't forget they're best friends, and friendship can be a wonderful and powerful thing.

—Deb Kelly

Chartbreaker
By Gillian Cross
(SLJ/C 1987)

After another fight with her mother's boyfriend, this time for skipping school, Janis just had to get away. It was pouring rain outside, but anything was better than staying indoors where *he* was, so she grabbed the nearest jacket and took off on her bicycle. She headed for her usual place, the truck stop cafe across the highway. Lots of times when she didn't feel like going home she'd linger at the cafe, just to sit and think in peace, while the cars droned past outside. The waitresses didn't appreciate her, but there wasn't much they could do except give her dirty looks. That day she had just enough change for a cup of coffee.

She was sitting there enjoying the warmth and dryness of the cafe when suddenly they came through the door, laughing and shouting so loudly that everyone turned to stare. That was Janis's first glimpse of Kelp, a band with no place to go but up.

She ran away from home to join the band, and they changed her name, from Janis Finch to just plain Finch. Dressed in a black ninja suit with her hair cut short and spiky, she was the perfect lead singer. But being a member of a band was much harder than Finch had ever imagined—even when she hit the top of the charts.

—Susan Dunn

Checking on the Moon
By Jenny Davis
(SLJ/C 1991)

I never expected to be spending the summer waitressing at a diner called EATS in the Pennsylvania coal country. I thought I'd be chatting with my friends at the pool in Blue Cloud, Texas, where I live. Or used to live, anyway.

It all began when my mother went to a reception for a famous concert pianist. Six weeks later, to the day, my mom and Jacob (the concert pianist) were married. (And she tells *me* not to be impulsive!) And now she's off touring Europe with him while my older brother Bill and I are stuck in Washco, Pennsylvania, at our grandmother's. I'm glad Mom's happy, and I even like Jacob, but I worry a lot about where I'm going to be living next year. I just can't see an internationally-known concert pianist settling down in Blue Cloud, Texas. But as long as Bill's around, I try not to let it get to me. Bill is the one person in my life I can always count on, who'll always be there for me.

So for now I'm living in Washco, which I have to admit is an OK place to be. I get along with my grandmother pretty well, and I've made at least one good friend. Even Bill seems to be feeling happier, now that he's found Jessica, who's just the right combination of pretty and nice for my favorite brother's girlfriend. The only bad thing is the crime— there's an awful lot of crime around here. The other night Mr. Johansson, who runs the shoe-repair shop, was mugged and beaten up. All my grandmother's friends are afraid they'll be next, but no one knows what to do. I just try not to think about it.

But now I have to. Because now it has happened to someone I really care about. Late last night the phone rang, and Bill got up to answer it. I heard him talking, and then his voice went all wrong. When he slammed down the receiver he moaned—a moan of anguish that I'd never heard before. I asked him what was wrong, and when he answered, his voice was hard, not like the voice of my brother Bill at all: Jessica had been raped.

—*Mary Fellows*

Children of the River
By Linda Crew
(Golden Kite Honor 1990, IRA 1990)

When the Khmer Rouge Army took over Cambodia in 1975, Sundara fled with her aunt's family to the United States. Now, four years later, Sundara is still trying to fit in at her new high school. Her aunt insists on following Cambodian ways, no matter how out-of-place they may seem here in Oregon, but Sundara is beginning to wonder whether it's possible to honor her family's traditions and become an American at the same time. She keeps getting caught in the middle, squeezed between the two cultures. In Cambodia, for example, all marriages are arranged by parents. There's no such thing as dating, and an unmarried girl is never supposed to be alone with a boy. But here in America, Jonathan McKinnon, star of the high school football team, insists on having lunch with Sundara and dropping by her house unexpectedly. Sundara loves spending time with Jonathan, but she can't seem to make him understand the customs her aunt adheres to. Her aunt doesn't want Sundara to so much as glance at a "whiteskin." And she's threatened to throw her out on the street if she "shames the family" again.

Can Sundara manage to be both Cambodian and American at the same time? Or will she and Jonathan have to keep their love a secret, even from each other?

—*Dara Finkelstein*

Chrysanthemum
By Kevin Henkes
(Notables 1991, SLJ/C 1991)

When she was born, her parents thought she was perfect, so they gave her a special name: Chrysanthemum. Chrysanthemum loved her name, until she started school. Then she discovered that all the other kids had names like Sue, Bill, Sam, and Rita, and they laughed when Mrs. Chud came to "Chrysanthemum!" in roll-call; in fact, the whole class spent the rest of the day giggling about Chrysanthemum's name. Her parents did their best to comfort her that night, but when Chrysanthemum went to school the next day, the same thing happened: everybody laughed at her name.

And it kept happening until Miss Twinkle arrived to teach music. All the kids loved Miss Twinkle, and guess what? She said that her name was Delphinium, and that "Chrysanthemum" was one of the names she had picked out for her new baby! Suddenly all the girls in the class wanted to be called after flowers too, and Chrysanthemum decided that her name was perfect.

—*Deb Kelly*

Class Dismissed II: More High School Poems
By Mel Glenn
(Christopher 1986, SLJ/C 1986)

Here's what Carolyn Warren has to say:

In class I often
Play my Walkman,
Polish my nails,
Scribble a few notes,

Talk to a friend,
Read Teen Romance,
Put on my makeup,
Drink my soda,
Munch on some chips,
Doodle in my notebook,
Plan my weekend.
I pass all my tests.
My teachers can't understand it,
But I do.
You just have to have something to do
While you're getting an education.

Sound familiar? Well, there's more—for instance, Craig Blanchard's story:

Because I had failing grades in history,
Because my father threatened loss of limb and other minor
inconveniences,
Because my teacher thought I had the intelligence of an ad-
vanced flea,
I stayed in my room and in the library,
And worked on this fantastic paper on
The Great Depression and the New Deal.
I felt in sympathy with Roosevelt
As he tried to put the country back together,
As I was trying to put my life back together.
When I turned in the paper I felt proud of myself.
When I got it back, I felt crushed.
My history teacher had written,
"I don't think you did this by yourself. It's too good."
The Depression isn't historical, it's personal.

If you've ever felt alone, read on. Listen while kids in high school talk about their lives and how they feel about themselves, their friends, their families, and their school. Find yourself in one of these poems, which express just about everything you could experience while living through high school.

—Susan Trimby

Come Sing, Jimmy Jo
By Katherine Paterson
(Notables 1985, SLJ/C 1985)

My name's Jimmy Jo Johnson, and I'm eleven years old. Actually, my name isn't really Jimmy Jo, it's James. Jimmy Jo is just what I go by on stage, because my mother says that your average country music fan can't warm up to a name like James. I didn't like having to change my name, but then I don't like a lot of the other things that have happened lately either.

It began on the night the Family came home from their latest tour—the Family being my mother, Olive; my father, Jerry Lee; my uncle Earl; and my grandpa. Up till then, I'd always stayed behind with Grandma when the Family took their singing act on the road, and as far as I knew, I'd be living on the farm with Grandma forever. But everything changed that night, when Eddie Switten heard me sing. He was going to be the Family's new manager and get them a spot on Countrytime TV. Once he heard me sing, he insisted that I join the act. I didn't want to, and I don't think my mother wanted me to either, but Eddie said it was either that or no deal.

So we packed up and moved, all except Grandma, and now we're living here in Tidewater, far away from Grandma and the farm. I miss her a lot. Oh, I like the singing well enough, and now that I'm used to the crowds, I even kind of enjoy the audiences, but I hate the school I go to, and there's this scary man who's been following me around in a rusty black pickup.

Some days I wish we'd never left the farm—like yesterday, when we tried to call Grandma and couldn't get an answer. We tried all evening, every half hour, until finally my father said he'd drive out there and make sure she was all right. I could hardly sit through school today, not knowing whether Grandma was alive or dead. At the end of the day I got a note saying my father wanted me to meet him in Anna's Chicken House after school. But when I walked in, it wasn't my father who was waiting for me there. It was the man from the black pickup truck.

—Mary Fellows

Come to the Edge
By Julia Cunningham
(Christopher 1978)

Life had found a way to sap the soul out of Gravel. His youngest years were a blur, a series of nights spent worrying about Father and days spent looking for him. But Father always turned up, usually in some gutter; they were never separated for long.

So even at the foster farm, Gravel waited longingly for those special Saturdays when his father wandered in for a visit. Gravel understood that his father needed to be free to build a new life for the two of them. That was why he'd left Gravel at the foster farm.

Then one day it all came tumbling down. Gravel's best friend, Slim, disappeared from the farm. He'd probably been placed with a real family, which would be good, but all Gravel could see was that he'd been left behind—again. He was so angry he did something unforgiveable: he attacked the principal. And then, when it seemed that things couldn't get any worse, his father came—and abandoned him to the farm's version of justice. "He would be like a stone around my neck," his father said. "The fact is, I don't want him." The words struck Gravel like bullets. As soon as the numbness wore off, he fled.

If you're wondering what could be out there for a fourteen-year-old boy who feels like "nothing," come to the edge.

—Bernice D. Crouse

The Cookcamp
By Gary Paulsen
(SLJ/C 1991)

The boy is only five years old. His father is away at war. Then Uncle Casey moves in. The boy doesn't really like him, so his mother sends the boy away. She pins a note to his jacket and puts him all by himself on a train to Canada, where his grandmother lives.

There are nine men there, as big as the trees they're clearing to build a road in the wilderness. His grandmother is their cook. There is the cooking, the big men and their trucks, and always, the loneliness of missing his mother.

—Cecilia Swanson

Cracker Jackson
By Betsy Byars
(Notables 1985, SLJ/C 1985)

How do you help someone who's being abused? That's Cracker's problem. He's already promised Alma, who used to babysit for him when he was a kid, that he won't mention her bruises or her fears to his mom, so now there's no one he can ask for advice.

When Alma's husband hurts her baby too, Alma gathers up the courage to leave him and go to a shelter for battered women. But halfway there, she makes Cracker turn around and go back.

And it doesn't end there. It never does.

Alma used to take care of Cracker. He was the baby, and she was the babysitter. Now he has to grow up fast.

—*Carol Kappelmann*

Crutches
By Peter Hartling
(Batchelder 1989, Notables 1989)

In the confusion among the mass of refugees, Thomas lost sight of his mother. The war was over now, the war that had killed his father and left Thomas and his mother seeking a place that would offer them food, shelter, and safety. They had agreed that, if they somehow became separated, they would meet in Vienna at Aunt Wanda's home. Thomas made it to Vienna, but at Aunt Wanda's address he found only the bombed-out shell of a building. No one seemed to have any idea what had happened to the people who had lived there. Thomas found his way to a shelter where he was able to sleep and get some food. He was afraid to stay there long—the Russian authorities were known to seize unaccompanied children—but he had to remain in the neighborhood so his mother would be able to find him.

Then Thomas saw a man who looked as if he knew how to survive. He had only one leg, yet he seemed to know where to find food and which people to hide from. Thomas began following him and copying what he did. When the man noticed, he told Thomas to go away, but Thomas suspected that he wasn't as gruff as he sounded. And Thomas was right: eventually the man offered him some food and listened to his story. They became a pair, struggling to survive. Thomas called his friend "Crutches." Together they searched for Thomas's mother in the brutal aftermath of war.

—*Helen Schlichting*

The Cuckoo Sister
By Vivien Alcock
(Notables 1986, SLJ/C 1986)

The doorbell rang and there she stood: the girl who would change Kate Seton's life forever. Who was she? The note claimed that she was Kate's long-lost sister Emma, who had been stolen from the carriage when she was only a baby. The note seemed to be from the woman who had snatched the baby away and now, years later, had sent her home again. But Kate didn't really believe it. *Her* sister wouldn't have spiked hair, heavy makeup, and flashy clothes. Kate had always dreamed that one day Emma would return, but this was *not* the Emma she had imagined.

Street-talking Rosie couldn't see herself as Emma either, but when her mother dumped her on the Setons' doorstep and fled, she didn't dare tell anyone the truth. Or what she thought was the truth.

Is Rosie Emma, come home after many years, or is she the cuckoo in the nest—the imposter who will push out the true fledgling?

—Mary Cosper

The Cybil War
By Betsy Byars
(Notables 1981)

Tony was Simon's best friend . . . sort of. He acted like a friend, but then somehow things would get twisted around and Simon would feel as if he'd been stabbed in the back. Like when Tony told Harriet that Simon had said Cybil's legs were like double popsicle sticks. Deep down, Simon thought Cybil was the most wonderful person on the whole earth. How could Tony say something like that and blame it on Simon?

Tony thought it was just a big joke. Anything for a laugh! But Simon wasn't laughing, and the day finally came when he realized that some changes would have to be made. He couldn't let Tony maneuver him into these embarrassing situations any longer. No friendship was worth it.

—Carol Kappelmann

Dakota Dugout
By Ann Turner
(Notables 1985)

Grandmother remembers how she first came to the Dakota Territory and how she cried when she saw what was to be her home—a sod house built into the side of a hill. The windows were made of greased paper, and the sun could barely filter through. Dirt often fell from the ceiling and so did bugs—and even snakes! It didn't seem like a home at all.

But sometimes, Grandmother says, when we think back to the days when we struggled just to put food on the table, we realize that those were probably the best times of our lives.

—*Carol Kappelmann*

Daphne's Book
By Mary Downing Hahn
(SLJ/C 1983)

Why, oh why had our English teacher chosen me to be Daphne's partner in the seventh-grade Write-a-Book Contest? He said it was because I was the best writer and she was the best artist, but it didn't seem fair! She was so strange! I mean, not only did she dress differently from the rest of us, she never smiled and she hardly even talked! OK, so maybe it was all the teasing she got, what with the other kids calling her Daffy Duck instead of Daphne, but I was afraid that next they'd start teasing me!

In fact, I'm still afraid, but not for myself any more. Just for Daphne and her little sister, Hope. You see, once I started to work with her, I discovered what a wonderful person Daphne is and how much we have in common. And more important, I've found out the terrible reason why she never smiles. Now I want more than anything to help her, but Daphne made me promise not to say a word to anyone, even though things are getting worse instead of better! Daphne will hate me if I let my mother know what's going on in her home, but I'll hate myself forever if I don't get someone to help! Would somebody please tell me what to do?!

—*Sister M. Anna Falbo, CSSF*

The Dark Is Rising
By Susan Cooper
(BGHG 1973, Newbery Honor 1974)

Strange things were happening to Will Stanton on the eve of his eleventh birthday. The radio, which had always worked fine, began to emit loud static whenever he stood near it. The rabbits, when he fed them, were jittery, and they cringed at his touch. As he walked over to Dawson's farm to fetch more hay, he noticed how the rooks were flying to and fro, agitated, instead of roosting in the trees. At the farm, Farmer Dawson had a warning for Will: "The Walker is abroad. And this night will be bad and tomorrow will be beyond imagining." Then he gave Will a gift—a flat circle made of iron, quartered by two crossed lines. Will felt a growing alarm.

That night in his attic bedroom, with snow falling thick and fast outside, Will looked again at the gift from Farmer Dawson. It was cold to the touch, so cold it numbed his fingertips. Suddenly and without warning, he was so frightened he could hardly breathe. He could hear Farmer Dawson's warning: "This night will be bad and tomorrow will be beyond imagining."

Will Stanton is the seventh son of a seventh son, and he is the last of the Old Ones. The Old Ones have been fighting the powers of The Dark from time immemorial. With his eleventh birthday, Will has come into his powers as an Old One. He will be joining the fight against evil. His first task will be to collect the six signs—circles quartered by two crossed lines. He already has one—there are only five to go. But he must find them all, or else The Dark will triumph.

—*Linda Olson*

The Day That Elvis Came to Town
By Jan Marino
(SLJ/C 1991)

Wanda's life has been turned upside down. She's had to give up her beloved attic bedroom to her crosspatch aunt, her best friend has gone away for the entire summer, and now her mother's expecting a baby, which means that Wanda will have more work to do. She tries as best she can to help her mother—she takes her father his lunch and even walks him home in the evening, so he won't be sidetracked by alcohol. But sometimes Wanda thinks her mother will drive her crazy: "When she wants me to do something, she treats me like I'm forty years old, but when she doesn't want me to do something, she tells me I'll be able to do that when I'm grown up."

Wanda's mother takes in boarders for extra money, and the latest one is Mercedes Washington, a glamorous singer who has a temporary gig in Savannah. Wanda loves to talk to Mercedes and listen to her stories about the music world. One day Mercedes mentions that she knew Elvis Presley, *the* Elvis Presley, back in high school! So when Elvis is scheduled for a concert in the city, Wanda writes to him, sure that he will remember Mercedes and send some free tickets. But Elvis doesn't send tickets; he doesn't even write back, and then Mercedes admits that she hardly knew him.

Wanda's angry—all her plans have gone up in smoke! What else is she going to discover, when Elvis comes to town?

—Deb Kelly

Days of Terror
By Barbara Claassen Smucker
(Canadian Governor General's 1980)

Peter and his family are Mennonites living in Russia in 1917. They are members of a farming community, and their life is good. They have plentiful harvests, close ties to friends and relations, and strong religious beliefs—everything they need for happiness . . . .

Until the Revolution starts, bringing with it chaos in the government, civil war, and ultimately starvation. The Mennonites are labeled enemies of the new state, and soldiers are sent to take everything from their farms. Some houses are burned, and some of Peter's friends are killed trying to save their homes and their livestock. Those who aren't killed are going to be very hungry.

Peter's family have no chance in Russia any more. Their only hope is to emigrate. They can try to escape to Canada, but it's a desperate move. They must leave everything they've ever known—their farm, their friends, even Grandfather—and take to the road. There is terror everywhere, and unforeseen dangers lie ahead. The sacrifices they must make will eat away at their confidence and their ability to keep going. Peter only hopes he will be strong enough to survive.

—Colleen Stinson

Dealing with Dragons
By Patricia Wrede
(SLJ/C 1990)

Princess Cimorene is bored and unhappy. She is the youngest of the seven daughters of the king of Linderwall. Her six older sisters are your basic generic princesses, dainty maidens with long golden hair and sweet dispositions. Cimorene is tall as a maypole, dark-haired, and as for her disposition—well, you *could* describe her as "strong-willed," but what you would really mean is "stubborn as a pig."

When Cimorene gets tired of regular princess lessons, she has the castle armsmaster give her fencing lessons. When her parents make her stop, she has the court magician give her magic lessons. Her parents stop that, too. Also Latin lessons, cooking lessons, and juggling lessons.

What do her parents want? Apparently they want her to marry the dull Prince Therandil, and that is absolutely the last straw! Cimorene decides that the only thing to do is to go and get herself captured by a dragon. After all, being a dragon's princess is a perfectly respectable occupation, so her parents can't complain, and it has to be more interesting than embroidery lessons or learning how to curtsey to ambassadors.

So Cimorene, following the advice of a helpful frog, sets off to find a more exciting life. She finds much more excitement than she bargained for, once she starts dealing with dragons.

—Sarah Flowers

Dear Bill, Remember Me? and Other Stories
By Norma Fox Mazer
(Christopher 1977)

Chrissy is mad for homemade chocolate pudding. She has a drunken father and uncle to deal with, but chocolate pudding makes up for it all.

Unlike Chrissy, Zoe's been over-protected. But one day, walking through the park, she meets Peter, a young man who will come to mean more to her and teach her more than the three supportive women with whom she lives.

Jessie, forced to keep a journal for several months as a school project, starts dating her first boyfriend, and all her roller-coaster emotions are expressed in her journal entries. And Kathy has just learned that her older sister's former boyfriend, on whom she once had a crush, is getting married. She tries to find just the right words to write him a letter: "Dear Bill, Remember me?"

And these are only four of the girls you will meet here—young women struggling to deal with all kinds of problems in their lives.

—*Colleen Stinson*

Dear Mr. Henshaw
By Beverly Cleary
(Newbery 1984, Notables 1983, SLJ/C 1983)

Mr. Henshaw is an author. He wrote a book called *Ways to Amuse a Dog*. Leigh's second-grade class read that book, and Leigh wrote to Mr. Henshaw to tell him how much he liked it, but he never got an answer. The next year, when Leigh was in third grade, he read *Ways to Amuse a Dog* again, all by himself this time, and he wrote to Mr. Henshaw again. This time he got a printed form-letter back.

In fourth grade Leigh made a diorama of *Ways to Amuse a Dog* and wrote to Mr. Henshaw again. In fifth grade he did a report on the book and wrote to Mr. Henshaw to tell him about it. This time Mr. Henshaw answered! He suggested Leigh read another book he had written. Leigh chose *Moose on Toast*, which was almost as good as *Ways to Amuse a Dog*.

Now Leigh is in sixth grade, and he has to write an author report. Naturally he chooses Mr. Henshaw, and writes him a letter with questions he needs answered for his report. What Leigh doesn't expect is that Mr. Henshaw will send back a list of questions of his own. Leigh doesn't want to answer Mr. Henshaw's questions, but his mom finds the letter and tells him he has to. So Leigh keeps writing letters to Mr. Henshaw. Sometimes Mr. Henshaw writes back, and Leigh discovers that he knows a lot more than just how to write good books.

—*Colleen Stinson*

The December Rose
By Leon Garfield
(SLJ/C 1987)

Climbing and clinging and soot—that was just about all he'd ever known. He'd started off as an orphan and then been apprenticed as a chimney sweep. Luckily for him, he had talent—as a climber, that is. Why, he could hold on to anything! In fact, that was how he got named Barnacle, for his amazing power to cling.

Oh, it wasn't an easy life, being a chimney sweep. Filthy black he was, day and night, from all that soot. And he wasn't allowed much to eat, either, for fear he'd grow fat and get stuck inside a chimney.

But sweeping out chimneys had its advantages, sometimes. He could eavesdrop on the conversations in the rooms below. He sure heard some interesting talk—so interesting that one day, trying to hear better, he leaned a little too far over and the next thing he knew he was falling, falling down the chimney, smack dab into the middle of a room full of conspirators. Well, of course poor Barnacle was terrified. So he ran (not a bad idea, considering). But then he made a mistake: in his panic, he grabbed a beautiful silver locket, a little bit of jewelry that meant all the world to the conspirators. Poor Barnacle! For now he was running for his life!

—Sister M. Anna Falbo, CSSF

Deep Wizardry
By Diane Duane
(SLJ/C 1985)

Nita and Kit became wizards when they were twelve. They had passed their first ordeal and were expecting to enjoy a quiet vacation at the shore, but there they met a dolphin who took them to S'reee, a wounded whale wizard. Suddenly they were involved in the Twelvesong, an ancient ceremony enacted by sharks and whale wizards to defeat the Lone Power and slow the death of the universe. To join in the Twelvesong, Nita and Kit became whales—and prepared for the ultimate sacrifice.

—Melanie L. Witulski

The Devil's Arithmetic
By Jane Yolen
(National Jewish 1989)

Hannah was tired of remembering. It seemed that on any Jewish holiday, and especially now at Passover time, all she ever had to do was remember things. Remember the family histories, remember the right answers in all the ceremonies, remember the Holocaust, and on and on.

That Passover evening, Hannah stepped through a doorway in her apartment that somehow took her back to Poland in the 1940s, where she was transformed into a girl named Chaya.

The longer she remained in the past, the more her memory of her present life faded. Because when Hannah walked through that doorway, she found herself starting down a path that stretched far into the past, to the gas chambers of a Nazi death camp.

—Jeff Blair

Devil's Donkey
By Bill Brittain
(Notables 1981, SLJ/C 1981)

When Dan'l Pitt came to live with me in my quarters above the Coven Tree General store, I had no idea what lay ahead for all of us. Dan'l was only nine. His widowed ma had just died, and I was his only living relative, me bein' a third cousin or so.

Well, Dan'l was a good lad and a good help in the store, but a bit headstrong when it came to buckin' tradition and listenin' to advice. There's things goin' on in Coven Tree that a person needs be aware of, things you can do and things you'd best leave alone.

There's a sayin' here in town, "Who sheds his blood by Coven Tree, under old Magda's spell will be."

And so when Dan'l cut branches from the old Coven Tree that stands at the crossroads and in so doin' cut his leg, he let loose powers that were beyond belief. I had tried to warn him, but he wouldn't listen.

Now we were both caught in old Magda's spell, and the Devil was about to demand his due. It would take all our cunning and then some, to outwit old Magda and break the spell.

How were we going to do it?

—*Carol Kappelmann*

The Diamond Tree: Jewish Tales from Around the World
Selected and retold by Howard Schwartz and Barbara Rush
(Notables 1991)

Diamonds don't grow on trees! But a poor man named Nissim finds a tree with very special jewels sparkling on its branches.

You probably already know the story of Noah and and the Ark. But have you heard about the giant who hitched a ride on the roof, or how Noah managed to feed his huge and hungry friend?

Have you ever seen a hoopoe? It's a striking bird with a colorful crest, and it can be wiser than Solomon himself.

Learn with Rabbi Hanina that honesty can be well rewarded, and see what happens when the foolish villagers of Chelm try to stay cool.

These are only a few of the strange and funny people you'll meet in these stories from all over the world.

—*Donna L. Scanlon*

Dicey's Song
By Cynthia Voigt
(BGHB 1983, Newbery 1983, Notables 1982)

You never knew where a road would end; you just knew that roads ended. The Tillerman's road had ended at Gram's house. So they were going to make a home with Gram. Home: a home with plenty of room for the four children in the shabby farmhouse, room inside, room outside, and room within Gram's heart too—the kind of room for love to grow that they really needed. That was one of the lessons the long journey had taught Dicey—how to figure out what they needed. That long summer's journey stretched behind them now. They'd made it through; they'd made it home. Dicey still felt a responsibility to worry about and watch over the three younger children. But she now wanted to be just a little selfish too. She found an old sailboat in the barn that she began to fix up. The boat was her lucky charm, her rabbit's foot, her horseshoe, her pot of gold; it was the prize she'd given herself for leading them from nowhere to somewhere. But Dicey couldn't help but worry about the little money they had; there were so many of them to feed. Dicey felt she must get a job to help out. She knew big troubles have little beginnings. She tried to reach out, to tell Gram to let her take over the responsibility, but it wasn't until Dicey learned that you can't reach out with closed fists that she was able to let go of the past and to build a future.

—Judy Druse

Dinosaur Mountain: Graveyard of the Past
By Caroline Arnold
(Notables 1989)

Curious about dinosaurs? What do the names Tyrannosaurus, Stegosaurus, and Apatosaurus bring to mind? Here is a book about the different species that once roamed North America, and the best place to see their fossil remains just as they are being uncovered—at Dinosaur National Monument in Utah.

Author Caroline Arnold takes you on a trip through time as she describes the important discoveries made at this site, beginning with the excavation in 1909 of the most complete Apatosaurus skeleton ever found. How did these creatures live? Why did they suddenly die out? What other, smaller animals lived at the same time? What plants? At Dinosaur National Monument, scientists continue to uncover answers—and also more questions.

You can observe these scientists at work. Imagine yourself in a visitors' center, where an entire side of the building is nothing but dinosaur fossils, still embedded in rock, still being carefully excavated as you watch. If you are curious about dinosaurs and how their skeletons are discovered and uncovered, *Dinosaur Mountain* can show you all about it.

—*Susan Perdaris*

Dixie Storms
By Barbara Hall
(Notables 1990, SLJ/C 1990)

Tobacco farming in Virginia demands ideal conditions, if the crop is going to flourish. And the summer Dutch Peyton was fourteen, conditions were anything but. Already the precious leaves were curling up from a lack of rain, and the males of the Peyton family seemed to be going a little crazy. Dutch's nine-year-old nephew was growing wilder every day, her older brother was turning sulky and mean-mouthed, and her father could think of nothing but the failing crop. They were all in need of something to perk them up, when Norma arrived.

Dutch had never met Norma before because of a feud between their fathers, and she'd always wondered what her city cousin was like. Although Norma was about her age, she seemed older and much more sophisticated. She had all kinds of advice to give Dutch about living, loving, and the pursuit of happiness.

As the brutally hot days dragged on without relief, Dutch learned the real reason for Norma's summer visit—a deep, dark family secret that threatened to burst upon them like a powerful Dixie storm.

—*Sue Padilla*

Dogsong
By Gary Paulsen
(Newbery Honor 1986, Notables 1985, SLJ/C 1985)

Russel climbed out from under the ledge. The storm had passed, and the wind was dying down. Steam rose from vents in the snow that covered the dogs. Russel pulled them out, righted the sled, and started home. The dogs ran for about thirty yards, then slowed to a walk and stopped. Russel made them go on. A man must run the dogs. The dogs tried to turn, but Russel forced them ahead. Twice more they veered to the right, but Russel controlled them until they followed his commands. They ran then several hours, but the lights of the village never appeared. He stopped the dogs to look around and found he had pushed them the wrong way. The huge ice-plate had moved, and the directions were changed. They were out on the ice, and they were lost!

—Cecilia Swanson

The Door in the Wall: A Story of Medieval London
By Marguerite De Angeli
(Newbery 1950)

Robin thinks his life is all set. His father has ridden off with the king's men to fight the Scots in the north, his mother has gone to be a lady-in-waiting to the queen, and Robin is going to live at the manor of Sir Peter, where he will serve as page. If he does well, in a few years he will become a squire and then a knight, and then he too can fight for the king.

But when Robin wakes up on the morning he is to leave, he cannot move his legs. After a month in bed he still cannot move. All around him servants and neighbors have begun dying of the plague, until finally no one comes, no matter how loudly Robin calls. He is alone. Everyone else has died or run away.

Then . . . he hears footsteps, and he is rescued by Brother Luke, who takes him to the hospice of St. Mark's. There Brother Luke nurses Robin back to health and teaches him how to strengthen his arms, since his legs are still useless. He also teaches Robin to read and to carve wood. But most important of all, Brother Luke tells Robin that any time you come up against a wall, you only have to follow it along far enough and eventually you will find a door.

Robin has no idea what that means. But as time goes on, he learns that his life is not as limited as he thought, that being a page or a soldier is not the only way to serve his king, and that you have only to keep looking to find the door in the wall.

—Sarah Flowers

Dragon of the Lost Sea
By Laurence Yep
(Notables 1982)

It was strong magic, old magic, and it carried a faint scent of the sea. It seemed to be coming from a nearby village, so the old lady stepped off the main road onto a path which led to the village.

Upon entering the village she saw a sedan chair surrounded by four creatures who looked like men. Near the inn's doorway was a guard with a cutlass. All reeked of the magic that had created them. It was Civet, the great enemy of Shimmer's clan, she who had stolen their entire sea and put it into an object the size of a pebble.

Shimmer went to the well where Thorn, the servant boy, was drawing water. He was being teased by the villagers for saying he had seen the Unicorn. When their teasing shifted to the beggar lady, he defended her by throwing water at them. He was hauled off to the inn to be beaten, but Shimmer filled his water bucket and took it after him. The boy Thorn fed her in return and asked her to stay the night at the inn.

Civet sent her guard to kill Thorn that night. As Shimmer wrestled with the creature, she suddenly found herself holding empty air while a paper cut-out of the guard drifted to the floor. The sedan chair and porters were also paper cut-outs.

Follow Shimmer and Thorn as they strive to recover the lost sea from the powerful magic of their enemy.

—*Eileen Gieswein*

The Duplicate
By William Sleator
(Notables 1988, SLJ/C 1988)

What would you do if there were two of you? Send the other you to school, then stay home and watch TV all day? Let the other you do homework while you play basketball? Sounds great, doesn't it.

That's what David thought, too, when he saw a second seagull mysteriously appear as the first touched a strange machine David had found on the beach. Then the machine worked a second time with David's fish. Now he was sure he had found the way out of his latest jam. He could make a duplicate of himself, send that other David to visit Grandma, and still keep his date with Angela, wonderful Angela, who had filled his dreams for weeks.

But having a double was more of a problem than David had expected. How do two Davids live in the house without Mom or Dad noticing something? What about clothes? (two Davids wear twice as much). Which David gets to eat meals at the dinner table? What happens when one does something the other doesn't know about? And most worrying of all, how does David get rid of the other David when he wants to be just his single self again?

—*Colleen Stinson*

Enchantress from the Stars
By Sylvia Louise Engdahl
(Newbery Honor 1971)

Elana was a young and naive member of the Federation, studying to become a field agent for the Anthropological Service. She should have been on the starship studying for her exams, but she didn't want to miss this chance to participate in a real mission, to save a world from invasion. So when her father and Evrek were sent to Andrecia on a dangerous mission, Elana stowed away on the landing craft. "Are you crazy, Elana?" demanded Evrek when they found her. "Did you think we were going on a picnic or something?" But Andrecia was such a beautiful, peaceful-looking planet that Elana didn't believe any serious danger could be lurking there.

Evrek and her father couldn't spend valuable time protecting her, so Elana was sworn into service. Her father even thought up a role she could play in the mission. Soon she was involved up to her eyebrows, and way beyond her limited training and experience.

Georyn saw the strange young woman as an enchantress. She was beautiful and tall. Her glowing face and silvery-green garments were like nothing he had ever seen on Andrecia. Elana also possessed powers Georyn couldn't begin to fathom—strange powers that she was not yet fully trained to use. Her father's new plan was for her to portray an enchantress and convey a small amount of her psychic ability to Georyn. Luckily, her father, as leader of the landing party, was on hand to provide lots of support and advice. But all too soon, Elana was forced to depend on her own wits and powers for survival. One misstep could mean the destruction of an entire civilization.

—Bernice D. Crouse

Eva
By Peter Dickinson
(BGHB 1989, Notables 1989, SLJ/C 1989)

Eva closes one eye. Now she can't see that blur of nose down in the corner. She holds her mother's hand—and feels that her own hand is suddenly too large, and her thumb all wrong. Her mother's voice sounds strained. Eva can hardly move, but she knows she has been in an accident. And she knows they're keeping something from her. She must be horribly disfigured, she thinks.

But when they finally give her a mirror, it's beyond imagination. Although she knows she's a girl named Eva, the face in the mirror belongs to a young female chimpanzee named Kelly.

While Eva's mangled body lay in an irreversible coma, her memory was transferred to the brain of Kelly, a chimp from the research pool where Eva's father works. This radical experiment is Eva's only chance. And the scientists are hopeful. If anyone can survive the shock of waking up in a different body, it will be Eva, for she has always lived around chimps and knows them better than most kids know their best friends.

Once the story gets out, Eva becomes a media icon: adored, hounded, marketed; set apart from everyone else. She knows that the only way to keep her sanity is to accept who she is: a chimp, but a chimp with human understanding and memory. She carries in her mind the ghost of her human body—the rhythms of walking, of riding a bike, of reaching overhead—but her new body is weighted differently and the proportions are changed, so that she has to relearn every action.

She also carries the ghost of a chimpanzee's mind. Although Kelly's memories were submerged by the flood of human intelligence, part of Kelly is still there, at the edge of Eva's consciousness: Kelly's instincts, Kelly's dreams of a green jungle patched with sunlight, and of a body swinging easily through the branches.

More and more, Eva finds herself drawn to the research chimps. Will she have to choose between animals and humans, or can she somehow live in both worlds? Can Eva's intelligence make Kelly's dream come true?

—Sarah Flowers

Everywhere
By Bruce Brooks
(Golden Kite Honor 1991, Notables 1990, SLJ/C 1990)

How far would you go to keep your grandfather alive?

This boy's grandfather had just had a heart attack. The town nurse arrived, talking about Grandfather as though he weren't there anymore. When her nephew, Dooley, emerged from behind his aunt's back, Grandmother told the boy to take Dooley outside and play. The boy didn't feel like playing with anyone—he wanted to stay close to his grandfather, in case anything happened—but he did what Grandmother said.

Dooley wasted no time in announcing that the old man would die, surely die—unless they could save him with something called a "soul switch." The boy had never heard of such a thing and wasn't sure they should try it, but Dooley was older and seemed to know what he was talking about. It sounded strange and scary, but wasn't it worth trying, to keep his grandfather alive?

The boy learned a lot that day, not only about "soul switching" but also about himself and the special love he had for his grandfather.

—*Judy McElwain*

Exploring the *Titanic*
By Robert D. Ballard
(SLJ/C 1988)

Fourteen years before the *Titanic* sank, even before it had been built, a writer named Morgan Robertson published a story called "The Wreck of the *Titan*." In his story, the passenger ship *Titan* sails from England for New York. Halfway across the Atlantic, it hits an iceberg. Although labeled "unsinkable," the *Titan* sinks very quickly, and most of its passengers go down with the ship because there aren't enough lifeboats to save them. Eerily, this story foretold what would happen to a real ship, the *Titanic*, fourteen years later.

"Titanic" means huge and giant-like, and that's what the *Titanic* was—one of the biggest passenger ships of all time. It was as long as three football fields, and its nine decks reached the height of an eleven-story building. And it too was supposed to be unsinkable. When the *Titanic* left Southampton, England, on April 10, 1912, for its first voyage across the Atlantic, it was carrying 2,200 people, passengers and crew, and not nearly enough lifeboats to hold them all. Toward midnight on the fourth day of the voyage, an iceberg loomed up, dead ahead. The *Titanic* swerved to avoid a direct collision but scraped against the ice anyway, with enough force to rip through the ship's hull. Cold sea water began to pour in. At 12:30 a.m., the captain gave orders to load the lifeboats, women and children first. The crew had had little practice in this maneuver, so the first boats to be lowered into the sea were less than half full. Crowds of people remained on deck. By 1:30, enough water had poured into the forward compartments of the ship to cause a noticeable slant. Shortly after 2:00 a.m., the passengers on deck heard muffled explosions from deep within the hold. Then the great ship slowly upended itself and slipped beneath the water. The unsinkable had sunk, with 1,500 people still on board.

In July of 1986, Robert Ballard and two members of his team descended two and a half miles to the ocean floor in their tiny submarine. One year earlier they had located the wreck of the *Titanic*. Now they wanted to explore the sunken liner at close range. As they shone their lights on the rusted wreck of the lost ship, the events of that night seventy-four years earlier seemed to come alive once again.

—*Linda Olson*

The Facts and Fictions of Minna Pratt
By Patricia MacLachlan
(Notables 1988)

Minna looks out the bus window and thinks about her life. Her present life. Right now she likes artichokes and blue fingernail polish, and Mozart played too fast. She loves baseball and the month of March (no one else much likes March) and every shade of brown she's ever seen. But this is only her present existence. Someday, she knows, she will have another like, a different one, a better one. McGrew knows this too. McGrew is ten years old. He knows nearly everything. He knows, for instance, that his big sister, eleven-year-old Minna, is sitting patiently next to her cello waiting to become a woman.

That day at practice, Minna meets Lucas. She watches Lucas's long fingers curl around his viola, one leg stretched out, one slid back to hook over a chair rung. Minna doesn't fall in love quickly. Most often she eases into love as she eases into a Bach cello suite, slowly and carefully, frowning all the while. "You have," she begins, and clears her throat, "you have a wonderful vibrato." "I learned it at music camp," he says solemnly. Then Lucas reaches into his jacket pocket and pulls out a frog! "I saved him from Biology lab," he explains. "I'm going to put him in the park pond . . . want to come?"   —*Deb Kelly*

Fallen Angels
By Walter Dean Myers
(King 1989)

Dear Mama,

I saw a man die today. We went out on patrol, looking for Viet Cong. We were on our way back to camp. The sergeant had a map, 'cause the enemy plants mines and booby traps all around the camp. We were only a hundred yards from camp, and I think I heard the noise, but I'm not sure. All of a sudden, Jenkins was on the ground, screaming and bleeding from a big piece of metal sticking out of his chest. A Cong had put a booby trap on the path. I never saw a dead person before, except Grandma at her funeral. I was prepared for that.

I won't mail this letter Mama. I don't want you to worry about me, but I hate it here. I want to go home. I don't want to see anyone else die.

Love,
Perry

Note: To present this, open the letter and read it; then tear it up at the end.

—*Cecilia Swanson*

A Family Project
By Sarah Ellis
(Notables 1988)

The Baby Project—to Jessica and Margaret, this sounded like the perfect title for their animal reseach assignment. They would study the human animal and learn all about the baby that Jessica's mother was going to have.

So they did. They studied heredity and baby food and people's attitudes to babies—they even interviewed strangers at the mall. But when the project was finished, they still had to wait for the baby. In fact, for Jessica and her family, the waiting had just begun.

—*Melanie L. Witulski*

The Fighting Ground
By Avi
(Notables 1984)

Jonathan looked over at the edge of the field where his father's flintlock musket leaned against a stump. The gun was primed, ready to be used. Jonathan knew how. Hadn't his father taught him, drilled him, told him that everyone had to be prepared? Hadn't he said, "We must all be soldiers now?"

Jonathan pictured himself in the New Jersey uniform. He saw himself dressed in the white leggings and the fancy blue jacket with red facings, a beautiful new gun snug against his cheek.

Down in the village the church bell began to ring, the signal for news—fire, danger . . . enemy troops! "Maybe you'd best get back to the house," his father said. "I'll need to know the news. Don't . . . go beyond!" Jonathan felt his stomach turn over as he saw the fear in his father's eyes.

Before the end of the day, he would know why his father was so frightened. For Jonathan would ignore his father's warning. He would go beyond the boundary—and meet the Hessian mercenaries face to face!

—*Diantha G. McCauley*

A Fine White Dust
By Cynthia Rylant
(Notables 1986, SLJ/C 1986)

The Preacher Man had eyes like a pick-ax murderer. Cold, steely-blue eyes that drilled into Pete's soul like a burning light. Those eyes, and that man, were unlike any he had ever seen before.

Those fiery eyes filled Pete with a holy fever that threatened to burn away all ties to his family and friends. Who was this man? And what happened between him and Pete that left the ceramic cross which Pete cherished more than anything ground into a fine white dust?

—*Jeff Blair*

The First Hard Times
By Doris Buchanan Smith
(Notables 1983)

I will *not* call him "Daddy." He's *not* my daddy. Zan, Lyddy, and Margaret can call him that all they want, but I won't. He's not my daddy and he never will be!

My daddy may still be alive. "Missing in action" doesn't mean dead. Even after ten years, he could still be alive. I know Mom's been lonely. I can understand that. But she didn't have to get married, and she sure didn't have to marry Harvey. If she couldn't stand being single, couldn't she have found someone who at least lived in the same town? No one should move four girls to a whole new town. Why couldn't he move in with us?

I don't know. This situation was doomed from the start. Maybe everyone else can adapt, but I can't. Harvey is not my father and never will be!

So there!

—*Carol Kappelmann*

The Fledgling
By Jane Langton
(Newbery Honor 1981)

They were all against Georgie, every one of them. Oh, they didn't oppose her to be mean—they simply didn't understand her. They told her she was confused, needed more friends, was likely to hurt herself in the process. In fact, Eleanor and Eddy even formed a new club, the Georgie Protection Society! But not even her mother's warnings could stop Georgie from trying to do what she wanted the most: to fly! To soar high above the trees whenever she wanted! To sail through the sky with the geese, who would be her teachers! She was sure that she could do it. So far, all she'd gotten for her efforts were scraped knees and elbows, but Georgie was sure that things were about to change. Hadn't that large, mysterious goose looked right at her as he flew overhead? And hadn't he left behind a single, shining feather? True, it didn't look like a special feather, but Georgie knew it was powerful and magical and the beginning of something wonderful.

A book for people who believe that dreams really can come true.

—*Sister M. Anna Falbo, CSSF*

For Laughing Out Loud: Poems to Tickle Your Funnybone
Selected by Jack Prelutsky
(SLJ/C 1991)

If you have got a funnybone,
and I've no doubt you do,
then this completely silly book
is sure to tickle you.
I've filled it full of dizzy rhymes,
the wildest I could find,
and if it makes you laugh out loud,
that's what I had in mind.

With that invitation, come into a world of silly stories, tongue-in-cheek tales, and goofy characters. Make fun of such serious and sober subjects as homework, parents, and hot dogs. Only strong and solemn souls will be able to keep straight faces when reading about Friendly Frederick Fuddlestone, who could fiddle on his funnybone, or Chester Lester Kirkenby Dale, who caught his sweater on a nail. For those whose hobbies run to recipes, there are "Rhinoceros Stew," "Snowflake Souffle," and "Garbage Delight." The weird, wild, and wonderful are waiting to be discovered in *For Laughing Out Loud: Poems to Tickle Your Funnybone.* You'll never think about poetry without laughing again!

—*Nancy L. Chu*

A Formal Feeling
By Zibby Oneal
(Christopher 1983, Notables 1982)

Anne is frozen in time. She doesn't care about anything except keeping her mother's memory alive. Her mother was the most wonderful and talented person in the whole world, and Anne can't understand how her father can remarry and her brother just go on with his stupid life. To Anne, her father has betrayed her mother, and her brother has forgotten her. She is the only one who remembers.

But what Anne doesn't realize is that her own life has stopped. She is stuck in the past; she refuses to look at the present or set goals for the future. There's no way for her to grow, change, or even survive, until she lets the ice melt, and lets her heart and mind truly feel the hurt she's been hiding from herself ever since the day she learned that her special, wonderful mother was dead.

—*J. R. B.*

Fran Ellen's House
By Marilyn Sachs
(Notables 1987)

I know I should be happy. After all, it's been three years since my family lived together—three years since Mama became ill and we kids had to be sent to foster homes. Now Mama is just fine and we're back together again, but everyone is so different! Take my beautiful baby sister Flora, for instance. Used to be *I* was the one she cared about. Now she cries whenever I go near her! And as for my other sisters, they may be older now but they're as bratty as ever. And my brother Fletcher is so busy with schoolwork and his part-time job that I hardly ever see him!

So here we are together again, at last, in our own little house. It's what I've been dreaming about for the past three years. It's just what I wanted, isn't it? So why do I feel so bad?

—*Sister M. Anna Falbo, CSSF*

Franklin Delano Roosevelt
By Russell Freedman
(Golden Kite Honor 1991, Notables 1990, SLJ/C 1990)

One summer afternoon, Franklin Roosevelt was out with his children at their island vacation home off the coast of Maine. They went sailing, helped to fight a forest fire on a nearby island, went swimming, jogged across their island, swam again, and raced to the house. Except for the fire, it wasn't that unusual a day for Franklin and his children to spend together.

But it was the last day that Franklin Roosevelt ever walked. He caught polio, and it left his legs paralyzed. His mother thought he should retire from public life and lead an invalid's life at his country house.

But Franklin and his wife Eleanor agreed that he must remain active. He had always been restless, but now he learned patience and how to wait for results. He said, "If you have spent two years in bed trying to wiggle your big toe, everything else seems easy."

So he didn't let something like paralysis stop him. He became Governor of New York and then President of the United States. He was elected to the presidency in 1932, in one of the darkest times in U.S. history—the depths of the Great Depression. Uncounted millions of Americans were out of work, and the whole country lived in fear. Poverty and hunger and failure loomed everywhere. But on the day he became President, Franklin Roosevelt told the American people, "The only thing we have to fear is fear itself," and he promised "action, and action now."

Not everyone liked the actions he took, but they changed forever the relationship between government and citizen. Franklin's energy, his ideas, and his personality made him both loved and hated—and got this complicated man elected to the presidency four times! To find out more about the man who was described by a close friend as "the most complicated human being I ever knew," read *Franklin Delano Roosevelt*, by Russell Freedman.

—Sarah Flowers

The Friendship
By Mildred D. Taylor
(BGHB 1988, King 1988, Notables 1987)

More than thirty years ago, a friendship had been forged between a young white boy and a black man. The boy, John Wallace, was traveling through the county when he became mired in some swampland. He was sinking fast when Tom Bee pulled him out of the muck and rescued him.

Soon after, John came down with a fever and Tom took care of him until his strength returned. John swore that Tom was like a daddy to him now and that nothing would make him forget all that he owed his friend.

Now, decades later, in 1933, that friendship has been shattered beyond repair. Tom Bee has committed an unpardonable sin for a black man in Mississippi, an act so awful that John Wallace has no choice but to deny the past and the man who saved his life.

What was the crime? Why was a thirty-year-old friendship destroyed?

—Jeff Blair

A Frog Prince
By Alix Berenzy
(SLJ/C 1989)

"The frog turned into a handsome prince, married the princess, and they all lived happily ever after."

Well, not quite.

The frog in this story isn't an enchanted prince in the shape of a frog. He's . . . well, a frog. He's a noble frog, mind you, but a frog nonetheless. And even though the king's daughter has rejected his friendship, the king likes him well enough to give him handsome clothes and a fine pony, just right for a frog-sized adventure.

The frog sets out toward the edge of the world, but when he gets there he discovers not the edge of the world but a wall, only a wall, surrounding a palace. Inside the palace sleeps a very special enchanted—and enchanting—princess. Will she too reject a noble-hearted frog?

—Donna L. Scanlon

The Frog Prince, Continued
By Jon Scieszka
(Notables 1991)

"And they lived happily ever after" . . . isn't that the way fairy tales are supposed to end? Well, it didn't end that way for the Frog Prince and his Princess. They weren't happy at all; they were miserable. The Princess nagged, and the Frog Prince wished he were home on his lily pad. Then he had an idea. He would find a witch to turn him back into a frog! So the Frog Prince went running into the forest to look for a witch. He found lots of different witches from lots of different fairy tales, but none could turn him back into a frog. So he gave up and went back to the palace to live unhappily ever after.

But when he kissed his Princess, the Frog Prince got a surprise. Maybe there *was* a chance for them to live hoppily ever after!

—*Colleen Stinson*

From the Mixed-Up Files of Mrs. Basil E. Frankweiler
By E. L. Konigsburg
(Newbery 1968)

Most of us, at one time or another, have thought about running away from home. Some of us actually started, but only reached the front yard or the end of the block. Maybe the reason we didn't get very far was that we had no idea where we were going.

I'd like to introduce you to Claudia Kincaid, a girl with a plan. She had good reasons for wanting to run away. As the eldest child and only girl in the family, Claudia got stuck with all the chores, while her little brothers got away with murder. It was so unfair! But unlike most runaways, Claudia didn't just take off for the wild blue yonder—she spent weeks making careful plans. First, she looked for a suitable destination: a place that could offer shelter, beauty, and comfort (she was a girl who liked comfort). After consulting several guidebooks, she decided on the Metropolitan Museum of Art in New York City. Next, money—to get there, she would need money. So she carefully saved her allowance, giving up all the things she usually bought during the week. She even gave up ice cream sundaes, unless, of course, they were on sale. And finally she chose a companion: Jamie, the best of her brothers. He could keep a secret, and what's more, he was rich.

So with twenty-eight dollars and sixty cents, a couple of clean shirts, and socks and underwear packed in their instrument cases, Claudia and Jamie caught the train to New York City and the Metropolitan Museum of Art. Find out what unexpected adventures you can have when you've planned ahead, very, very carefully!

—*Linda Olson*

Garbage Delight
By Dennis Lee
(CLA 1978)

Now, I'm not the one
To say No to a bun,
And I always can manage some jelly;
If somebody gurgles,
"Please eat my hamburgles,"
I try to make room in my belly.

I seem, if they scream,
Not to gag on ice cream,
And with fudge I can choke down my fright;
But none is enticing
Or even worth slicing
Compared with Garbage Delight.

With a nip and a nibble
A drip and a dribble
A dollop, wolloping bite:
If you want to see grins
All the way to my shins,
Then give me some Garbage Delight!

—*Colleen Stinson*

The Gathering
By Virginia Hamilton
(Notables 1981)

They are the four children of power: Justice, who carries the Watcher within herself; her older twin brothers Thomas, a magician, and Levi, a telepath; and their friend Dorian Jefferson, a healer. When their minds are joined, they become a single entity known as First Unit, which has the power to travel through time.

In the first novel of the Justice trilogy, *Justice and Her Brothers,* the children learn about their powers and how they are to use them. In *Dustland,* First Unit travels to the future and finds that Earth has become a grim and dust-choked place, populated by weary, stunted humans and strange curious creatures. They also encounter their foe, the entity Mal, which brings sickness wherever it goes and threatens their lives.

In this book, *The Gathering,* First Unit returns to Dustland. This time they meet Duster, the leader of a "packen" of young people not much older than the twins. Duster and his packen wander like nomads through the dusty waste and struggle to survive; whenever they try to find their way out of the dust, they are threatened by Mal.

Now, with the help of First Unit, they see a chance to escape. But is the place they're going any better? What is the true mission of First Unit? Will Justice and her brothers get home safely, or will Mal defeat them at last?

—*Donna L. Scanlon*

A Gathering of Days: A New England Girl's Journal, 1830-32
By Joan W. Blos
(ABA 1980, Newbery 1980)

Thursday, November 4, 1830

Returning home from school this day I had a dreadful fright! Clearly I saw presented to me the dark silhouette of a lanky man, his coat all tattered against the sky, his bony hand above his eyes as if to give them shade.

Although I quickly pointed him out, so swiftly did he vanish away that nothing remained when Cassie and Asa obeyed my pointing finger.

Wednesday, November 10, 1830

I saw my phantom again today—this time it stayed a longer while, peering and peering into the dusk, and in the same location, over by Piper's Woods.

I am resolved to examine the spot.

Monday, November 29, 1830

I have searched just everywhere! Today I carried my writing book home—Father had said he wished to see it, and Teacher Holt had granted permission exactly on that account. Now neither I nor Matty can find it.

I have not yet told Father of this.

Thursday, December 2, 1830

Lo! My lesson book is returned, and in the queerest way!

There is a nobbly boundary stone that separates the schoolhouse lot from the woods that belong to Wally Piper . . . My book was there at the close of school, just as plain as anything, as if it had been set down.

Then on the cover's inner side, just below my name and place, a stranger had left a message: PLEEZ MISS TAKE PITY I AM COLD.

Who left that message in my writing book? Who is the phantom haunting Piper's Woods? I am determined to find out!

—*Linda Olson*

Note: The entries are adapted from pages 9-20 of the hardcover edition.

Gentlehands
By M. E. Kerr
(Christopher 1979)

Love and death. The best of life and the end of it. It would have been hard for Barney to imagine that summer without them both, intertwined as they were.

Love took the form of Skye Pennington. Barney knew he was in over his head the first time he heard her name. Girls like that never had names like Elsie or Mary. They always had those special names, to be spoken in their particular tones and accents.

Death came in the form of Gentlehands—a nightmare from a Nazi deathcamp that awakened after forty years to hover over Barney's life and threaten all he knew.

And all he knew that summer was Skye.

—*Jeff Blair*

The Ghost Drum: A Cat's Tale
By Susan Price
(SLJ/C 1987)

This story takes place long ago and far away, in a distant northern land where the winter is a cold half-year of darkness. It tells of two children, a boy and girl, one born with great good luck and the other with none at all.

The boy, whose name is Safa, is the only son of the czar, a wealthy and powerful ruler. The girl, whose name is Chingis, is the daughter of a slave woman and doomed by her birth to a life of poverty, toil, and servitude.

Contrary to what you might think, Chingis is the lucky one. Soon after her birth, her mother is approached by a shaman, a good witch of great wisdom. The shaman wants to take baby Chingis away and raise her to be her apprentice; she promises the baby's mother that if she will make this sacrifice, Chingis will become a woman of power instead of a slave and mother of slaves. And after some hesitation, Chingis's mother gives her baby to the witch, for she wants her beloved child to be happy in the future.

Safa, on the other hand, is considered a threat by his father. The czar is so sure that his son will seize the throne for himself that he has Safa locked in a tiny stone room without even a window to the outside world. The door is guarded by soldiers, and Safa is never allowed leave. As he grows up, he wants desperately to see what's beyond that door. The young prince has never seen the sun, or a tree, or his father's palace, or any people other than the woman who cared for him when he was very small and the soldiers who stand outside the door. After his nurse dies, he passes his days in darkness, utterly alone. He howls, he screams, he hurls himself at the walls and tears everything in his room to shreds. Finally all agree that the czar's son has become a madman. All, that is, except one.

Chingis hears Safa's cries and recognizes the infinite sadness of his spirit. And she is determined to help him.

—Jo Berkman

A Girl from Yamhill: A Memoir
By Beverly Cleary
(Notables 1988)

Beverly Bunn sat in her seventh-grade library class as Miss Smith began to read aloud from a student's story. With the opening sentences, Beverly felt her mouth go dry and her stomach twist—this was *her* story the teacher had chosen to read to the whole class. "When Beverly grows up, she should write books," Miss Smith announced. The author who would one day be known as Beverly Cleary was dumbfounded—no one had ever praised her imagination and creativity before.

Of course, in the Depression years people tended to focus not on the creative side of life but on the practical—how to make ends meet when there was almost no money to be had. Beverly's parents scrimped in all kinds of ways. Her mother used almond extract instead of the more expensive vanilla to flavor desserts; the whole family used plain baking soda for brushing their teeth, and when the last of the tea was gone, Beverly's parents drank steaming cups of hot water. Regretfully (for they liked the cartoons and short stories), they gave up their subscription to the *Saturday Evening Post* magazine. Books were precious and impossibly expensive to buy (thank goodness for the Portland Public Library!).

But in spite of the Great Depression, life in the little house near Klickitat Street was far from depressing. Beverly enjoyed school and being with her friends. Occasionally she spent the night at her friend Claudine's, listening to the radio and reading romances. Beverly's mother would have disapproved if she had known. It wasn't an easy time to grow up, or an easy family to grow up in, but Beverly survived—and she succeeded as well! As her grandfather proudly told the customers in his general store, "Yes sir, she's the only granddaughter I got, and she's a crackerjack!" You'll think so too.

—Vicki Reutter

The Girl Who Cried Flowers, and Other Tales
By Jane Yolen
(Golden Kite 1975)

A girl who cries flowers: now, *that's* unusual. Olivia, who was found in the crook of an olive tree, never cried tears; she wept flowers of gold, blue, silver, and snow white. The villagers were proud of their treasure and boasted to strangers. Olivia would produce a tiny tear-blossom for each of them, and her fame spread far and wide. Soon, instead of a single flower, people were requesting elaborate bouquets, decorations for the altar, garlands for the dance. Their greed and Olivia's generosity led to tragedy.

It is Dawn-Strider who brings the sun early each day. At least, he did until he met Night-Walker, the giant who prowls around in the dark. Night Walker was puzzled by this child who showed no fear. He laid plans to capture Dawn-Strider, the child who brings the light.

Vera longed to know the future. At first she was satisfied with a simple outline of things to come, but soon she wanted more. In her quest for greater and greater detail, she met the Weaver of Tomorrow and became his apprentice—and part of the future, in ways she never expected.

These are only some of the haunting, mysterious tales you'll find in *The Girl Who Cried Flowers.*

—Nancy Bardole Hanaman

The Goats
By Brock Cole
(Notables 1987, SLJ/C 1987)

Most kids have the time of their lives at summer camp. And no wonder: they get to escape from their parents and their little brothers and sisters, and spend the whole summer swimming and riding horses and meeting new people from all over. But for a lot of kids, going to camp for the very first time can be a little scary. All the other kids in the cabin already know each other; they're friends with the counselors too. They talk about funny things that happened last summer, things that mean nothing to a new camper, who won't even know the words to all the camp songs.

Laura and Howie were both new at camp that summer, and neither of them liked it very much. Both had been dumped there by parents who didn't want to be bothered with their children while school was out. Laura called her mother collect at work every day to ask if she could please come home. She wasn't athletic, she didn't like the outdoors, and the other girls in her cabin were being mean to her. It was pretty much the same for Howie. He and Laura both wore glasses and were "socially retarded." That's why they were chosen to be the goats.

Howie's cabinmates told him they were going to the island for a cookout. Laura's told her they were going to go skinny-dipping. But what they really had planned was to take Laura and Howie's clothes and leave them marooned on the island overnight. Everyone thought it would be a great joke—"the goats" were a camp tradition that had been around for years. Some of the counselors had been goats back when they were campers. But for Laura and Howie, it wasn't funny at all. It was just one more message telling them they weren't good enough, didn't fit in, didn't measure up. They knew that their cabinmates would be back to pick them up the next day—and then spend the rest of the summer laughing at them. So Howie and Laura, tired of being picked on, decided to play a little joke of their own. They sneaked off the island that night and swam away—not back to camp, as everyone expected, but to the mainland, where they disappeared into thin air.

Nobody, not even Laura and Howie, thought these goats were capable of such an adventure, but from someplace deep inside they found the courage to prove to themselves, their families, and the other campers that they were valuable human beings, not throw-away kids.

—Susan Dunn

The Gold Cadillac
By Mildred D. Taylor
(Christopher 1987)

"We got us a Cadillac: We got us a Cadillac! Come on see!" the girls called as they ran through the apartment building. Their daddy had come home driving a new Cadillac—a *Gold* one! "I just couldn't resist it" he said. Everyone in the neighborhood and all the aunts, uncles, and cousins oohed and ahhed over the beautiful car—everyone, that is, except their mother. "We're supposed to be saving for a new house," she reminded their father. And Mother refused to ride in the car, until the day Daddy announced that he would drive from Ohio, where they lived, to Mississippi to see his parents, Wilma and Lois's grandparents.

The uncles warned that a trip to Mississippi in *that* car would be terribly dangerous, but Daddy argued, "It's my car; I paid for it, and I'm driving it south to Mississippi." "Then the girls and I'll be going too," said Mother. And when the uncles decided they'd *all* go, to look out for each other, Mother and the aunts began to get the food together: fried chicken, baked ham, home-made cakes, pies, and potato salad. They filled jugs with water, punch, and coffee; they packed picnic baskets with bread, hard-boiled eggs, fruit, napkins, dishes, spoons, and cups. "It's like a grand, grand picnic," Lois thought to herself.

But it wasn't long before Lois began to realize that it might not be such a "grand, grand picnic." As they crossed the Ohio River into Kentucky, Daddy told Lois and her sister not to say anything to anybody. "Let your mother and me do all the talking."

Than they began to see signs everywhere, signs Lois didn't like, signs that said, "White Only—Colored not allowed." The signs were above water fountains, in restaurant windows, in ice cream parlors, at hamburger stands, on the restroom doors of service station.

Even though Wilma and Lois didn't understand the signs, they made the girls feel uncomfortable, as though they were in a foreign land. Daddy explained that they were not allowed in any of those places: the restaurants, the water fountains, the hotels, and motels. So *this* was why their mother and their aunts brought all that food along. The picnic wasn't so grand after all.

Then, just after they crossed the Mississippi state line, a policemen stopped the car; he called Daddy a liar when he said the car was his. The trooper searched Daddy—and took him to *jail!*

—Dorothy Davidson

A Good Courage
By Stephanie Tolan
(SLJ/C 1988)

Ty knows he's going into The Cage. He was caught teaching the small children how to read—the work of Satan, or so Brother Daniel has told the rest of the commune. Ty's mother had been so sure that this religious community would be the answer, but she hadn't realized how little contact she'd have with her son once she joined. The children of the community are separated from their parents and sent to do field work seven days a week, sick or well. Brother Daniel makes the rules. But Ty won't conform.

What Ty doesn't understand now is why Brother Daniel is leading him not to The Cage but to the animal shed, the only part of Ty's life in the commune that's tolerable. As they enter, Ty's stomach lurches; he looks around for a shovel, a stick, any weapon, but realizes that nothing is going to stop what's about to happen. Daniel picks up Ophelia, Ty's pet rabbit, in his huge hands. In the darkened shed, the snap of this helpless rabbit's backbone is like a gunshot. "So is Satan conquered!" The soft, heavy body lands against Ty's feet. It will take more than "a good courage" for Ty to understand how the senseless killing of an animal can have anything to do with God.

—Colleen Macklin

Good Night, Mr. Tom
By Michelle Magorian
(Greenaway 1982, IRA 1982, Notables 1982)

Old Tom picked up a poker and walked to the fire. Little Will thought, "Now I'm really going to get it!" He clutched the seat of the stool tightly. Tom looked down on him. "About Sammy," Will heard him say. He knew he should listen to what Tom was saying, but he couldn't keep his eyes off the poker. He saw Tom's brown wrinkled hand lift it out of the fire—the tip was red, almost white in places, and Will was certain he was to be branded with it. The room seemed to spin, he watched the tip of the poker come closer, and then it all went dark!

Will was an abused child of a single parent, and he had been evacuated from London to the safety of the English countryside just prior to the outbreak of World War II. He had never known kindness or love and was at first terrified of every strange country sound and sight.

Mr. Tom had lived alone for a long time, but his heart went out to Will. He and his dog, Sammy, taught Will about a world he had never imagined existed before—a world of friendship and affection.

Just when he was becoming comfortable with Mr. Tom, Sammy, and a new friend Zack, who helped him to laugh again, a telegram arrived from his mother. She said she was ill, and wanted him to return to London. Mr. Tom tried to get her to come to the country, but to no avail. He spoke to the billeting officer, but got nowhere. Mothers had the legal right to their children, and Will was sent back on the train to the life he had tried so hard to forget.

It was a sad moment when the two said goodbye and Will boarded the train. The whistle blew, and Mr. Tom watched the train puff away out of sight. When Mr. Tom didn't hear from Will, he began to worry. He couldn't ignore that sick feeling he got every time he thought of the frightened and bruised little boy who had arrived at his door so many months before. Finally he made up his mind. He and Sammy would go to London to find Will!

—Beverly Montgomery

The Great American Gold Rush
By Rhoda Blumberg
(Notables 1989, SLJ/C 1989)

Have you ever wished you were a millionaire? Most people have dreamed about suddenly becoming rich. It's not surprising, then, that when a piece of gold the size of a dime was found in California, people from all over the world caught "gold fever" and set out to make their fortunes. Some people did become rich, most didn't.

In 1848, a sawmill worker found the small piece of gold that changed the whole country in only four years. The population of California grew from 15,000 to 250,00 during that time, and thanks to the Gold Rush, the United States became one of the richest, most powerful nations in the world.

Do you think you would have packed up and headed for California too? Find out what might have happened if you had.

—Cecilia Swanson

The Great Gilly Hopkins
By Katherine Paterson
(Christopher 1979, Newbery Honor 1979)

Gilly carefully spread her gum on the underside of the car door handle—a sticky little surprise for the next person to get in the car and pull the door shut, compliments of The Great Gilly Hopkins. Then she turned her attention back to the lecture coming from the driver's seat. Miss Ellis was delivering the old "please make an effort to get along" speech while taking Gilly to yet another foster home. Gilly had the speech about memorized by now. She knew what they called her at Social Services—"Gruesome Gilly"—and, if anything, she was proud of her reputation: she was unmanageable, and so clever that no one wanted to tangle with her.

If Gilly had her druthers, she wouldn't be messing around with this foster placement stuff anyway. Her real mother would come back and take her away from this Grade-B existence. Gilly carries her mother's picture, somewhat faded now, to every foster home she's assigned to, and at night she'll pull it out from the bottom of her suitcase and wish for her real family to take her away.

There's an old proverb that advises you to be careful what you wish for, because you just might get it. Gilly doesn't know it, but at this latest placement things will happen that will teach her what "family" really means. What is it that finally gets the best of The Great Gilly Hopkins?

—*Jeff Blair*

The Great Little Madison
By Jean Fritz
(BGHB 1990, Notables 1989, SLJ/C 1989)

James Madison was not tall—only about five-foot-six—and he had a light build. He was sickly and shy, and had such a soft voice that when he spoke in public, it was difficult for people to hear him unless they crowded close. And crowd close they did, for everyone wanted to know what "The Great Little Madison," as he came to be called, had to say.

Madison hated slavery and hated to see people punished for their religious beliefs. As one of the framers of the Constitution, he worked hard to specify *freedom* of religion in the Bill of Rights—"toleration" was not enough. When the Constitution was finished, he worked hard to persuade people to vote for it, explaining carefully, in a series of essays, just how the new government would work and what dangers the framers had tried to avoid. As a result, a lot of people who had been outraged over the Constitution at first (it *wasn't* very popular!) decided to take a second look, and ended up voting for this new type of government.

Small and sickly though he was, Madison won the respect of his contemporaries. Twice he was elected to the Presidency, carrying the weight of war upon his shoulders as he led the nation to victory in the War of 1812. He lived in an exciting time and knew most of the great men who helped shape our country—Washington, Jefferson, Hamilton, Jackson—as well as some of the not-so great, like Aaron Burr. Meet "The Great Little Madison"—and his wife, Dolley, who did a lot more for our country than lend her name to some cupcakes!

—*Melinda Waugh*

The Green Futures of Tycho
By William Sleator
(SLJ/C 1981)

Only a brontosaurus saw the beings drop the object into the swamp. It wasn't edible, so the brontosaurus let it be. For several million years, the object sank deeper into the mud. It lay under an ocean for eighty million years, until an earthquake made a mountain and the mountain rounded with age. A glacier carried the object thousands of miles. Then it lay undisturbed for many centuries more, until Tycho Tithonous dug it up in the process of making a vegetable garden.

Its metallic sheen caught Tycho's eye, and he absently picked up the object and stuffed it in his pocket. But his brother Leonardo had seen it too, and they started to argue, bringing Tamara and Ludwig over to see what was going on. Reluctantly, Tycho pulled out the object out for all to see.

It was shaped like a small egg, with thin, barely visible, etched dials. Ludwig reached for it, but as Tycho backed away he involuntarily squeezed the thing—and Ludwig, Tamara, and Leonardo vanished.

Tycho blinked. It was now suddenly sunset, and his parents were seated on the lounge chairs. He could hear Ludwig playing the piano. Tycho began digging in the garden again, thinking about what had just happened. The silver egg! He had squeezed it just before his brothers and sister had vanished.

After dinner Tycho decided to test his theory. He locked himself in the bathroom and studied the egg. Its etchings were really tiny dials, one inside the other. He turned them and squeezed, and suddenly sunlight was pouring through the window and Tamara was sitting in the bathtub.

"You monster! Get out!" she shrieked.

Tycho spun the dials and squeezed the egg, and his father was at the sink shaving. His father saw him and cut himself as he jumped in fright.

"What a rotten trick, Tycho!" And Tycho spun and squeezed.

The bathroom was a wreck. There were gaping holes in the walls, ceiling, and floor. Outside was a horrible green glow and terrible, unearthly stench. Tycho spun the dials in the opposite direction and squeezed again.

He was back in the old bathroom. Someone was taking a shower. When the water stopped the shower curtain rustled, and Tycho looked up to see himself stepping out of the shower.

—Diantha G. McCauley

The Grey King
By Susan Cooper
(Newbery 1976)

As the youngest of the Old Ones of Light, Will Stanton has an important part to play in the final struggle between the powers of Light and Dark. He must locate one of the symbols of the Light—a golden harp—and his success is crucial to the Light's victory.

But after a severe case of hepatitis, Will has forgotten not only who and what he is, but also his quest. Now he's just a boy recuperating from an illness, staying with his aunt and uncle on their small farm in Wales. It's a pleasant place, but somehow he can't relax. Something keeps tugging at his memory—something important he can't quite recall.

Then Will stumbles onto the old pilgrims' road once know as Cadfan's Way. There he meets Bran, a boy with white hair and golden eyes of a raven, and Bran's dog, Cafall, with silver eyes, and his own other identity comes flooding back. As the boys begin searching for the golden harp, the presence of the Dark grows stronger in the valley. Together Will and Bran must unravel past mysteries and face very present dangers if they hope to succeed in their quest.

—Evette Pearson

Hatchet
By Gary Paulsen
(Notables 1987)

Someone was screaming. High tight, animal screams of fear and pain echoed through the cabin as the plane plummeted out of the sky and crashed through the trees and into the lake. He didn't recognize his own voice, but it was Brian who was screaming. He was the only person on the plane who could have screamed—he was the only one alive.

The pilot had died of a heart attack hours ago and the plane had flown on automatic pilot until it ran out of gas and dropped like a rock from the sky over the Canadian forest, hundreds of miles off its course.

When Brian awoke, he was more alone than he had ever been in his life—alone in a wilderness with nothing to eat, no shelter, and only the clothes on his back. All he had to help him survive was the hatchet that his mother had given him before he left. A hatchet versus the wilderness: what kind of odds were those?   —*Jeff Blair*

The Haunting
By Margaret Mahy
(Carnegie 1983, SLJ/C 1982)

"Barnaby's dead! Barnaby's dead! I'm going to be very lonely." The day Barnaby kept hearing that over and over in his head was a terrible day. "Barnaby's dead! Barnaby's dead!" the voice kept saying. But *he* was Barnaby, and he wasn't dead at all. What could it mean? And where was this voice coming from? Was it Barnaby's own voice—was he talking to himself? Or was it the voice of one of the friends that Barnaby, and only Barnaby could see when he was younger? Or was it the voice of the shadowy figure who now appeared beside him, like . . . a ghost! Could *Barnaby* be haunted?

—*Colleen Stinson*

The Headless Cupid
By Zilpha Keatley Snyder
(Newbery Honor 1972)

Suddenly acquiring an older sister, or stepsister, would make anyone curious, and David had a sneaking suspicion that Amanda might not be your average stepsister. And he was right: there was nothing average about Amanda.

The day she arrived, she brought in two big suitcases, several cardboard boxes, and a bad-tempered crow. She was wearing a black dress that ended well below her knees in a crooked hem, and a huge, bright-colored shawl with a shaggy fringe. Her hair was braided into dozens of long, snaky locks, some looped to the back of her head. In the middle of her forehead was a triangular spot that caught the light like a tiny mirror when she moved. As a witch in training, Amanda dressed the part.

Amanda's familiarity with the supernatural seemed harmless at first, even entertaining, especially after she offered to teach David and his younger brother and sisters some elementary tricks. But things got serious when something began tossing rocks through the halls and throwing plants down the stairs. Was there really a spirit loose in the house? Years ago, a poltergeist was supposed to have invaded the old house, and some even blamed it for the broken, headless cupid on the carved staircase. Certainly the cupid was broken, and the head had never been found, nor the culprit— human or otherwise—identified. Had Amanda, by dabbling in witchcraft, called the spirit back?

—Evette Pearson

Healer
By Peter Dickinson
(Notables 1985, SLJ/C 1985)

I'll never forget the day I met her. I was at school sitting in the hallway outside the secretary's office, waiting for her to finish up with some kid who'd skinned his knee. I could barely wait for her to finish. My head was throbbing, and I needed two aspirin.

"You've got a nasty head," she said.

I looked down and saw a fat little girl with glasses. She couldn't have been more than six. I tried to shrug it off, saying "I'm all right."

She replied, "Not now, but you will be soon."

Then she reached out and took my hand. Though I tried to grab it away, she held on tight and reached for the other one. Her hands were chilly, yet I felt this heat on the back of my neck and between my shoulder blades. The heat made me drowsy and I could feel myself nodding off.

She whispered, "Better now?" and I was.

That's how I, Barry Evans, met Pinkie Proudfoot.

And now, after two years of not knowing what had happened to her, I was seeing her again. She was the reason I was at the Hall of Harmony with a self-induced migraine. It was the only way I could get near her, see if she was all right, and make sure she wasn't being exploited as "The Healer."

—*Pam Spencer*

Heartbeats, and Other Stories
By Peter Sieruta
(SLJ/C 1989)

I'm fifteen, and I've got all these hormones going crazy on me, so you probably know what that means. I met Molly in Driver's Ed. She's perfect, or *almost* perfect—she's tall; I'm not. When we stood next to each other that first day, we looked like an ostrich and a hummingbird. Of course everyone laughed. I like to *make* a joke, not *be* one, so when the teacher asked Molly where she was from, I said, "From the valley of the Jolly Green Giant, ho, ho, ho." Now she won't talk to me. If you have any ideas about how I can get her to like me, I'd appreciate your help. I've already tried several things, but so far I'm just making it all worse. I could really use some help!

—*Cecilia Swanson*

The Hero and the Crown
By Robin McKinley
(Newbery 1985, Notables 1984, SLJ/C 1984)

My name is Aerin, and my father is the king. For as long as I can remember, there have been rumors about my parentage. Everyone believes that my mother, the king's second wife, was a witch who tricked my father into marriage and then died of disappointment when I was born a girl instead of a boy. And some (especially my cousins) whisper that that the king was not my father at all.

Cousin Galanna particularly enjoys tormenting me, and once dared me to eat leaves from the surka plant. I nearly died. During my convalescence, I went out one day to the pasture where my father's injured warhorse, Talat, was kept. Talat had been badly wounded in battle and could use only three legs. My father kept him for breeding, although he was so ill-tempered he'd often attack the mares. I hadn't planned to tame the stallion, but gradually we became friends. I even learned to ride him, and with exercise his weak leg became stronger.

I also discovered an old history of the kingdom, with lots of information about dragons in it. Since dragons were still a dangerous nuisance, I was interested. There was even a recipe for an ointment that would protect the wearer from dragon fire. Unfortunately, only the ingredients were given, without any specific amounts. But I began to experiment, and finally I discovered a combination that would allow me to walk through a bonfire without being burned. Then all I had to do was wait for the next report of a dragon attack.

And now my time has come. A dragon is ravaging a village, and I ride out on Talat with my ointment and my spear. I am betting my life, and Talat's, that this smelly stuff will work. When I find the dragon, he runs straight at me, but fortunately Talat knows what to do, because I am paralyzed with fright—the dragon is faster and more dangerous than I had ever imagined. My career as a dragon-killer may be over before it's begun.

—Abbie V. Landry

Hey World, Here I Am!
By Jean Little
(Notables 1989, SLJ/C 1989)

If you had Kate Bloomfield in your class, you'd either love her or hate her, but you would certainly know she was there. She has very definite opinions about lot of things, including Dominic Tantardini, who looks like a Greek god to Kate (even though he's Italian); old people; her parents and her big sister; this year's English class; notebooks, journals, and mosquitoes.

In this book, Kate tells what she thinks about all these things and more. It's as though you'd been allowed to peek at her most private journal. She shows us her serious, thoughtful side, for instance, with the four-line poem titled "Surprise":

I feel like the ground in winter,
Hard, cold, dark, dead, unyielding . . .
Then hope pokes through me
Like a crocus.

And she shows us her funny side in the longer poem "Smart Remark," which she ends by comparing her sister to a caterpillar, her father to a spider, and her mother to a queen bee. She writes about her best friend Emily and about writing poems. She writes about the mean substitute teacher she had for one day, and about an old woman she has known all her life.

If you've ever kept a private journal for your teacher, you'll empathize with Kate when she tells about "My Journals." If you've ever had a friend with whom you've shared very special moments, you'll know what Kate means by "Not Enough Emilys." Sure, Kate is Canadian, Jewish, and a girl, but even if you aren't those things, you'll understand what Kate means in another poem, called "Yesterday":

> Yesterday I knew what was Right and what was Wrong.
> But today . . . everything's changing.
> Life is harder now . . . and yet easier . . .
> And more and more exciting!

Hey world, here's Kate!

—*JoEllen Rice*

Hide Crawford Quick!
By Margaret Walden Froehlich
(Notables 1983)

Nothing was right at our house. Worst of all, I didn't know what was the matter. Mama was fine, she'd had the baby. But Daddy was so crabby, Huie cried all the time, and Roberta and Lizzie were awful! And on top of that, Daddy got this mean woman to come and stay with us.

But finally, that long week was over, and Daddy brought Mama and the new baby home.

"They're here," Lizzie shrieked. "Let's have a look at the new baby."

Watching sleeping babies wasn't too interesting, but in a little while, Crawford awoke with a loud demanding cry. All four of us girls crowded around to see him.

Suddenly, Lizzie's voice rang out above Crawford's crying: "How come this baby is broke? You should take him back and get a new one."

In the next few days, I kept remembering my sister's words. And why not? I thought. We had wanted a perfect little brother, one that Father would call Robert Charles Prather, Jr., not "Crawford." Where did that name come from, anyway?

We had expected a perfect baby, one to cuddle and powder and show off. This was a family problem, Mama said, so I couldn't even tell Nanny Olive, my best friend. And Nanny Olive was making a present for the baby!

Crawford had a lot of colic, mostly in the evenings around dinner-time. One evening, the potatoes were scorched and the scorch spread over the whole house. Dinner was spoiled and Crawford was wailing. Roberta said she couldn't eat. The baby made her sick. "I can't stand him, him and his one foot."

Daddy stood up and said, "Do you think anyone can stand it?" He walked out, slamming the door. He left without his coat, even though it was December.

I was terrified. What if Daddy decided to go away for good? What would Mama do? What would become of us all?

Find out what Gracie does in *Hide Crawford Quick!*, by Margaret Froehlich.

—*Linda Henderson*

The High King
By Lloyd Alexander
(Newbery 1969)

Taran Wandering—the assistant pig-keeper, weaver, potter, swordsmith, and gardener—has finally reached his home at Caer Dalben, and even the pig Hen Wen, who can prophesy the future, is pleased to see him.

But the person Taran wants to see is Princess Eilonwy. No matter how foolish it may seem, he's decided to ask her to marry him, even though he is not of noble birth. As he greets the other guests and learns that he's not the last to arrive—they are still waiting for Prince Gwydion and the bard Fflam—he rehearses his proposal in his mind.

Then suddenly the door is flung open, and Fflam bursts in with a badly wounded Gwydion. The murderous Huntsmen of Annuvin, servants of Arawn Death-Lord, ambushed them on their way to this gathering, with Arawn himself, disguised as Taran, luring them into the trap. Prince Gwydion will live, but Arawn has captured his sword. At all costs it must be recovered.

Taran puts his dreams of marriage aside as he and his friends prepare for the final battle against the forces of darkness. He knows that the road ahead will be the most dangerous he has ever traveled—already there are signs of ill-luck and even of treachery. But he cannot abandon the fight. Can he and his rag-tag companions defeat the Death-Lord? Or will Taran lose everything—his love and his life?

—*Abbie V. Landry*

Hiroshima No Pika
By Toshi Maruki
(Addams 1983, BGHB 1982, Batchelder 1983, Notables 1982)

Seven-year-old Mii was eating sweet potatoes with her mother and father when the atomic flash devastated Hiroshima.

Every year on August 6th, the people of Hiroshima print the names of loved ones who died from the bomb on lanterns. Then they light the lanterns and set them adrift on the seven rivers that flow through Hiroshima. As Mii's mother put it: "It can't happen again if no one drops the bomb."

—Paul H. Rockwell

Note: This book should be used with discretion and is best read in the company of a teacher or parent. I never booktalk *Hiroshima No Pika* without permission from the teacher.*—P.H.R.*

Hit and Run
By Joan Phipson
(Notables 1985)

Roland heard a thud! when the Ferrari hit the baby carriage, but he didn't feel a thing. He caught a glimpse of a bundle with two fat legs sticking out, flying through the air, and then it was all behind him. Maybe it hadn't really happened, maybe he'd just grazed something, or the wind from the speeding car had pushed it over. Yeah, that was probably it, because he *was* speeding—you don't borrow a Ferrari so you can poke through town at twenty-five miles an hour. And then he saw the police behind him, and he knew it was true.

Instinctively, Roland stepped on the accelerator and tried to get away. He cornered onto a dirt road that turned into a rough path, too rough for a panicked, inexperienced driver. When the car skidded out of control and flipped over, Roland knew he should lie there and wait for the police—at this point he was lucky to be alive. But something made him run, deep into the brush, with blood streaming from the cuts on his back. Something pushed him on. Something told him the smashed Ferrari was only the beginning of this nightmare. And Something was right!

—Colleen Stinson

Hold Fast
By Kevin Major
(CLA 1979)

How would they know? People tried to tell me they understood and they knew what I was feeling, but how could they, unless they were fourteen too and both their parents had just been killed in a car accident? Accident, my foot! The other guy was drunk, and now my parents are gone.

I figured Brent and me would just move in with Aunt Flo and Grandfather. I know they're old, but they live right here in town and we've always spent time at their place. That's why it was such a shock when I found out only Brent would be staying. As soon as school started, I would be moving to St. Albert, a piece away, to live with Aunt Ellen and Uncle Ted—people I'd hardly even met. They have a kid my age—Curtis—maybe that's supposed to make it all right.

Curtis and I didn't get along too well at first. We didn't have much in common . . . until his old man started laying into me the same way he does Curtis, yelling and screaming and ordering me around. Once he threatened to hit me, but he'd better not try. Things are better for Curtis now that I'm here taking most of the heat, but he still doesn't like it and that's why he wants to come with me. Because I'm getting out of here. The plans are all made, we're ready. And we're leaving.

—*Colleen Stinson*

How It Feels To Be Adopted
By Jill Krementz
(Notables 1982)

Barbara knows nothing of her biological parents. They gave her up right after she was born, and she stayed in a foster home until she was about a year old, when she was adopted. Although she loves her adoptive parents wholeheartedly, Barbara feels embarrassed when curious people ask questions about her background. She'd like to know the answers herself; she'd like to know how and why she was put up for adoption. Not knowing makes her angry.

The other kids in this book agree—finding out about your birth mother is important. Maybe you would even want to meet her. But at the same time, most also feel that the mother they have now, the one who takes care of them when they're sick and is there when they need her, is their *real* mother. As Sue, aged thirteen, says, "Finding your birth mother is just filling up a gap."

What would it feel like to be adopted? Listen to the stories of kids who are, and find out.

—Carol Kappelmann

How It Feels When a Parent Dies
By Jill Krementz
(Notables 1981, SLJ/C 1981)

You always think it won't ever happen to you, but when it does, you have to learn to deal with it. Your family isn't complete any more—one of your parents has died.

How do teenagers cope? How do they survive? Gardner, sixteen, says, "Crying has never been an outlet for me. . . . I do other things—like lie on my bed, go for a walk, or write." Others wonder why it happened to them, not to someone else: "Why is God picking on me?" Mother's Day or Father's Day becomes painful, and so does Parents' Night at school.

Listen to these teenagers who had to learn how to do something they'd never thought they'd have to do—live without one of their parents.

—Carol Kappelmann and J. R. B.

How It Feels When Parents Divorce
By Jill Krementz
(Notables 1984)

I used to dream they'd marry again.
They didn't.
I used to dream everything was all right.
It wasn't.
I used to dream I was happy.
I wasn't.

Most teenagers today have encountered divorce, maybe more than once. Some never see their fathers afterwards, or see them only occasionally. Others live with both parents but not at the same time, staying for a week at Mom's house and then a week at Dad's. In at least one family, the kids live in the same house all the time, while the parents take turns moving in and out.

Is divorce ever easy, or is it always hard and painful? Listen to the voices of these teens as they describe living with divorce.

—*Carol Kappelmann*

How Many Spots Does a Leopard Have? and Other Tales
By Julius Lester
(Notables 1989)

"Long before this time we call today, and before that time called yesterday, and even before 'What time is it?' the world wasn't like it is now." No, it was a time of curiosity, of questions like, Why do dogs chase cats? Why do monkeys live in trees? and How many spots does a leopard have? People all over the world puzzled over these mysteries and told stories to try to explain them—tales of crafty animals and cruel monsters, quick-witted, brave heroes and dastardly cowards, tales that give you answers to all those questions about why animals are the way they are today.

—*Pamela A. Todd*

Howl's Moving Castle
By Diana Wynne Jones
(BGHB 1986, Notables 1986)

In an instant Sophie was turned into a ninety-year-old hag, all because the Witch of the Waste didn't like the hat that Sophie had made for her. Her career as a hatter finished, Sophie had no choice but to seek her fortune elsewhere.

As she made her way out of town, Sophie came upon the wizard Howl's moving castle. Since the night was getting darker and colder and her bones were aching, Sophie hobbled right up to the castle, raised her walking stick, and shrieked, "Stop!"

And the castle stopped.

That's how Sophie came to be Howl's house- or castle-keeper.

Inside the castle, Sophie met Howl and Michael, the wizard's apprentice, and Calcifer, the blue fire demon. She soon decided that Howl was self-centered, cowardly, and a lady's man. And she learned that he had a *terrible* temper. When Howl didn't get his own way, he howled, moaned, groaned, shrieked, and cried so loudly that you could hear him all the way back in town—which is why he was named Howl. And if he was *really* angry, he'd slime himself—horrendous quantities of green goo would drip off his nose and puddle around his feet.

But Sophie discovered that, in spite of his temper, Howl had a good heart and that he too was under a spell.

Would Sophie and Howl be able to break each other's spells? Could this turn into a love story?

—*Diantha G. McCauley*

In a Dark, Dark Room, and Other Scary Stories
Retold by Alvin Schwartz
(Notables 1984, SLJ/C 1984)

Do you like scary stories? Do you like to sit in front of the fire while the wind howls outside and read scary stories? Stories about three-inch-long teeth? Stories about heads falling off? Stories about ghosts? Then *In a Dark, Dark Room, and Other Scary Stories* is for you. But only if you're very brave. And only if you're not ever afraid when someone yells, "Boo!".

—*Colleen Stinson*

In Summer Light
By Zibby Oneal
(Notables 1985, SLJ/C 1985)

Kate's father is a famous painter. Everyone wants to meet him and spend time with him. Everyone except Kate.

Fortunately she doesn't have to spend much time with him. She's away at boarding school most of the year, and during the summers she can usually find a job that will allow her some life of her own. But this year is different. This year she caught mono at school, so now, when all her friends are arranging for great summer jobs, she has to go home and recuperate.

What a prospect: a whole summer with a father who dominates everybody with his genius, his demands, and his artistic temperament. He absorbs all her mother's energy, and her little sister's—the great Marcus Brewer has to be the center of everything. When Kate learns that a graduate student will be spending the summer with them, cataloging her father's life-work, she knows what to expect: one more person's energy will be flowing Marcus's way. Ian's awe of the famous painter, the hero-worship in his eyes, seem to confirm her expectations.

But to her surprise, some of Ian's attention is directed her way. She didn't expect that; she didn't expect him to notice her, or her own tentative paintings. And she's not sure she's ready for the new way she's beginning to feel—about Ian, about herself, and maybe even about her father. —*Colleen Stinson*

In the Year of the Boar and Jackie Robinson
By Bette Bao Lord
(SLJ/C 1984)

Wham! The first punch hurt her eye terribly, but Shirley knew she was too puny to fight the tallest and strongest and scariest girl in the whole fifth grade. Instead, Shirley used a few choice words she had heard the rickshaw pullers use to insult riders who left no tips. And then, wham! Now the other eye hurt horribly too, but Shirley could not flee. A child of emperors and the ancient House of Wong could not flee. Hadn't Shirley's mother told her that she was to be China's little ambassador and that the reputation of all the Chinese rested on her shoulders? But five hundred million Chinese was a pretty heavy burden!

Shirley didn't have these problems when she still lived in Chungking with her mother, aunts and uncles, grandparents, and all the cousins. But in Chungking she was never told anything and was always treated like an ignorant child. Then the wonderful letter from Father had come, and she and her mother made the long journey across the ocean, then another long journey across the new country by train to arrive in Brooklyn, New York.

Once there, Shirley was so anxious to impress her father with her cleverness, and how she could find her way around in the new city after only one day, that she had begged and pleaded to be allowed to go to the tobacco shop by herself to buy cigarettes for him and his friends. She got there just fine (Father would be so pleased!) but the shopkeeper did not understand Shirley until she puffed on an imaginary cigarette and said the only two English words she knew: "Rukee Sike! Rukee Sike!" She had to go to still another store to purchase the cigarettes, and instead of a triumphant return home, she got terribly lost. And that was only the beginning.

Shirley had no friends among all the black, brown, spotted, and very tall kids in her class. She was not asked to play any games with them because she was always bowing to anybody who let her do anything. Shirley tried, but couldn't even learn to roller-skate. And now the best baseball player in the fifth grade—a very big, very black girl named Mabel—was furious with her for ruining the baseball game.

Would nothing ever go right for Shirley Temple Wong in the United States? Maybe she should never have come to this new country. Maybe she should have stayed in Chungking. Maybe . . . you should read this book yourself to find out if Shirley survived Brooklyn in 1947.

—*Susan Bogart*

The Incident at Hawk's Hill
By Allan W. Eckert
(Newbery Honor Book 1972)

Hawk's Hill is the knoll where the McDonalds build their home in Canada, on a sprawling prairie near Winnipeg, in the 1870s. They have four children, the youngest being Ben, a shy, withdrawn, undersized child who rarely speaks to people, even in his own family. He is clearly not an ordinary boy, and no one knows quite what to make of him. He has developed a kind of kinship with the farm animals and wildlife in the fields, even to the point of being able to mimic their sounds and actions with amazing accuracy. Some people believe he can talk to animals, and even wild creatures accept his voice and hand. When the McDonald's new neighbor, George Burton, arrives one day with his ferocious dog Lobo, to get permission to set badger traps on the farm, Ben is terrified by the rough, burly Burton, but he is able to subdue Lobo by imitating the dog's whines and movements!

Several miles away, a female badger has dug a burrow to raise her family in. Badgers are fierce fighters, and this one has a battle scar, a notched right ear. While out exploring the area, Ben spots the badger rustling in the grass. He gets down on all fours and imitates her chattering. Then he feeds her, and before he leaves, she actually allows him to touch her cheek and ear! Ben returns home smiling about his exciting encounter.

After the badger's babies are born, her mate is trapped and captured by Burton. The female badger, too, eventually becomes ensnared in the trap, and her babies starve while she struggles to free herself. She finally bites herself loose with her foot badly injured, but it's too late—the babies die.

Shortly after this, Ben is once again wandering the prairie, but this time he roams too far and becomes lost, just when a thunderstorm strikes. He takes refuge in a badger hole. Half asleep, he hears "a strange sound approaching, an intermingled wheezing and grumbling." The deep, solid bulk of something is entering the hole, and Ben is vulnerable and terrified. The female badger snarls viciously, and Ben screams.

Then he snarls, mimicking her, and lashing at her with his hands. He tries chattering at her, as he did with the badger he met before, not realizing this is the same one. The badger leaves, but that's not the end of the story. She returns and gradually comes to trust the boy, as he starts to trust her. The McDonald family continue to search for Ben long after their neighbors give him up for dead. What happens between Ben and the badger once they accept each other? Find out in *The Incident at Hawk's Hill*, an incident that really did happen.

—Patricia Farr

Indian Chiefs
By Russell Freedman
(Notables 1987, SLJ/C 1987)

The word "chief" meant different things to whites and Indians. To the whites, a chief was a leader, *the* leader, the person in charge, who commanded the group. But in Indian societies, there could be several chiefs at once, each with a different responsibility. War chiefs were the military leaders, civil chiefs supervised day-to-day life, and so on. A chief did not command; instead, he advised, with all the weight of his reputation and experience, and each chief shared his authority with the other chiefs in his tribe.

Some chieftainships were hereditary, passed down from father to son, but most had to be earned. Personal loyalties and people's respect determined who would become a chief.

All the chiefs in this book were called upon by their people to lead in a time of crisis.

Each man met the challenge in his own way.

There was Red Cloud, the first Indian leader to win a war with the United States (and the last); Quanah Parker, the half-white Comanche who ended his days as a major railroad stockholder and friend of presidents and congressmen; Washakie, who tried to lead the Shoshonis down the white man's path; Sitting Bull, who helped engineer the two worst defeats the U.S. Army suffered in the Indian Wars; and many others. Meet the chiefs—the Indian chiefs.

—Jeff Blair

Interstellar Pig
By William Sleator
(Notables 1984, SLJ/C 1984)

Stuck in a cabin at the beach in the middle of nowhere, with nobody to connect with but his parents—this was shaping up to be the worst vacation of Barney's life. When the most interesting thing around was his own bedroom, where a crazy sailor had lived for twenty years, you can see the depths Barney's summer had reached.

The stories about that mad sailor were actually sort of interesting. The landlord said that all the sailor had ever done was mew like a sick cat and claw at the walls. Even now, years later, Barney could trace the gouges in the wood around the window. They were deep and somewhat organized, as if there had been some method to the sailor's madness.

The summer perked up when three new people moved into the cabin next door. They were easily as strange as the mad sailor must have been. For some reason, they were obsessed with Barney's room and with those gouges by the window—they spent a lot of time studying them.

They also spent a lot of time with a role-playing game called Interstellar Pig. To play it you assumed the role of one of an assortment of alien beings traveling around the cosmos in search of an object, the Interstellar Pig. When Barney got invited to join the game, he didn't realize that it might be more than an afternoon's diversion. That invitation was the first step towards putting Barney's life, and the life of every creature on Earth, in line for total annihilation.

—Jeff Blair

Into a Strange Land: Unaccompanied Refugee Youth in America
By Brent Ashabranner and Melissa Ashabranner
(Christopher 1987, Notables 1987, SLJ/C 1987)

Many of us take our homes and our lives for granted. But what would you do if you had to leave everything you loved—your family, your friends, your home, and almost all your possessions—and move to another country where you couldn't even speak the language, and where no one cared for or about you? That's what hundreds of children and teenagers from Vietnam, Cambodia, Laos, Ethiopia, and Central America have had to do. Listen to some of their stories.

Lan was only eleven when his family sent him away from Vietnam—
it took him three tries just to get onto a refugee boat, but he wasn't
caught, and he survived. Tung's father, a soldier in the South Vietnamese army, had spent eight years in a North Vietnamese prison. When
he finally came home, Tung saw what had happened to him while he
was a prisoner, and told his family that he wanted to leave. His parents
agreed. It cost him two gold bars to get onto the boat, and he spent eight
months in refugee camps before he was able to find a foster family in
the United States. Tung and Hieu now live in Tucson with their foster
family, but for ten months after they left Vietnam they lived in a Malay-
sian refugee camp. Now they help the "new ones," who have just arrived, find their way in their new homeland.

What makes teenagers decide to leave their native lands and come
to the United States? How do they do it? How do they find foster families, and how do they survive in this country where they arrive as
strangers? Read *Into a Strange Land* and find out.

—*J. R. B.*

Invincible Louisa: The Story of the Author of *Little Women*
By Cornelia Meigs
(Newbery 1934)

You don't have to be rich to have a full life. Take Louisa May Alcott,
whose family were poor as churchmice. As a little girl, she lived in half
a dozen places, including a communal farm and a house so rickety it
was nearly condemned. She played in the fields, climbed trees, and
helped with chores. She rubbed pepper in her own eyes (on a dare), and
once nearly drowned in a pond. One afternoon, at the home of some
Quaker friends, she opened an oven door and found a runaway slave
crouched inside—the house was a stop on the Underground Railroad.

At sixteen, Louisa decided that her family had been too poor too
long. She started writing books, mostly wild, romantic tales that she
published under another name—even her family didn't know that she
was the author of stories like "Perilous Play" or "The Abbot's Ghost."
Soon she was her family's main support, and when she put her own
name on an account of her experiences as a volunteer nurse in a gruesome Civil War hospital, she became famous. But not as famous as she
would be later on, when she described her own family's dreams, joys,
and heartbreaks in *Little Women*.

—*J. R. B.*

Island of the Blue Dolphins
By Scott O'Dell
(Newbery 1961)

Karana, a young Indian girl, lived alone for eighteen years on the Island of the Blue Dolphins. This is her story of courage and survival.

"I went back for my little brother Ramo. He was left behind when the white men came in their ship to take my tribe across the sea. What else was I to do? Surely someone would return for us. In the meantime we had to survive. Our enemies were marauding Aleuts, and the wild dogs that roamed the island. After my brother was killed by the dogs, I had to go on alone. I was afraid. It was against our tribal law for women to make or use weapons, yet I would have to do these things. Would the four winds blow in from the four directions of the world and smother me as I made the weapons? Would the earth tremble and bury me beneath its falling rocks? Or, as some had predicted, would the sea rise over the island in a terrible flood? Would the weapons break in my hands at the moment when my life was in danger, as my father had once said? Soon I will try to leave this island. I must see my people again. I will use a canoe that was left behind. The way will be hard, but I will try, for I am Karana, the daughter of a chief."

—Anne Liebst

Note: The passage in quotation marks is adapted from the book.

The Island on Bird Street
By Uri Orlev
(Batchelder 1985, Notables 1984)

I am all alone, except for my mouse. My only chance for survival is to hide like a mouse, to make myself very small in the world, so no one will notice me, so I will not disappear into one of the camps, or be killed by the Nazi soldiers that march through the ghetto. I must survive, for I am sure that someday my father will return, and I must be here waiting for him.

My name is Alex, and I am eleven years old. I live at 78 Bird Street, in an abandoned house that was bombed out at the beginning of the war. The windows and the doors are boarded up, but I have a rope ladder so I can get out at night to search for food and water and coal. Living here isn't easy—any moment I could be captured and snatched away. But I must survive. My father said he would return as soon as he could, and he will—I know he will.

And so Snow and I wait, two mice in our hole, peeking out at the world and hoping for a happy ending.

—J. R. B.

Jacob Have I Loved
By Katherine Paterson
(Newbery 1981)

It's difficult living in the shadow of your sister—especially when she's your twin! Caroline is the one who is beautiful, talented, and smart, the one who gets all the attention and praise. Louise is forever in the background, never quite measuring up.

For years Louise's only friend was Call, who is fat and nearsighted—no one else would look at him twice. But nothing is safe from Caroline, not even her sister's best friend.

About the only time Louise can relax is when she's out on the water, working alongside her father. Then she can see herself as a separate person, good at her work, with a future of her own. Will her dreams be enough to carry her beyond the bitterness of her childhood, to fulfillment as a woman? Or will she always live in Caroline's shadow?

—Judy McElwain

Jenny of the Tetons
By Kristiana Gregory
(Golden Kite 1990)

In July of 1875, what was left of our wagon train pulled into Fort Hall, Idaho territory. My head ached terribly, and a bandage covered a deep wound on my forehead. I rested for a week, gradually remembering the Indian attack that had killed my family and left me a scarred orphan.

The wagon train was ready to move on, but I wasn't ready to go with them, nor could I stay at the fort. It was arranged that I stay with Beaver Dick, an English trapper, and help care for his family. As we neared his cabin, I could see their faces, and a chill went through me. His wife was an Indian!

—Cecilia Swanson

Jeremy Visick
By David Wiseman
(Notables 1981, SLJ/C 1981)

Matthew thought history was rubbish. Unfortunately, he expressed this opinion in history class one day, loudly enough for the teacher to hear. Now he had a special assignment: to visit the village graveyard and copy down what was written on the Martin family tombstone.

Well, he wasn't afraid to go into the graveyard. But after he found the Martins' plot and wrote down what was written on their stone, it was hard to leave. He found himself walking among the other graves, almost as though he were being guided, until he came to the Visick family tombstone. And there he stopped. According to the weathered letters on the stone, it was dedicated to the memory of Reuben Visick and his two sons, killed in the Wheal Maid mine cave-in on July 21, 1852. Matthew turned to leave, but his feet seemed frozen. Looking back at the stone, he noticed something else written at the bottom, almost obscured by grass. As he slowly deciphered the words, he heard a voice that wasn't his own reading aloud: "And to Jeremy Visick, his son, aged 12 years, whose body still lies in Wheal Maid."

From then on, Matthew was haunted by the thought of Jeremy Visick lying sealed in some cave underground. He began learning everything he could about Cornwall and its historic mines, and its long series of mine disasters. The Wheal Maid cave-in was one of the worst.

Then one morning Matthew woke up early and went downstairs to the kitchen. He noticed a light burning in the old storage shed in the back yard, and stepped out to investigate. But he stopped short—frozen—when the shed's door opened. Through the door came a woman holding a candle, followed by a man who stopped to talk with her for a few minutes. Somehow Matthew knew who they were—Mr. and Mrs. Visick. Mr. Visick kissed his wife goodbye and walked off down the path. Then his two older sons appeared at the door, kissed their mother, and followed.

And then, as Matthew watched, a boy about his own age came to the door. Jeremy Visick kissed his mother goodbye but didn't immediately set off down the path. Instead, he walked over to Matthew and took his hand.

Matthew would follow Jeremy Visick into Wheal Maid mine that day, to relive the cave-in disaster. Would he bring back Jeremy's body? Or would he lie beside it, sealed in an underground tomb?

—Diantha G. McCauley

Johnny Tremain: A Novel for Old and Young
By Esther Forbes
(Newbery 1944)

Johnny Tremain is fourteen and apprenticed to a silversmith in Boston. He's good at what he does, and he's proud of himself. Too proud, maybe, when he bosses around the other apprentices or when he decides to break the Sabbath to work on a special silver bowl for Mr. John Hancock. While he is working on the bowl, a crucible of molten silver breaks, and the hot metal burns Johnny's right hand so badly that it fuses his thumb to his hand. He can never work silver again.

What is a poor boy to do? Silversmithing is the only thing Johnny knows, and he can't learn a new trade with only one good hand. Johnny wanders the streets of Boston, angry, hungry, frustrated, feeling worse and worse about himself and his possibilities for the future.

Then he meets Rab, who works for a printer, and slowly things begin to change for Johnny. Rab becomes his friend and helps Johnny find work. And then, through Rab, Johnny becomes involved in the secret goings-on of the Sons of Liberty—Sam Adams, James Otis, Paul Revere, and the other leaders of the Revolution in Boston. Johnny may be just a poor boy with a crippled hand, but he finds a place for himself in the creation of a new country and a new way of life.

—Sarah Flowers

The Josie Gambit
By Mary Frances Shura
(Notables 1986)

I was the new kid on the block, here to live with my grandmother for six months. Maybe that's why I was objective enough to notice that something not quite right was in the air.

Tory was a chess player, just like Josie and me. She knew all the strategy that Josie's grandfather had taught me during my vacations over the years. But Tory was different from Josie and me. She had no scruples. I could see something evil in her eyes, even when she was acting like Josie's loyal friend. I knew she hated me the moment we met. Although I'm not a great-looking guy, very few people call me a freak at first sight.

Josie couldn't see the cruel streak in Tory. She knew Tory had big problems with her parents, and for Josie that explained and excused everything. But as I played chess with Tory at school, I began to wonder if she wasn't playing something more than a board game. Some rather strange things had begun to happen in the neighborhood. Tory was heading toward a "queen's gambit," the most daring move in chess. But she was playing with real people's feeling—and their lives.

—Bernice D. Crouse

The Journey: Japanese Americans, Racism, and Renewal
By Sheila Hamanaka
(Notables 1990, SLJ/C 1990)

I wish this book were twenty-five feet long and eight feet high. That's how big the mural called *The Journey* is. I would love to walk along slowly, looking very closely at every bit of color, every face, and feel the excitement as one scene flows into another. But even if the mural were that big, it still wouldn't be big enough to contain the emotion that the artist has put into it. For Sheila Hamanaka, *The Journey* is the story of her life and story of her people, the Nisei [Nee-say], the Japanese living in America.

To get the painting started, there's a wide golden road that means promise—the promise of a good life in a new country. A strong farmer reaches out and offers you a peach. A wise woman stretches and looks to the future. But why is she worried?

Gun ablaze, and a man hanging from a tree. Life has turned upside down for the Japanese-Americans. The world is at war, and the empire of Japan has attacked the United States at Pearl Harbor. The U.S. government has said, "Japan and the Japanese people are the enemy! Doesn't matter where they live! Throw the Nisei in Jail!"

Now you're at the middle of the mural, and there are crowds and crowds of people screaming, their faces blurred with tears. A son hugs his father and says, "Be strong." Then all the Japanese-Americans stand and say, "We must be free!".

A little boy runs to chase a ball, and the colors are bright again. People are shouting. They laugh. They demand to be heard: "We are Americans too!"

You walk to the end of the mural, and the color you see is that of hope for the future, a life of hard work, success, and peace. Raise your hand, reach up, finish the mural with the colors of your own imagination.

—Mark Anderson

Joyful Noise: Poems for Two Voices
By Paul Fleischman
(BGHB 1988, Newbery 1989, Notables 1988)

Did you see that grasshopper jump, or that water-strider skate across the pond? Did you hear the drone of the honeybee? Look over there— it's a firefly gleaming in the night. Soon you may hear the pulse of the cicada. You'll see and hear all this and much more as Paul Fleischman leads you into a world of insect life and celebration. Soar, creep, and spin with your new insect friends. Find the one you like best, and make a joyful noise.

—*Nancy Bardole Hanaman*

Julie of the Wolves
By Jean Craighead George
(Newbery 1973)

Julie knew she had to make the wolves her friends—if she didn't, she would die. She was lost on the Alaskan tundra, without food or protection. When she began her journey, she thought she had taken everything she'd need, but she didn't remember the compass—the one thing she shouldn't have forgotten. Now she was lost, and her food was gone. There was no way she could figure out how to get to San Francisco and no way she could survive—unless she made friends with the wolves.

—*Deb Kelly and J. R. B.*

Jumanji
By Chris Van Allsburg
(BGHB 1981, Caldecott 1982)

Their parents had left them alone for the afternoon, with strict instructions not to mess up the house. But after Peter and Judy had played with all their toys, they couldn't think of anything else to do. And then, there it was: a new toy—a board game they'd never seen before. It was called Jumanji, and it looked like some kind of jungle adventure game. Just what they needed to liven up the afternoon! They opened the box with great excitement, set up the board, and started to play—they hardly looked at the instructions, and they certainly didn't take them very seriously. And that was a mistake, as they soon discovered when a lion jumped down from the top of the piano and chased them around the house. In fact, each time the children threw the dice, another jungle animal appeared, and most of those animals were hungry! Too late they grabbed the instructions and learned that they couldn't just stop—to end the game, either Peter or Judy would have to play it through and reach the Golden City. And they'd have to do it fast, or they'd never see their parents again!

—Anne Liebst

Justin and the Best Biscuits in the World
By Mildred Pitts Walter
(King 1987)

It's hard being the only boy in the house, living with a mother and two sisters, especially if you can't seem to do anything right.

That's how Justin feels. He can't keep his room as clean as his sisters', no matter how hard he tries. He can't cook or do the dishes—he always drops something, or maybe he burns the pan. Why should he even try? It's woman's work, and he's tired of it.

Naturally he jumps at the chance to get away from all this and visit his grandpa on the ranch. He'll ride his favorite horse, help Grandpa fix the fences, and see the rodeo—man's work!

Well, Justin has always known his grandpa was special, but at the ranch he learns some things he didn't know before, about Grandpa, about cowboy days, and about "man's work" and "woman's work."

—Judy McElwain

Justin Morgan Had a Horse
By Marguerite Henry
(Newbery Honor 1946)

My name is Joel Gross, and I knew the schoolmaster Justin Morgan. And I knew his horse, almost from when it was born. I was the one who went with Justin to Massachusetts, to collect some money he was owed. Farmer Beane, who owed the money, was short of cash, so he gave Justin two colts instead. One was a big fine colt named Ebenezer, the other was a runt named Bub. I fell in love with Bub. Justin allowed me to train the colt, who learned faster and better than any horse I'd ever seen, but once Bub was grown, he rented him out to a farmer. I was afraid that Bub would be overworked, but in fact he became famous: he was so successful at pulling bees that after a while no one would pull against him, and he also won a name for racing, beating two fancy thoroughbreds from New York. Not bad for a poor schoolteacher's horse!

I was glad when Justin took the little stallion back, to ride on the rounds of his teaching circuit—Bub would have the easier life of a saddle horse. And I kept saving every penny, hoping that eventually I'd be able to own the horse myself. But Justin Morgan, who had always been sickly, fell ill and died, and Bub went to Sheriff Rice, who sold him to Farmer Evans, who put him up for auction. I didn't have the money to buy him, and though I knew the man who outbid me, he turned around and sold Bub again, to a stranger who took him away. It was the saddest day of my life. Would I ever find Bub again?

—*Abbie V. Landry*

The Keeper
By Phyllis Reynolds Naylor
(Notables 1986)

It was almost as though a stranger had moved into his father's body. Before, Nick's father had been neat, precise, organized almost to a fault. Now, this "new" father left papers strewn around the apartment, letters unopened, and bills unpaid. The man who had lived according to an unvarying ritual—rising at the same time every morning, going through a seven-minute performance with the shaving cream and the safety razor—now kept erratic hours and went days without taking a shower, let alone shaving. He spent hours pacing back and forth, pausing to stare intently out the window, as though he were watching for something. Nick didn't know what to think, or what to do.

He didn't know what to do the night his father took the bathroom apart, either. The clinking sounds woke Nick around 3:00 a.m. When he went in to see what was going on, he found his father sitting on the edge of the tub with newspapers spread all around him. The float from the toilet, the sink drain cover, and both faucet handles lay in pieces on the floor.

"Dad, what are you doing?"

His father silenced him with a "shh" and a warning finger to the lips.

"Looking for microphones" was his whispered reply.

"Microphones?! Dad, who would put microphones in our toilet?"

Leaning toward Nick's ear, his father whispered, "The Communists. Don't tell your mother; they're out to get me."

"He's crazy." The thought lodged in Nick's brain like a bullet. He had never known anyone who was mentally ill, but this sure wasn't the type of behavior he would have expected from someone who was. He'd have expected gibberish and vacant stares, not conversations like this.

His dad *was* crazy. It was a secret that Nick and his mother had to keep from the rest of the world. They couldn't commit his father to an institution unless he threatened to harm either himself or them, and he had never done that. Never, until the night he brought home a package—a long, thin package . . . like a rifle.

—Jeff Blair

The Kestrel
By Lloyd Alexander
(Notables 1982)

I am traveling around the kingdom of Westmark. You see, I am engaged to Princess Augusta (or Mickle, as I first knew her), and her father the king thinks I should get to know the land I will one day serve as prince. Meanwhile, of course, Mickle's mother hopes that while I am gone she can convince her daughter to select a more suitable husband, because I am just Theo, the former printer's devil. I know Mickle loves me, but I do not know what pressures she may be subjected to.

In my travels around the kingdom, I'm learning some things I didn't want to know. The friends from my apprentice days may be right—they used to say that the aristocracy and even the monarchy had done great harm to our country, and that our present institutions of government should be abolished. Now I have seen the evidence of harm myself, but I'm not sure of the remedy; however, Florian, Justin, and Luther are all engaged to some degree in revolutionary activities. Luther collects information; he tells me to warn Mickle against General Erzcour, but he won't tell me why.

Suddenly a commotion breaks out at the inn. A traveler has brought shocking news. King Augustine has died . . . and Mickle is now the ruler of Westmark! My one thought is to ride for the capital and give her my support. But no sooner am I on the road than my horse loses a shoe. As I walk back to the inn I'm accosted by a man I haven't seen for years: Skeit, the servant of the evil Carrabus. He draws his pistol and fires.

I wake up in Florian's camp, in the middle of a war. Troops from the Regian kingdom have invaded Westmark, aided by the turncoat General Erzcour. Mickle's army is in confusion; no one even seems to know where she is. But it is now clear that Florian and Justin have forces of their own, mostly guerrilla fighters. They oppose the Regian invaders even more hotly than they opposed the aristocrats. They can help Mickle, and they will—but the price may be her throne. Can Westmark afford the price of Florian's help? Can Mickle afford to refuse? And will I ever find her again?

—*Abbie V. Landry*

The Kid in the Red Jacket
By Barbara Park
(SLJ/C 1987)

Howard's been mad at his parents for weeks. Did they ask *him* if he wanted to move? No! Did they tell him how great it was going to be, even though he knew it'd be the end of the world? Of course they did.

Howard remembers a new kid at his old school. No one wanted to help that kid. They never even bothered to learn his name; they just called him by what he was wearing, "the kid in the green shirt" or whatever. Even when the kid had his name on his shirt, everyone called him "the kid in the Kenneth shirt."

Now Howard is the new kid—no name, no friends. Worse, there's a little girl from across the street who keeps hanging around. Can you imagine? A firstgrader tagging along with a fifth-grader! The very worst was when he tried running away from her so no one would see them walking to school together. She yelled across the playground, right in front of practically the whole school, "Why are you running? Do you have to go to the potty?"

It's hard to fit in, and Howard doesn't want to be known as "the kid in the red jacket" forever.

—*Cecilia Swanson*

The Kidnapping of Christina Lattimore
By Joan Lowery Nixon
(Poe 1980)

One day the most important thing in Christina Lattimore's life is getting her parent's permission for a school trip to France. The next day the most important thing in Christina Lattimore's life is survival!

Christina was kidnapped as she was getting out of her car in the driveway. A hand covered her mouth so she couldn't scream, and a needle was jabbed into her arm. When Christina woke up she was locked in a damp basement. She doesn't know why she was kidnapped or who is holding her prisoner. But she learns. By listening and watching, Christina learns more about her captors than she ever wanted to. And she learns that they have a plan, a plan that will make Christina look like the mastermind behind her own kidnapping.

—Colleen Stinson

King of the Wind
By Marguerite Henry
(Newbery 1949)

Agba was a horseboy in the stables of the Sultan of Morocco. The Sultan had many, many horses, and Agba, a mute, had charge of ten, one a bay mare in foal. During the holy month of Ramadan, the Sultan decided that every living thing in his palace would have to observe the fast, so the horses went without food or water from sun-up to sundown. The pregnant mare suffered more than the others. Weakened by the long fast, she managed to deliver her colt, but she did not survive. When the Chief of the Grooms came to her stall, he found her dead, and the mute boy Agba cradling a newborn foal. Pushing Agba aside, the Chief Groom inspected the animal, and then he drew his sword: on the chest of the colt he saw the sign of the wheat ear, the sign of bad luck and evil fate. But Agba threw himself on the colt and showed the Chief Groom the white spot on its hind foot—a hopeful sign, promising speed and strength. Grumbling, the Chief Groom put up his sword. The tiny colt could live—if Agba could find a way to feed it. So Agba sought out a camel driver and, with signs and gestures, got camel's milk to give the hungry orphan. He named the colt Sham, which means sun, and nursed it night and day. The colt flourished under Agba's care, and became the fastest horse in the Sultan's stable.

That was why Sham was chosen, with five other horses, when the Sultan decided to send a gift to the King of France. Agba would accompany his horse (the Sultan was pleased to learn that the boy was mute and could tell no tales). They would travel by ship to France. But the ship's master cheated the Sultan. He took the money that was meant to buy food for the horses and kept it for himself. By the time the horses got to France they looked like skeletons, and the King of France was highly insulted. He thought the Sultan was making fun of him. So he gave the starved horses to the army, except for Sham, who was put to work hauling carts of groceries for the royal kitchen—a purebred Arabian stallion pulling bags of cabbages and flour! Agba was ready to despair. How could he rescue the horse he loved when he couldn't even speak? Would Sham be worked to death as a carthorse? Or could he somehow, finally, outrun the bad-luck sign?

—Abbie V. Landry

Knights of the Kitchen Table
By Jon Scieszka
(SLJ/C 1991)

Joe is having a perfectly normal birthday with his friends Fred and Sam when, all of a sudden, a poof of smoke comes out of the book that Joe's uncle, a magician, gave him for a present. Instantly Joe, Fred, and Sam are transported back to the time of knights and dragons. Even worse, the Black Knight is pointing a long and very sharp spear at them.

After escaping from that little predicament Joe, Fred, and Sam have to face Smaug the Dragon and Bleob the Giant. And even if they don't get squashed or barbecued, they're still trapped—they've lost the book that brought them to the Dark Ages in the first place. Now they may never get back to the kitchen table to finish celebrating Joe's birthday. They may be trapped as knights of the Round Table forever!

—Colleen Stinson

Konrad
By Christine Nostlinger
(Batcheldor 1979)

One morning, Mrs. Bertie Bartolotti answers her door to find a delivery man with a heavy white parcel. Inside the package there is a huge, gleaming, silvery can. Thinking it must contain corned beef, Mrs. Bartolotti pulls the metal pull-ring and finds a creature crouching inside the can. It is sort of a crumpled-looking dwarf; it has a crumpled-up head with a very wrinkled face, and crumpled-up arms, and a crumpled-up throat and chest. After mixing the nutrient solution and pouring it over the creature, Mrs. Bartolotti learns what the parcel really contains—a factory-produced boy name Konrad. Being the product of highly developed technology, he is quite free of those faults and defects that children usually have. In fact, Konrad is trained and educated and guaranteed to please in every way.

So on the one hand we have Konrad, who knows all the rules—the "should do's" and the "shouldn't do's" of seven-year-old boys. On the other hand we have Mrs. Bartolotti, who has no idea what's proper or what isn't, and wouldn't care if she did. For example, when she dresses herself before going downtown shopping, she grabs a pair of jeans and a T-shirt off the line, but since they are unironed she covers them up with a thick fur coat—even though it's a warm day. And, of course, since she is wearing her fur coat she might as well wear her fur cap too. If she dresses herself like this, can you imagine the kind of clothes she picks out for Konrad?

But after a few weeks Konrad and Mrs. Bartolotti do adjust to each other. It is with great distress that they read the letter from the factory that explains that Konrad was sent to Mrs. Bartolotti by mistake, that it was really someone else who had ordered him, and that factory agents will be coming to collect him. Since neither of them want Konrad to leave, they must devise a plan to avoid the recall. Desperate situations call for desperate remedies—and that is exactly what Konrad and Mrs. Bartolotti come up with!

—*Lynda Smith*

The Land I Lost: Adventures of a Boy in Vietnam
By Quang Nhuong Huynh
(Notables 1982)

It's hard to imagine growing up in a land like Vietnam. There's really no way to compare it with our life in the United States. This is Quang Nhuong Huynh's story.

He lived in a remote village in the central highlands of Vietnam. His home was made of bamboo poles, with a roof of coconut leaves. Each house in his village was ringed with a deep trench to keep wild animals out, for the surrounding forest was full of wild hogs, monkeys, snakes, and even tigers! The villagers, who were mostly farmers, used water buffaloes to till the soil. Buffaloes were almost like wild animals themselves. They could be fierce and difficult to handle, so farmers tried to select the most docile calves, in the hopes that they would grow up to be gentle, obedient workers. This rarely happened. Quang Nhuong's family had one buffalo that topped all the others in the village—for size, strength, and toughness. When he charged into another water buffalo, the impact was tremendous. He was called Tank because of his looks and his style of combat—when Tank hit you, you knew you'd been hit!

Share Quang Nhuong's and Tank's adventures in a world beyond our imagination—*The Land I Lost.*

—*Carol Kappelmann*

Lester's Turn
By Jan Slepian
(Notables 1981)

Alfie was dead. Alfie, my friend, a good boy, a good person—best of all, my friend.

The question that was eating my heart out was, is Alfie dead because of me? Did my taking him out of the hospital cause his death?

All I wanted was for Alfie to be happy, to be free. How could he be happy in that awful hospital? I knew Alfie better than they did. I knew what he liked. So I went ahead with my plans and brought Alfie home.

Now he's dead.

Was it because of me?

—Carol Kappelmann

Let the Circle Be Unbroken
By Mildred D. Taylor
(Notables 1981)

Cassie Logan and her three brothers—older, serious Stacey, and younger, fun-loving Christopher-John and Little Man—belong to one of the most prosperous black families around Strawberry, Mississippi. The Logans are well-off because they have a five-room house with fireplaces instead of a one-room, tar-papered dirt-floor shack like many of their neighbors. They have several cows and horses, and the hired man Mr. Morrison to help work their land. Their land—that's the most important thing, because the Logans own all two hundred acres of it themselves. That means that what ever small profit they make from selling their cotton crop, they can keep. Their sharecropper neighbors aren't so lucky; their crops go first to the greedy white landowners who skim all the items they bought on credit right off the top, leaving very little behind. We see this world through eleven-year-old Cassie's eyes in 1934, in the middle of the Depression. Cassie has a hard time keeping her mouth shut about things that don't seem right, and there is so much she doesn't understand, such as:

—why the government folks up in Washington make the farmers plow up acres of beautiful blooming cotton to keep cotton prices up, promising to send government checks for the loss, money the farmers never see, since the white plantation owners keep it for themselves.

—why young black neighbor T.J. is hanged for the murder of a white store owner, after a trial by white folks in which all the evidence points to the white Simms brothers, boys who used to be T.J.'s "friends."

—why pretty black Jacey Peters gets in trouble for talking to a white boy, and why Uncle Hammer throws Cassie's photo of her white friend Jeremy into the fire.

—why Uncle Hammer hates Cousin Bud for marrying a white woman in New York.

—why everybody loves Bud's daughter Suzella when she visits, so pretty and light-skinned she could pass for white.

—why Suzella refuses to call herself black.

—and most of all, why her favorite brother, fourteen-year-old Stacey, doesn't want her to hang around him anymore, and why one morning he leaves a note saying he has run away to make money for the family to pay the new cotton tax.

How can Cassie grow in this hard, confusing, unfair world? Well, there are marble games to play in the red dust, fishing in the pond, chewing sweet gum peeled right off the tree, smelling all the green, growing things around her, munching on warm peanuts. And basking in the understanding love of wise Papa, respected by the whole black community, the warm love of Mama and Big Mama, who would do anything for their children; feeling the unspoken bond with hot-tempered Uncle Hammer, so much like Cassie herself, and the loyalty and companionship of her brothers, who always stick by her.

—Cathi Dunn MacRae

Libby on Wednesday
By Zilpha Keatley Snyder
(SLJ/C 1990)

Wednesday. The peak of the week. You've crawled all the way through Monday and Tuesday, made it to the middle, and now it should be an easy slide to the weekend. That's what Wednesday is to most people.

But to Libby, Wednesday is the writers' workshop. Libby and four other students, all winners of a writing contest, meet every Wednesday after school to read each other's writings, offer constructive criticism, and generally extend the torture of the school day.

This is Libby's first year in school, even though she's in eighth grade. She was always schooled at home before, with adults and books and her collections.

Now she's got to get used to other kids, like obnoxious Gary Greene with his evil smirk; Alex, who mainly writes parodies; Wendy, a student cheerleader on the student council; and Tierney with her strange punk clothes. Libby can't wait until she's "socialized" enough for her mother, so she can get away from all these Future Famous Writers, these weirdos!

—*Colleen Stinson*

A Light in the Attic
By Shel Silverstein
(Notables 1981, SLJ/C 1981)

Do you hate drying dishes? I do too. Wouldn't it be easier to let them sit in the sink and dry all by themselves? The next time you're asked to dry the dishes, there is a great poem that may help you get out of it:

> If you have to dry the dishes
> (Such an awful, boring chore)
> If you have to dry the dishes
> And you drop one on the floor—
> Maybe they won't let you
> Dry the dishes anymore.

How about sports? Does anyone like sports? Hockey? Baseball? Skating? What about diving?

> The fanciest dive that ever was dove
> Was done by Melissa of Coconut Grove.
> She bounced on the board and flew into the air
> With a twist of her head and a twirl of her hair.
> She did thirty-four jackknives, backflipped and spun,
> Quadruple gainered, and reached for the sun,
> And then somersaulted nine times and a quarter—
> And looked down and saw that the pool had no water.

Or, if you like milkshakes, here is a way you should never make one:

> Geraldine now, stop shaking that cow,
> For heaven's sake, for your sake and for the cow's sake!
> That's the dumbest way I've seen
> To make a milk shake.

No matter what you like, or what you don't like, there's a funny poem about it in this book.

—*Colleen Stinson*

Like Jake and Me
By Mavis Jukes
(BGHB 1985, Newbery Honor 1985, Notables 1984, SLJ/C 1984)

Alex's step-dad, Jake, doesn't seem to think that Alex is old enough or big enough or strong enough to help out with anything—to split the wood, carry the axe, stack the logs, light the fire—not anything.

But the time comes when Jake needs help, Alex's help. No one else can possibly know what to do or how to go about doing it, except Alex.

—Carol Kappelmann

Lincoln: A Photobiography
By Russell Freedman
(Newbery 1988, Notables 1987, SLJ/C 1987)

Everyone knows who Abraham Lincoln was—he was President during the Civil War, he freed the slaves, kept the United States united, and was assassinated by John Wilkes Booth. But who was the man behind the legend? Who was the boy behind the man?

Lincoln was a person made of opposites. He grew up in a log cabin, yet even before he was President, he was a wealthy lawyer, widely known for his skill in the courtroom. He spoke like a country farmer, yet he was one of our county's finest writers. He had a great sense of humor and loved telling stories, yet he was also moody and often depressed. He was logical, thinking through his actions carefully, yet he was also superstitious—he believed in omens, dreams, and visions.

Today we know him as an American hero, but when he was President, he was called a tyrant, a hick, and an ignorant baboon who was a disgrace to the nation. So who was he, and how did his friends and his enemies describe him?

Meet Abraham Lincoln—the boy, the man, the lawyer, the President, and finally the martyr who died for his country and for his unshakable belief in its future greatness.

—J. R. B.

Little by Little: A Writer's Education
By Jean Little
(BGHB 1988, Notables 1988)

What makes a person into a writer? Sometimes it's a piece of extraordinary luck, or a private experience that sets you apart and makes you think—hard—about yourself and others. And always it's the ability to remember how you felt, and to recreate those feelings for the people who will read your books.

Jean Little was born in Taiwan, where her parents worked as missionary doctors. At birth she was blind, and although she eventually gained partial vision, her eyes never worked well enough to allow for an easy, normal life. She didn't feel particularly sorry for herself—she was pleased that she could see at all—but she knew she was different from the other kids, who sometimes made fun of her. Jean had a solid, loving family, but she longed for friends. In the end she made up her own—and they came alive in books like *Sneaker Hill, Mine for Keeps, Hey World!*, and *Mama's Going to Buy You a Mockingbird*—books like this. —*Colleen Stinson and J. R. B.*

Little Town on the Prairie
By Laura Ingalls Wilder
(Newbery Honor 1942)

It was spring. The long, hard winter that had kept them cold, hungry, and cramped up in the kitchen of their house in town was finally over. It was wonderful to go out to the claim again! The sun was so warm and bright that it did not seem possible that the prairie had ever been scoured by freezing winds and buried in snow. Laura felt as though she could never get enough sunshine soaked into her bones.

Then one evening Pa brought home news. He had found Laura a job in town. Many of the men coming out to Dakota had no one to sew their clothes for them, and no idea of how to do it themselves. They paid Mrs. White to make their shirts, and now Laura was to work for her.

Each morning Laura milked and watered Ellen, her cow. Then, after a quick breakfast, she and Pa walked to town. They had to be at work by seven o'clock. At Mrs. White's, Laura would start off by basting or hand-sewing the shirts together. Then Mrs. White would stitch them tight on the sewing machine. Her feet flew up and down on the treadle that made the machine work—there was no electricity then. Next Laura sewed on the collars, made the buttonholes, and attached the buttons. Her shoulders and neck ached from sitting still so long. And her eyes grew tired and blurry. Sometimes the needle in her hand would slip and prick her fingers. But she kept on until the end of the day, when she and Pa would walk back home as the sun was setting.

Laura missed being out on the prairie in the sunshine, with the wildflowers growing everywhere, but she knew her work was important. Each payday she gave Ma her money to put towards Mary's college fund. The whole family was determined that Mary would have the chance to finish her education at the college for the blind.

But as determined as Laura was to help Mary and then to become a teacher herself, she was put to the test when handsome Almanzo Wilder began seeing her home. Laura was only fifteen, but she soon realized that she'd have to decide now what she wanted for the rest of her life.

—Linda Olson and Colleen Stinson

The Lives of Christopher Chant
By Diana Wynne Jones
(Notables 1988)

All that Christopher Chant wants is to be an ordinary boy. He wants to go to school, have friends, and play cricket. But does he ever get a chance? Oh no, not Christopher. He had to be born with nine lives and some of the most powerful magical abilities in the world! Various adults, including evil Uncle Ralph, know about Christopher's powers and try to use them for their own purposes. So instead of the normal childhood that he craves, Christopher has to spend his time exploring different worlds and dealing with the likes of mermaids and goddesses.

And now, on top of all that, the government had decided that he is to be the future Chrestomanci. The Chrestomanci is one of the most powerful figures in Christopher's world, sort of like the head of the FBI, except that his job is to find and punish those who misuse magic. As far as Christopher is concerned, this is the worst thing that could happen to him. He has to live in the castle of the current Chrestomanci and spend his days learning his future job. Christopher is bored by his magic lessons, and he can never remember the spells. He doesn't like living with a bunch of adults, watching him all the time and telling him what to do. So he tries to liven things up by overdoing the magic that he does know. Instead of moving a sandwich from one room to another, he'll move part of the table that it's sitting on too; instead of raising a chair, he'll push the roof off the house.

But soon Christopher doesn't have to try to make things exciting anymore. Life in the castle gets about as exciting as it can when war breaks out between the forces of the Chrestomanci and a gang of smugglers, and suddenly Christopher finds himself in charge!

—*Jo Berkman*

Lon Po Po: A Red-Riding-Hood Story from China
Retold by Ed Young
(BGHB 1990, Caldecott 1990, Notables 1989, SLJ/C 1989)

"Po Po" means "Grandma" in Chinese, but "Lon Po Po" is the Wolf-Grandma—the Big Bad Wolf, dressed up in Grandma's clothes! And how can you tell it's the Big Bad Wolf, even in the dark? Well, there are certain sure clues, like the long sharp teeth and the thick scratchy fur, and the hot, wolfish breath.

But don't worry. The Big Bad Wolf is no match for three clever little girls. They've seen through his disguise, and they know a trick to play. Let's hope it works—because Lon Po Po is getting hungry!

—*J. R. B.*

Loving Ben
By Elizabeth Laird
(SLJ/C 1989)

Ben was special, special because he was my baby brother, special because I loved him with all my heart, and special because he was handicapped.

I was twelve when Ben was born. Mom didn't even make it to the hospital to have him. He was born at home. At first I thought he'd been born dead—I hadn't heard him crying. Then the ambulance men left with a funny box-thing—a special incubator for babies—and Ben was inside. So Ben was alive, but there was definitely something wrong with him. His head was really big, twice as big as it should have been. The doctors called it hydrocephalus and said even though they could drain some of the fluid from his head periodically, he would always be handicapped by the damage done to his brain.

I loved Ben so much that I wanted to protect him. That's why I never invited the kids at school to my house after Ben was born—I knew what they'd think, and I knew what they'd say. I wanted to protect Ben, yes, but I think I also wanted to protect me. Mom's world revolved around

Ben and keeping him alive. It seemed as though he caught every germ there was. Many nights Mom only got a couple of hours' sleep. Dad was gone more and more of the time. But that wasn't Ben's fault. He was a happy baby. I'd taught him to kiss and clap his hands. He would laugh and laugh. Somehow I understood that it was best to love Ben just for himself. Wishing wouldn't make him any better, but loving him would make him happy. And then came the Saturday when I was in Mrs. Chapman's shop with Ben in his stroller and I ran into Miranda and her current boyfriend.

I knew when I saw their faces that my secret was out. For two years no one at school had known about Ben's handicap, but now everyone would know. I dreaded going to school Monday. I heard Miranda even before I saw her, surrounded by her friends. "I've never seen anything like it," she was saying. "I mean, this great big head, like a monster in a weird cartoon."

This was my beloved brother they were talking about. I felt as if I were going to explode.

—*Carol Kappelmann*

Lyddie
By Katherine Paterson
(Notables 1991, SLJ/C 1991)

Papa had been gone for three years, and in all that time they'd not heard a word. After he left, Mama changed—she couldn't seem to handle the responsibilities of the farm, and finally she just took the younger children and moved to her sister's place. Lyddie and Charles stayed behind, hoping they could keep the farm going until Papa returned. Mama might have given up hope, but Charles and Lyddie would not, not even when they got the message that Mama had hired them out—Lyddie to a tavern-owner and Charles to a mill-owner.

Lyddie had always been a hard worker, but it was soon clear to her that she would be little more than a slave at Cutler's Tavern. No matter how hard she worked, she'd never earn enough money to help pay off the debts on the farm. Then a young woman passing through on her way home for vacation told Lyddie about Lowell, Massachusetts, where new factories had opened, that paid young people well.

As soon as Lyddie was fired by the tavern-owner, she headed for Lowell to become a factory girl. The pay was better, but the life was so different—and so hard: long hours, choking dust, and dangers Lyddie had never even thought of. Was there any hope for the future? There had to be, because Lyddie would never give up!

—Helen Schlichting

M. C. Higgins, the Great
By Virginia Hamilton
(BGHB 1974, Newbery 1975)

I suppose you're wondering about this pole I'm sitting on. Well, this pole was my prize for swimming the Ohio River. It's forty feet of cold steel and the best kind of ride you want. My Dad got it for me, and I attached the bicycle seat at the top along with the pedals. Real comfortable.

Me, I'm M. C. Higgins, and up here I feel like anything's possible. It's when I climb back down that things don't look so good. Like, right behind our home there's an ugly spoil-heap left by the mining company.

And it's sliding down the mountain, heading straight for our house! I tell you, it's dangerous living up here on Sarah's Mountain! But my folks don't want to leave. They say our roots are here, that this is where we belong. If only they'd agree to move somewhere safe. There's got to be a way, and I'm going to find it!

—Sister M. Anna Falbo, CSSF

The Machine Gunners
By Robert Westall
(BGHB 1977, Carnegie 1976)

Chas McGill was sixteen and lived in Garmouth, England, during World War II. Garmouth was on the coast of England, and suffered nightly from fierce German air raids; during the day all the townspeople could talk about were the rumors that Hitler and his troops would soon be invading. Bodser Brown had the best collection of war souvenirs in all of Garmouth; besides the normal shrapnel and bullets, he had the nose cone of an anti-aircraft shell and the flying helmet he had taken from a dead German pilot. Chas had the second-best collection, and he would've done anything to beat Bodser and have the best—and he knew he could, as soon as he saw the downed German aircraft, a Heinkel 111, with its machine gun still intact.

Although the police soon found the plane and launched a huge search for its missing weapon, Chas organized a gang that hid the gun in a fortress they built in the garden of a bombed-out home. They planned carefully to use the gun to shoot down the German hit-and-run bombers. They didn't plan to let a war orphan live in the fortress, and they never expected to actually capture a German flyer and hold him prisoner, but when these things happened, that just made the group more determined to continue as a military unit. Until the night of the great invasion, when a foreign army advanced upon the fortress—and at last the machine gunners swung into action.

—Elizabeth Overmyer

Maggie by My Side
By Beverly Butler
(Notables 1987)

Una had been with me six years when cancer took her. Overnight she was gone, out of my life forever. It wasn't that I hadn't lived through similar losses before. I'd spent my whole adult life with a series of guide dogs, and I can tell you, a dog's only real failing is that its lifespan is so much shorter than a human's, shorter than that of the person who loves it and, in my case, depends upon it.

My name is Beverly Butler, and I am blind. Sister, my first dog, opened up a whole new world for me. I couldn't let go of my hard-won freedom now, despite my grief over Una. It was time to search for a new guide dog. I was pretty picky, but I got results sooner than I'd expected. "We have a beautiful German shepherd ready for you."

Her name was Maggie. That was perfect. No one else in my life had that name. I already knew how difficult it could be having a guide dog with a popular human name.

But I still missed Una terribly. Turning to another dog so soon seemed like a betrayal of our partnership. I knew that Una wouldn't have agreed, though; I had to move forward or my life would become paralyzed. Two weeks at Pilot Dogs training school lay ahead of me. Then there would be months of building a strong relationship with Maggie, getting used to her ways and getting her used to mine. As any experienced guide-dog owner can tell you, it takes at least six months to become a working team.

Will Maggie and I be up to it? We'd better be!

—Bernice D. Crouse

The Magical Adventures of Pretty Pearl
By Virginia Hamilton
(Notables 1983)

The gods of Mount Highness in Africa were too busy with their god-business to pay much mind to what was going on down on the plains. Only Pretty Pearl god-child and her big brother, best-god John de Conquer, seemed to care that strangers were carrying off the dark humans from the way-low grounds below the mountain. Even though he was troubled, best-god John de Conquer said it wasn't wise to interfere with human bein's too long, because "they grow on you. You can't fool around de human bein's too long, else you commence actin' human yourself." But Pretty Pearl wasn't satisfied. She just had to go down and find out where these humans were being taken. So she and John de Conquer followed them to America and discovered that the dark ones had become slaves.

Pretty Pearl was anxious to help, and to try out her powers, but she had to wait for the right time. And when that time came, a personal test came with it: she could help the dark humans but she had to do it by the rules. She held the power to help or harm both the slaves and herself. If she succeeded within the rules, she would grow into a god-woman. If she failed, she too would become a mortal—and a slave.

—Pamela A. Todd

Maniac Magee
By Jerry Spinelli
(BGHB 1990, Newbery 1991, Notables 1990)

Who was Maniac Magee? He wasn't always called Maniac, you know. He started out in life as Jeffrey Lionel Magee. His parents died when he was three, and he lived with his aunt and uncle until the day he ran. He ran to get away from the fighting, and he ran until he found a friend. Amanda Beale was the first person he talked to after he ran away from his aunt and uncle. She loaned him a book. And that's how the whole thing started.

He ran everywhere, from the East Side, which was black, to the West Side, which was white.

He made friends with black kids. He made friends with white kids.

He rescued Arnold Jones from Finsterwald's back yard.

He tattooed Giant John McNab's fast ball for half a dozen home runs, and bunted for the first homer ever made on a frog ball.

He kissed a baby buffalo.

He untied the Cobble's Knot.

He ran everywhere he went—he even ran on the rails of the railroad tracks!

He was no ordinary kid. He was Maniac Magee!

> Ma-niac, Ma-niac
> He's so cool!
> Ma-niac, Ma-niac,
> Don't go to school.
> Runs all day,
> Runs all night.
> Ma-niac, Ma-niac,
> Kissed a bull.

Who *was* Maniac? Why was he a legend on the East Side and a legend on the West Side? How did he change that town and the people who lived there in ways no one had ever thought possible? Find out, in *Maniac Magee.*

—*J. R. B*

(from talks by Sue Padilla, Melanie Witulski, and Marvia Boettcher)

Martin's Mice
By Dick King-Smith
(Notables 1989)

It's unthinkable! Quite preposterous! Who ever heard of a cat who won't eat mice? Martin comes from a long line of venerable mousers. To his mother and his siblings, he's an embarrassment, a failure. But Martin just doesn't have a taste for mice, or for anything else he has to catch alive and eat. Actually, Martin would love to have a mouse for a pet. Drusilla, the mouse he catches, at first thinks this is just an elaborate game—surely Martin is only toying with her before he has her for dinner. But Martin installs Drusilla and the little ones she gives birth to in a bathtub in the hayloft of the farm where he lives. The mice can't escape, but at least they're safe in the tub from Martin's prowling relatives. Drusilla, making the best of a bad situation, keeps Martin at her beck and call. Not only must he find her food but, in time, a new husband. Martin has a hard time understanding Drusilla's discontent. She's not really his prisoner, she's his pet! However, when a city lady visiting the farm decides that Martin would make the perfect pet for *her*, he learns how the other half feels. He vows to win back his freedom. Once again, Martin proves that there is no other cat quite like him.

—*Maureen Whalen*

Me, Mop, and the Moondance Kid
By Walter Dean Myers
(Notables 1988)

Do you like sports? Do you like helping your friends, even when they don't think they need your help? Do you like beating the odds and winning against great obstacles? Then you would fit right into our Little League team, the Elks.

Me (Tommy Jackson—that's TJ, please) and my little brother Billy, the Moondance Kid, are members of the Elks, although we'd really rather play on practically any other team. The Elks always lose. But that could change, because Miss Olivia Parrish—Mop, of the Dominican Academy—is joining the team, and she's a top-notch catcher, unless her temper interferes. And if I have my way, we'll win the championship and get Mop adopted, all in one summer. I know what she's feeling right now—me and Moondance were adopted just six months ago.

Of course, we do have to overcome the shortcomings of the rest of the team, and since the Academy might be closing soon, we have to find parents for Mop fast. If she just wouldn't be so prickly when she meets prospective parents, and if she would just do—hey, I gotta go. I got practice. I think Billy might be improving faster than me, and if there's anything I *don't* need it's a little brother who's better at baseball than I am. Not that I'm not proud, but who can he look up to, unless I'm the best?

Oh, and by the way, look around for Taffy, will you? That's the Academy's llama, and it's disappeared.

—*Susan Trimby*

Megan's Island
By Willo Davis Roberts
(Poe 1989)

"Megan, look! Somebody's been here," Sandy yelled to his sister. Sure enough, there was a footprint in the sand. It was a bare footprint like their own, but it was bigger!

They were exploring the island near their grandfather's lakeside cabin, where their mother had brought them even before school let out for the summer. It was very odd, the way she did it—she just threw some clothes into a bag and said they were going to Grandpa's; she didn't even give Megan time to call her best friend, Annie, and tell her they were leaving. Then, as soon as they got to Grandpa's, Mother took off again, by herself this time, without telling them why, or where she was going, or how long she'd be away.

But she was certainly coming back. Megan and Sandy spent the time exploring the island and working on their secret hideout, made of pine branches and well stocked with emergency supplies. Only, the hideout wasn't a secret any more, not if those footprints meant anything. Someone had found it—and eaten half the supplies!

That someone turned out to be an older boy named Ben, who was spending the summer with his father in a cottage not far from Grandpa's. Once he understood about the hideout, Ben had an even better idea: together, they could build a treehouse, where they could *really* hide—and at the same time watch everything that was happening down below.

The treehouse was just about finished when the first suspicious character showed up: a new customer at the general store, asking questions about Megan and Sandy. He said he was their uncle.

Megan and Sandy didn't *have* an uncle!

—*Dorothy Davidson*

Merlin Dreams
By Peter Dickinson
(Notables 1988)

Have you ever wondered about your dreams? What are they, anyway, and what, if anything, do they mean? Usually dreams seem to be nothing more than a jumbled kaleidoscope of selected memories from the past, but then there is the rare dream that almost carries the aura of a vision or glimpse into the future. Why, some people even claim that certain types of dreams can actually shape or alter events in the waking world.

Let me tell you about some of Merlin's dreams. You remember Merlin, don't you? He was the legendary wizard who brought King Arthur to the throne and then finally met his doom when he was trapped forever under an unmarked stone on the English moors. Under that rock, Merlin still dreams.

Some of his dreams, such as the tale of Sir Tremalin, appear to be nothing more than straightforward memories of past adventures. Sir Tremalin, a sorry excuse for a knight, who had never met a challenge or done a noble deed in his life, was suddenly forced to accept a perilous quest that not only involved fighting two hardy and undefeated warriors but a deadly invisible foe as well. To all outward appearances, Sir Tremalin was a disastrous choice for such a quest; in Merlin's dreams, however, appearances can be deceiving—things are never quite what they seem. This is what Prince Alexander also discovered, in another of Merlin's dreams. When Alexander decided to hunt down and destroy the evil dragon that was terrorizing his country, he discovered—just as Sir Tremalin had on his quest—that the enemy was not quite what he had expected.

But perhaps I shouldn't tell you any more of Merlin's dreams, especially not the strange tale of the beautiful enchantress who held an entire country under her spell. Listening to a wizard's dreams can be dangerous. Dreaming itself can be dangerous because, as Merlin once said, "Dreams are their own masters." So don't treat dreams lightly; if you do, you might just find yourself mastered by your own or someone else's dreams. After all, look what happened to Merlin.

—*Margie Reitsma*

The Midnight Horse
By Sid Fleischman
(Notables 1990, SLJ/C 1990)

Have you ever heard of the Great Chaffalo and his world-famous horse trick? Well, I hadn't either, until I traveled to Cricklewood to see if my great-uncle would take me in. The Red Raven Inn in Cricklewood even has an autographed poster of the Great Chaffalo himself.

Chaffalo was a tall man with a broad red sash across his chest and an equally broad smile on his face. He was born in Cricklewood, but traveled the world performing his act. He was given a beautiful chiming watch by the King of Prussia. He always came back here, though, to rest after his travels, in the summer house he had built.

He was a great magician, and I'd heard that he'd even pinched a Chinese coin off a young boy's nose! And his most famous trick of all was his horse trick. He could snap his fingers and turn a pile of straw into a horse. But even though he had an exciting life, the great Chaffalo didn't live long. He was shot and went to an early grave. Only his ghost lives in the old summer house now. At least, I hope it does—I'm going to need some help real soon.

You see, my great-uncle is an old grouch. He wouldn't take me in, and now he's trying to take my inheritance away from me, and the Red Raven Inn away from Miss Sally. We could really use some help, but I'm not sure what the Great Chaffalo and his horse can do now— they're only ghosts. Can a ghost still work magic?

—*C. Allen Nichols*

Midnight Hour Encores
By Bruce Brooks
(SLJ/C 1986)

Sibilance T. Spooner is a sixteen-year-old cello player—one of the top cellists in the world. She lives in Washington, D.C., with her father, Taxi. Sib and Taxi have a pretty mellow relationship, giving each other lots of space and still taking each other seriously. For instance, Sib never asks Taxi to show her anything unless she really wants to be shown. "Taxi cares about anything you ask him about," Sib says. "Put him in motion, and you just can't turn him off." And so Sib only asks him to show her things that seem really important. "He doesn't fool around, and he doesn't give up, and he doesn't let go even when you would just as soon skip the inquiry midway through."

Sib knew that about Taxi. So she should have known what she was in for on the day she asked Taxi to take her to meet her mother.

—*Sarah Flowers*

Mississippi Bridge
By Mildred D. Taylor
(Christopher 1991)

Jeremy was not your typical poor-white boy in 1930s rural Mississippi. His father and most of the white folks he knew hated the colored folks. They especially resented any who owned property or had jobs. Jeremy didn't feel that way, which is why he wasn't typical.

Jobs were mighty scarce in Mississippi after the crash of 1929, when the bottom fell out of the cotton market. And on this particular day, a pouring rain had driven all those unemployed men and boys indoors. Most of them whiled away the hours talking around the pot-bellied stove at the Wallace general store.

That's how Jeremy, his pa, and his brothers came to be there when the bus pulled up out front. Seemed like everybody and his brother was wanting to go someplace that day, white and colored alike.

One of the people waiting to board the bus was Jeremy's colored friend Josias. Josias was all spruced up for a new job. That didn't sit too well with Jeremy's pa, who made some ugly remarks. Jeremy was disgusted with the way his pa was acting. So when Josias headed out to board the bus, Jeremy followed and stood on the porch.

Miss Hattie and her granddaughter got the front seats on the bus, them being white. The colored folk moved to the back. But at the last minute Josias was booted off by the driver, who said there wouldn't be enough seats for late-coming white folks. Josias wound up sprawled in the red mud. Jeremy was shocked.

But what came next was even more shocking, though some said it had a strange justice. Josias and Jeremy were the only witnesses to what happened on that Mississippi bridge.

—Bernice D. Crouse

Monday in Odessa
By Eileen Bluestone Sherman
(National Jewish 1987)

Imagine yourself trapped in a society that persecutes you for practicing your religion. To survive, you will either have to give up your beliefs or move to a more tolerant place—but there's a catch: you won't be allowed to leave without permission, and as soon as you apply for permission, you will be branded as a traitor!

You might not want to live in a society like that, and neither do Marina Birger's parents. They are beginning to talk about leaving the Soviet Union, about applying for an exit visa, in spite of the danger. Marina is determined to keep them from going ahead with this plan. It's insane, it just doesn't make sense! Her mother and father have good jobs; they are both valued employees at the city's largest hospital. But once they apply for a visa, they won't be valued anymore. Instead, they'll become pariahs, avoided by all but their bravest friends, and subject to constant harrassment, even arrest. And it's not as if her parents are particularly religious. Although they're Jews, they don't seem to care about religion, and they've taught Marina nothing about Judaism—except that it's a subject not to be mentioned in public.

So Marina makes a plan of her own. If she can be chosen for the city-wide finals of the storytelling contest, then surely her parents will give up this crazy idea of moving to another land. There's no doubt that she's the best storyteller in her school; it's just that no Jewish girl has ever been chosen before. Marina has undeniable talent, and she practices very hard. She *does* win the contest—and the attentions of the charming Misha Pasternack! Her parents are very proud of her, and drop their dangerous plan.

And then the trouble starts.

—*J. R. B.*

Monkey Island
By Paula Fox
(Notables 1991)

Clay lived in a run-down hotel with his mother. They had one small room where his mother cooked on a hotplate and Clay slept on a cot. They shared a bathroom (that didn't lock) with the neighbors down the hall. The stairways and hallways were smelly and littered with trash, and the elevator was a trap, where muggers and druggies could lie in wait. Nobody stayed in this hotel because they wanted to; it was where social services put families who couldn't afford to rent apartments.

Clay's mother had been gone five days when Mrs. Larkin caught him rummaging through her trash. "What's going on here?" she asked. "Where's your mother?" Fear kept Clay from saying anything.

"Come on in," Mrs. Larkin invited. "I'm going to give you a bit of supper, and you're going to tell me what's up."

So Clay had his first good meal in five days. He was so hungry that he ate everything she offered. But when it came time to tell his story, there wasn't much to say.

"Clay, I think we have to do something. Your mother's going to have a baby. She shouldn't be out there wandering the streets."

Clay knew what Mrs. Larkin had in mind. The social services people had messed with his life before. That's how his family had wound up in this crummy hotel in the first place. Fear coursed through him. Once Mrs. Larkin called the police, Clay would never see his mother again.

He made a phony excuse and went back to their room. He put on the best clothes he owned and stuffed his mother's money into his pockets. He made sure he still had his key to the room—he would check back every day to see if his mother had returned.

Then he hit the streets. As the November night wore on and the temperature dropped, he wandered from one small refuge to another, seeking whatever warmth and comfort he could find.

Somewhere in the maze of streets he discovered Monkey Island.

—*Bernice D. Crouse*

More Stories Julian Tells
By Ann Cameron
(Notables 1986,SLJ/C 1986)

I could hardly see my brother Huey's face behind that bloody Kleenex. It was all my fault. You see, I get great ideas. Now, some people can see those little sparks that mean trouble is on the way, but I can't. That's why it's my fault my little brother tried to be Superboy and got a bloody nose. Read my stories and I'll tell you all about it. I'll also tell you about my dad, the day frogs wore shoes, and all kinds of other things.

—Cecilia Swanson

The Moves Make the Man
By Bruce Brooks
(BGHB 1985, Newbery Honor 1985, Notables 1984, SLJ/C 1984)

The first time Jerome sees Bix, he knows that the two of them could be friends. He watches Bix play baseball, and even though Jerome doesn't much like baseball, he sees that Bix is one of those natural shortstops who knows just what he is doing. He always knows where to be and how to move his body. Bix plays baseball, in fact, the way Jerome plays basketball, so Jerome knows they have something in common. But Bix leaves before Jerome has a chance to meet him.

Eventually they do meet, although they've had some major changes in their lives in the meantime. But Jerome was right, Bix is the kind of person he wants for a friend, even though Bix does some pretty strange things at times and even though he has some pretty weird moods. Like, Bix believes in truth with a capital T, always telling the truth, never lying, never faking anything. Which is fine until Jerome begins to teach Bix to play basketball.

At first it's great. That wonderful shortstop's body understands the ball, and Bix learns fast: dribble, both hands, move, lay-up, jump, all the fundamentals. Then one day Jerome realizes that Bix is all set with everything he needs, everything but moves, fakes. "Oh," thinks Jerome, "I never thought to teach him how to fake." And so he does—or he tries to. Bix refuses to learn. "No moves," he says, "no fakes. That's lying and I don't lie, and I don't need to lie." "But you need fakes if you're gonna win this game," Jerome tells him. "No I don't," says Bix.

But Jerome knows he's wrong. How can he convince Bix that in basketball—and sometimes in life—fakes are part of the game? You've got to learn the moves if you want things to happen. You've got to learn the moves so you can spot the other guy's moves. But does the man make the moves, or do the moves make the man?

—*Sarah Flowers*

The Mozart Season
By Virginia Euwer Wolff
(Notables 1991)

Allegra hadn't expected that summer to become the Mozart season. She'd almost forgotten about the tape Mr. Kaplan had made of her performance of Mozart's Fourth Violin Concerto, so the news that the tape had qualified her to play in the Bloch Competition came as a complete surprise. Now, even though she wasn't yet thirteen, she would have to spend the next three months with Mozart, trying to bring her performance to perfection for the competition. Allegra hardly hesitated before agreeing to enter the contest, but as the summer progressed she began to wonder if she truly the talent and the courage to take on this challenge. And Allegra had more to think about than just Mozart—she'd been drawn into the lives and tragedies of those around her. All of these things would become a part of who she was and, also, a part of her Mozart season.

—*Helen Schlichting*

Mr. Popper's Penguins
By Richard Atwater and Florence Atwater
(Newbery Honor 1939)

Mr. Popper is a painter. He paints the outsides of houses and decorates the insides. He works hard and he likes to paint, but secretly he's always wanted to be an explorer. The best times for Mr. Popper are when he can stay home and read about explorers and their expeditions and listen to their reports on the radio. His favorite place to read about is the South Pole. The North Pole is nice too, but the South Pole has penguins!

One day Mr. Popper writes a letter to Admiral Drake, an explorer at the South Pole. Mr. Popper doesn't expect to hear from Admiral Drake; he certainly doesn't expect Admiral Drake to speak directly to him on a radio broadcast and tell him to watch for a surprise. But when the big box arrives by Air Express from the South Pole, Mr. Popper can't wait to open it. Who would have guessed that Admiral Drake would send Mr. Popper a penguin?

Life with a penguin is interesting for Mr. Popper and his family, especially after they get another penguin, and then—baby penguins. But it's expensive, keeping so many penguins happy. So Mr. Popper must come up with an idea—an idea that will bring in enough money to keep the penguins cool and happy, and the rest of the family comfortable.

—*Colleen Stinson*

Mrs. Frisby and the Rats of NIMH
By Robert C. O'Brien
(BGHB 1971, Newbery 1972)

Imagine for a minute that you are a mouse. You don't deliberately do anything to bother humans, but for some reason they seem to hate you. It can be quite a challenge, avoiding their traps and surviving the cold, lean winter days. Mrs. Frisby, despite being a widow, has survived. In fact, by being a resourceful mouse, she's managed to bring all three of her children safely through the winter too. They have lived in relative comfort during the cold weather inside a cinder block buried in Mr. Fitzgibbon's garden.

Now temperatures are beginning to rise, and that means moving day is just around the corner. The Frisby family must be out of their garden home before plowing time, or die!

But Timothy Frisby is suddenly quite sick. He has never been as strong as his brother and sister, but this time the diagnosis is pneumonia. Timmy will take at least a month to recover fully. In the meantime he has to stay inside where it is warm and dry.

What's a mother to do? If Timothy stays put, he'll probably get plowed under, but if he leaves the cinder block, he'll die of exposure. Mrs. Frisby has always seen Timothy as special—indeed, all her children seem far above average. Somehow she must protect her family. The crisis demands that Mrs. Frisby act, no matter how dangerous that may be. Her friends direct her to the rats under the rosebush. Mrs. Frisby has noticed that they sometimes do rather unratly things, but what could a rat do that a mouse couldn't? The owl says the rats could move her whole house to a safer place. Mrs. Frisby has her doubts—she's not sure the rats will even want to help her. But she'll just have to risk their anger. Timothy's life is at stake!

And risk she does, facing not only the owl, who could well have eaten her, and the mysterious rats of NIMH, but Dragon the cat as well. And in the process Mrs. Frisby is shocked to discover how her dead husband and her children came to be so special.

—*Bernice D. Crouse*

The Mummy, the Will, and the Crypt
By John Bellairs
(SLJ/C 1983)

What did a fancy chess set, an ancient Greek newspaper, and a weathered signboard have in common? The tour guide said that together the pieces of this odd collection would lead to the will of a very wealthy dead man.

Some members of Mr. Glomis's family were determined that the will should never be found. But others had offered a $10,000 reward to the finder of the will. Johnny loved a good puzzle, and the reward was an added incentive to check out the clues.

When Johnny's grandmother fell sick and the medical bills started to pile up, Johnny focused more attention on the puzzle. He had already formed some ideas when, by some twist of fate, he attended a camp right next to the Glomis country estate. The gloomy old mansion at Staunton Harold was impossible to resist—until the night that strange Glomis boy disappeared.

That was the night Fergie and Johnny sneaked into the estate grounds. After a long, wet tramp through the dark forest they eventually reached Staunton Harold. Standing in its gateway was Chad, a young Glomis, armed with a gun. Chad was one very mixed-up young man, but he relented enough to take the boys on a tour of the mansion's secret passage. But he drew the line at taking them into the family crypt under the chapel.

Johnny was very disappointed to be so close to the mansion and still not be able to check out his ideas. He didn't get a chance to complain, though, because suddenly Chad just disappeared into the darkness.

Fergie and Johnny decided to head back to camp the wet woods. But they hadn't gotten far when screams stopped them in their tracks. Something had happened to Chad! They turned and ran toward the hideous sounds. They found only Chad's rather expensive flashlight lying in the road. Maybe the danger was human or animal, but after Chad's hair-raising story about "The Guardian," neither Johnny nor Fergie had the courage to continue the search. Fergie decided to give up the hunt for the will forever, but Johnny's business with the Guardian wasn't finished.

—Bernice D. Crouse

My Brother Sam Is Dead
By James Lincoln Collier and Christopher Collier
(Newbery Honor 1975)

"You're a boy, Sam, a boy dressed up in a gaudy soldier's suit." Father was not at all happy that Sam was quitting college to join the Continental Army and fight the British. How I hated to hear them argue! All I wanted was to have Sam sidle up to my bed and tell his stories about the pretty girls at Yale and the "telling points" he had scored in debates with his buddies. When he confessed he was going to steal Father's gun, I could barely believe it! He said Americans had to fight for their freedom, and Loyalists like Father would only serve to make the king richer. I didn't much care who was right or wrong as long as Sam came home safe and sound.

But it was dangerous now. Patriots stopped Father and me as we drove the cattle to market. "I suppose this cattle is going to end up in Lobsterback stomachs," one of the men said, and another took out his pistol and knocked Father right off his horse. "I'm all right, Tim," he said, but I knew they would have shot him if a band of Loyalists hadn't come charging toward us to break it up. No, it just wasn't safe anywhere. And with food so scarce, our cattle made us a prime target for rustlers on both sides. I know I should have butchered the cattle like Sam said to do, and hid the meat in the barn. I might have saved Sam's life if I had. Yes, I might have saved his life.

—Vicki Reutter

My Grandmother's Stories: A Collection of Jewish Folk Tales
By Adele Geras
(National Jewish 1991)

I love to visit my grandmother. She lives in an apartment full of all kinds of interesting things. I like to help her in the kitchen, because she cooks all kinds of wonderful things to eat, too.

But best of all are her stories. I think my grandmother knows more stories than anyone else in the world. No matter what I find in her apartment—a pair of shoes, a button, some embroidery—my grandmother knows a story to go with it.

She's told me stories about the wise men of Chelm, a village where everyone is foolish. The "wisest" man in Chelm wears golden shoes—on his hands! (He's also the one who decided that heavy wooden chests should not be equipped with wheels—and he had a wise reason you'll never guess).

But not all her stories are about Chelm. She's told me how the great King Solomon taught a selfish merchant a lesson in generosity, and how a poor farmer outwitted the czar. And she has a wonderful tale about a man and his wife who found a way to make their house bigger—without using tools or lumber!

My grandmother's stories—you'll have to hear them yourself!

—*Donna L. Scanlon*

My Name Is Sus5an Smith. The 5 Is Silent
By Louise Plummer
(SLJ/C 1991)

When people ask about the name she signs at the bottom of her paintings, she tells them, "My name is Sus5an Smith. The 5 is silent." Sus5an is an artist, eager to prove herself. She's bored with small-town Utah, and she dreads the long, utterly predictable summer days ahead. When her Aunt Libby invites her to spend the summer in Boston, Sus5an feels that her real life is finally beginning.

But Sus5an is looking for more than excitement in Boston; she's looking for someone special. She was only seven when her Uncle Willy walked out on her Aunt Marianne. Everyone else in the family said he was a liar and a cheat, but Sus5an thought Willy was the greatest, and she still wears the silver necklace he sent her for her eighth birthday. Her family just never saw the real Willy, the warm, thoughtful person she remembers.

So this summer Sus5an will be looking for big-city excitement and for recognition as an artist—and for her long-lost uncle. The summer will be a time of growing and learning. Will it be a summer of joy, or of sorrow?

—*Helen Schlichting*

My Prairie Year: Based on the Diary of Elenore Plaisted
By Brett Harvey
(Notables 1986)

Elenore was just a child when her family moved to a farm on the prairie. The prairie is beautiful, with long green grass waving like an ocean all around the little white house on the hill. The prairie is beautiful, but it is also hard work, and it can be dangerous. Blizzards in winter, tornadoes in the spring, and huge grass fires in summer. *My Prairie Year.*

—*Cecilia Swanson*

My Side of the Mountain
By Jean Craighead George
(Newbery Honor 1960)

Sam Gribley had turned his back on civilization. Sharing an apartment with eight brothers and sisters in busy New York City was not how he wanted to spend his life, so he walked out. He left New York with the clothes on his back, a penknife, a ball of cord, an ax, forty dollars, and some flint and steel. He ran away to the Catskill Mountains, into the wilderness with no companions, no tent, and no instant food.

After the first night in the rain, he was almost ready to quit, but he learned—he adapted to the forest. That summer he taught himself to catch fish with a string, start a fire with flint and steel, and make clothes from deerskin. He captured a baby falcon that he named Frightful and trained to be his companion and help him search for food. And he burned out a six-foot room in a gigantic hemlock tree—his new home.

But living in the wilderness had its problems. Sam had to hide from hunters and hikers and to endure the months of bitter ice and snow. Also, being always alone made him realize how important human contact and conversation are. But even though there were hardships, Sam came to love and cherish the life he'd made for himself. Unfortunately, he could do nothing to stop the rumors about a wild boy who lived in the mountains. Journalists and reporters began to look for him. Could Sam hold on to the life he'd come to love? Or would he be discovered and returned to the city?

—*Mary Cosper*

My War with Goggle-Eyes
By Anne Fine
(Notable 1989, SLJ/C 1989)

Kitty's mother had had boyfriends before. That wasn't the problem. It was *this* boyfriend, so much worse than any of the others. His name was Gerald Faulkner, but Kitty called him Goggle-Eyes because he goggled at her mother like a dog drooling over a bone. He was old too, much older than her mother—over fifty, with gray hair and a little on the chubby side. Kitty hated him on sight. And she hated him even more when he wouldn't stop goggling at her mother. *And* telling her what to wear on their dates *and* trying to bribe Kitty and her little sister with chocolates *and* even having the nerve to nag Kitty about cleaning up her room. He acted as if he lived in their house already; he even helped himself to whatever he wanted in the refrigerator without asking anybody. Of course Kitty's mom got mad at her when she wasn't polite to Gerald, and that started *more* fights.

Kitty was very strongly against nuclear weapons—she even belonged to a group that went out and picketed—so when Goggle-Eyes laughed at her beliefs, that was final straw. This was war! When Goggle-Eyes telephoned, Kitty never passed on his messages; she wouldn't touch the chocolates he brought every week; and she talked about her mother's old boyfriends in front of him every chance she got.

Kitty was determined to break up her mother and Goggle-Eyes, no matter what! could she do it?

—*Susan Dunn*

Nekomah Creek
By Linda Crew
(Notables 1991)

What was I going to do? The school counselor wanted to see me. The teacher had told her that I wasn't behaving right in class and was just reading during recess. But I like to read—I'd much rather read than play four-square or soccer.

Then Mrs. Van Gent started in with those seemingly harmless questions and comments—like about my dad staying home and cooking and taking care of the twins, like about Mom going to work every day. And then the bombshell: didn't I feel resentful about the twins, after having been an only child so long?

How could I ever make her understand that I loved my family just the way they were? My mom wants to work. She designs greeting cards. And my dad loves cooking and staying home and spending time with the twins and me. It seemed as thought everything I said got turned the wrong way around. Mrs. Van Gent thought there were something weird about my family.

How could I set her straight?

—*Carol Kappelmann*

Never to Forget: The Jews of the Holocaust
By Milton Meltzer
(Addams 1977, BGHB 1976, Taylor 1977)

Bergen-Belsen. Treblinka. Sobibor. Auschwitz. Buchenwald. Chelmno. Theresienstadt. Death camps. Genocide. Holocaust. Five million, nine hundred and eighty-seven thousand. Names and statistics.

But this is not just a book of names and statistics. It is a book of survival—true stories told by those who survived the horrors of the Holocaust. Their stories are shocking and tragic—"I was praying for death to come. I was praying for the grave to be opened and to swallow me alive. Blood was spurting from the grave in many places, like a well of water, and whenever I pass a spring now, I remember the blood which spurted from the ground, from the grave. I was digging with my fingernails, trying to join the dead in that grave."

Why must these stories be told? Why cause the survivors the pain of remembering? Hear the words of a survivor: "Then for the first time we become aware that our language lacks words to express this offense, the demolition of man. In a moment, with almost prophetic intuition, the reality was revealed to us: we had reached the bottom. It is not possible to sink lower than this, nor could it conceivably be so. Nothing belongs to us anymore; they have taken away our clothes, our shoes, even our hair; if we speak, they will not listen to us, and if they listen, they will not understand. They will even take away our name, and if we want to keep it, we will have to find in ourselves the strength to do so, to manage somehow so that behind the name, something of us, of us as we were, still remains."

These stories must be told so that we will never forget the people who lived them.

—*Anne Sushko*

Note: The quoted passages are from pages 70 and 121.

The New Kid on the Block
By Jack Prelutsky
(Notables 1984, SLJ/C 1984)

Slimy-faced creatures beneath the stair,
Snillies who hop and skip here and there,
Floradora Doe who talks to her plants,
And Uncanny Colleen who got washed with the pants,
These are just a few of the sights that will shock
You, when you read *The New Kid on the Block.*
(And just be glad your nose is on your face!)

—*Pam Swafford*

Next-Door Neighbors
By Sarah Ellis
(SLJ/C 1990)

Everyone has neighbors. The couple across the street, the family next door, the old man with the dog two doors down. When Peggy's family moved to the city, she never thought that one neighbor would become so important to her.

Mrs. Manning was the rich lady who lived next door. But it was Sing, the Chinese man who worked for her, who interested Peggy. He told stories, he listened to her problems, and he taught Peggy and George how to make shadow puppets from cut-outs. Peggy never would have thought that one person could make such a difference in her life—especially when that person was as unlikely a friend as Sing.

—*Colleen Stinson*

Night Cry
By Phyllis Reynolds Naylor
(Poe 1985)

It's amazing what you can be afraid of. The spooky stories Granny Bo told, superstitions, an old horse, animal noises in the night.

It's amazing what you *should* be afraid of. Dad's new job as a traveling salesman, which leaves Ellen alone at night; the stranger who appears out of nowhere, asking to trade work for a meal; the TV breakdown, which means almost no contact with the outside world, no news about the kidnapping.

There are strange things happening around Ellen—lots of things that make her nervous. But which ones are just silly imaginings, and which ones should she really be scared of?

—Colleen Stinson

The Night Swimmers
By Betsy Byars
(ABA 1981, BGHB 1980)

Roy woke up in the middle of the night and realized that Retta and Johnny were gone. He was alone in the house. "They went night swimming without me," he said to himself.

That had to be it. Even though they'd been caught before and warned not to use the Colonel's pool, Roy was sure that was where they'd gone. He crept out of the house and moved quickly through the deserted streets to the Colonel's home. As he neared the pool, he heard the splashing of water.

He'd show them. He'd sneak up on the diving board and jump right in on top of them. They'd really be surprised.

The only problem was, Roy had never jumped off a diving board before.

And Roy couldn't swim.

And Retta and Johnny were *not* there in the pool to pull him out.

—Carol Kappelmann

Nilda
By Nicholasa Mohr
(Addams 1974)

Nilda just couldn't figure out whom to believe. On the one hand there was her mother. A deeply religious person, she urged Nilda to hold on to the faith, to say her prayers, go to church, and believe in God, who would somehow always provide. Her stepfather said just the opposite. He'd have nothing to do with religion. "Superstition" was what he called it, said it didn't do people any good to have God reward them after death when they needed help right here on earth. And Nilda ought to know that herself. Couldn't she see how hard it was for the family to survive?

It *was* hard for the family—tough enough just being Puerto Rican, getting called "spick" and treated like dirt, without being poor besides. Life in the New York City *barrio* in the 1940s was far from easy, but it was all that Nilda knew—all she knew, that is, until by chance she stumbled upon her own secret garden and felt at last the first stirrings of real happiness.

Go with Nilda as she journeys from the darkness and poverty of the barrio into the bright light of personal peace.

—*Sister M. Anna Falbo, CSSF*

No Kidding
By Bruce Brooks
(SLJ/C 1989)

It's the 21st Century. Seventy percent of the adult population are alcoholics, which means kids have more responsibility than ever before. Sam is fourteen. He is responsible for his own life—he works in a printer's shop—and also for his alcoholic mother and his ten-year-old brother Ollie. His dad is long gone.

When Sam was twelve and a half, he decided he couldn't handle things at home any longer, so he had his mother committed to a sobriety center, a drying-out hospital. He had Ollie put in foster care. Now he thinks it's time for some changes. Ollie's foster parents want to adopt him; one way or another, a decision will have to be made. Sam thinks his mother should have another chance, so he arranges to have her released. He fixes her up with an apartment and a job; he arranges everything.

But in one short week, things start getting away from Sam again. Ollie is keeping secrets, their mother isn't behaving the way Sam expected, Ollie's foster parents have a very frank discussion with Sam, and suddenly he's having trouble keeping everything under control. It's an eye-opening week for this fourteen-year-old grown-up. No kidding!

—*Sarah Flowers*

Nothing but the Truth: A Documentary Novel
By Avi
(Newbery Honor 1991, Notables 1991, SLJ/C 1991)

When you read a newspaper article, do you assume that every word in it is true? If you've ever had a newspaper story written about you, you probably know better. Philip Malloy certainly does. He learned all about being a celebrity, the hard way.

Before the newspapers got hold of him, Philip was mainly famous for getting lousy grades in English—so bad he couldn't even try out for track—and for inventing sneaky new ways of annoying the teacher, whom he really disliked. Miss Narwin was Philip's teacher for homeroom as well as for English, so he had plenty of opportunities.

During homeroom at Harrison High, students were required to stand at respectful, silent attention for three minutes every morning while the national anthem was played over the PA system—this was a school rule. Philip decided to stand at respectful attention and hum along. Loudly. He'd tried this before, in his other homeroom, and no one had reacted. But Miss Narwin did. She sent him to the assistant principal. And after he'd refused for the third time to stop humming, Philip was suspended.

The local newspaper picked up the story and reported that Philip had been carried away by patriotic feeling. By the time the media circus—including the national networks—got through with him, Philip had become the Uncle Sam of Harrison High. He was famous! But was he happy?

—Jo Berkman

Number the Stars
By Lois Lowry
(National Jewish 1990, Newbery 1990, Notables 1989, SLJ/C 1989)

Life stopped being simple for Annemarie the day she and her friend Ellen were racing each other home from school. They were running as fast as they could when the German soldier stopped them. Rough and threatening, he demanded to know who they were and what they were running from. At that moment the girls would have liked to have run away from *him*, but they didn't dare. They knew, of course, that there was a war going on and that Nazi troops had occupied their Denmark, but never before had they felt this in their own lives. When the soldier finally let them go, they walked home very quietly. Their parents were upset, and angry at them for foolishly attracting the Germans' attention.

Soon word got out that the Germans were planning to round up all the Jews in Denmark and ship them away. Ellen's parents decided that it would be wise to disappear. They went into hiding, and they sent Ellen to live with Annemarie's family, as though she belonged there. Ellen and Annemarie had been friends for so long it was easy for them to pretend to be sisters, but now it was more than a game. When German soldiers burst into Annemarie's house in the middle of the night, pushing their way into the girls' bedroom and refusing to believe that the Johansens could have a daughter with black hair like Ellen's, what could the girls do to outwit them? How could they fool these intruders, until Ellen could escape?

—Helen Schlichting

Old Yeller
By Fred Gipson
(Newbery Honor 1957)

He wasn't much to look at—a big yeller dog with a mutilated ear and a tail that was only a stump. And not only was he ugly, he was also a thief. The day I found him, he had just stolen and devoured the last of our middling meat.

But maybe he wasn't as bad as I first thought. Papa had just left with other Salt Licks farmers to drive their cattle to Abilene, Kansas, where the big cattle market was. With him gone for who knew how long, maybe a big ugly dog could be useful. Maybe—if we could feed him enough to keep him from stealing from us and all the neighbors as well!

Surely he could help keep the coons and skunks out of the corn, find lost cows, and fight off the bar hogs.

Surely he could earn his keep.

Maybe I'd even get so I liked him!

—Carol Kappelmann

On My Honor
By Marion Dane Bauer
(Notables 1986, SLJ/C 1986)

Joel scrubbed until he thought he would bleed, but the smell stayed in his nostrils—the river smell, that dead fish smell, the dead smell. Dead like his friend Tony was now.

They had both sworn, on their honor, that they wouldn't go to the river. They crossed their hearts for Joel's dad, but they crossed the bridge anyway. And Tony was still there in the river.

They were supposed to be riding their bikes to the state park, but who could stop Tony when he wanted to do something? Tony was the kind of guy who made all your other friends seem a little boring. He was vibrant, reckless, full of life. Except he wasn't full of life anymore.

How was Joel supposed to know that Tony couldn't swim? That he'd be sucked under the muddy water? That he'd be dead? And what was Joel supposed to do now with the questions piling up around him? He couldn't tell the truth, not to anyone. After all, he'd sworn on his honor.

—Jeff Blair

The One Hundredth Thing about Caroline
By Lois Lowry
(Notables 1983)

Caroline Tate is on to something! She and her best friend Stacy have been conducting an undercover investigation of the mysterious new tenant on the fifth floor of her apartment building, and the evidence they've found is truly alarming. It seems that Fred is planning to get rid of Caroline and her brother JP so that he can marry their mother!

Normally, JP is a total pain, but now Caroline needs even his talents if she is to defeat this horrible plot! Together they must get hold of the evidence and arrange a gathering in the Tate apartment, where they will expose Fred's scheme in front of their mother and Mr. Keretsky, Caroline's friend from the Museum of Natural History. It's the only way to stop Fred from poisoning JP and Caroline!

—Judy McElwain

One More Flight
By Eve Bunting
(Golden Kite 1977)

Sometimes I feel like a leaf in the wind
A leaf from a weeping tree.
And I cry and I cry to the wild, lonely wind,
Won't anyone listen to me?

The first time Dobby heard this song on the radio, he knew that this was his song. It fit him to a T. He was the leaf in the wind, running away again, blowing in the wind, drifting anywhere.

They had told him that if he ran away again, either from the Residential Treatment Center or from one of the foster homes, it would mean Juvenile Hall for him. He had used up all his options.

But this time he'd found Timmer and the birds. The birds were in cages, but only temporarily. Timmer rehabilitated hurt and maimed eagles and hawks, then returned them to the wild.

Could he do the same thing for Dobby—heal his wounds and set him free? Or was it already too late?

—Carol Kappelmann

One-Eyed Cat
By Paula Fox
(Christopher 1984, Newbery Honor 1983, Notables 1984)

Uncle Hilary had given Ned a gun for his birthday that year—a real boy's present. But Ned's father, a minister, made him put the gun in the attic. He would not be allowed to use it until he turned fourteen.

But Ned knew he had to try the gun, just once. Late one night, after everyone had gone to bed, he crept up the attic stairs, found the gun, took it out of its case, and carried it outside.

The night was quiet. Ned lifted the gun to his shoulder and sighted along its barrel. He pointed the gun at the pine trees, then slowly turned in a circle, following the mountains, the river, the Makepeace mansion, to the old stable. As he blinked, he saw a shadow against the stable. Before he realized what he was doing, he pulled the trigger.

No one punished Ned for his disobedience—except Ned! He was consumed by quilt. He was sure that someone had been watching him from a window that night.

And then a cat turned up next door in the old man's woodshed—a one-eyed cat that kept shaking its head, as if it were in some kind of trouble. Had he shot the cat? Was that what the shadow against the stable had been? Was Ned responsible?

—Diantha G. McCauley

Onion John
By Joseph Krumgold
(Newbery 1960)

My dad was impressed, I think, that Onion John had four bathtubs in his house. My dad hadn't really expected too much at Onion John's place, since it was pretty much a shack. Those bathtubs had him close to speechless. Of course Onion John, being Onion John, might have four bathtubs in the house, but he kept them all in the living room and used them for storing vegetables, dust rags from the church, and newspapers in.

Onion John was what you'd call our town character. He was also my best friend. I was the only person in town who could understand him. When he talked, people just heard sounds like "Mayaglubpany," but I understood him plain as day.

As I was saying, my dad was close to speechless up there at John's shack. All he could say was, "We'll build him a new place" and "The Rotary needs a project." And sure enough, pretty soon folks from all over town chipped in and built Onion John a new place with a stove, running water, and only one bathtub, in the bathroom this time.

That one tub was a big part of the problem. You see, we all expected Onion John to act like everyone else. And some people just can't be changed.

—Jeff Blair

The Other Side of Dark
By Joan Lowery Nixon
(Poe 1987)

Stacey heard a noise. She was in the backyard when she heard something in the house. Then she saw him and knew he was scared. He ran out the door, pointed the gun, and shot her.

When she woke up, Stacey remembered. She remembered her mother's cry from the house, she remembered the gun, and she remembered the shot. But she didn't remember his face, she didn't remember her mother's death, and she didn't remember the last four years of her life—four years that went by while she was unconscious, as her friends matured, and her own thirteen-year-old body grew into a seventeen-year-old body that seemed to belong to someone else.

She doesn't remember his face. But he remembers hers. And he can't let her remember any more.

—Colleen Stinson

Our Eddie
By Sulamith Ish-Kishor
(Newbery Honor 1970)

The children in my father's school thought the world of Papa. They thought we were *so* lucky to have him for a father. But that was because in school he was compassionate, patient, understanding. His students didn't know that when Papa left the school building, he also left behind those kindly traits that made him so popular. They didn't realize that with us, his family, he was a real tyrant, demanding service and obedience and never taking "no" for an answer. All he cared about was his mission. Oh, yes, our father had a mission in life, an all-important mission that sapped all his time and energy, a mission to teach the Hebrew language to poor Jewish children. But while he was open to their need and wants, Papa was oblivious to our own! We were poorer than the poorest children in his school, but he simply did not care. And so we suffered, all of us, and Eddie, my oldest brother, tried hard to make up for it. Only there wasn't much he could do, and even that little brought nothing but trouble.

Our Eddie. He tried so hard to help us. If only he could have helped himself!

—*Sister M. Anna Falbo, CSSF*

Our Sixth-Grade Sugar Babies
By Eve Bunting
(SLJ/C 1990)

Have you ever tried carrying a five-pound bag of sugar all day long? Well, neither had any of us sixth-graders until our teacher decided to teach us Responsibility. She had us each dress up a bag of sugar to look like a baby and told us to watch over it as though it were a real baby—for an entire week! At first it was kind of fun. But then this new boy moved in across the street, a guy so gorgeous that we referred to him as "Thunk," short for "The Hunk"! I mean, how could I let a boy who was that good-looking see me walking around with a dressed-up bag of sugar? Honest, I didn't mean to cheat. I really wanted to do the assignment and prove that I'm a responsible person. But when I saw Thunk riding his bike toward me, I just had to hide my sugar baby! You understand, don't you? It's just that while I was trailing Thunk, my sugar baby vanished. Now I'm in real trouble, and all on account of our sixth-grade sugar babies.

—*Sister M. Anna Falbo, CSSF*

Outlaws of Sherwood
By Robin McKinley
(Notables 1988)

They keep coming—people who are in trouble, who have been thrown off their land, who are looking for adventure—they keep coming to Sherwood, to me, hoping the great Robin Hood will help them. What would they say if they knew I was an outlaw by accident? I aimed at Tom Moody's leg and killed him with an arrow to the chest because I'm such a bad shot. I cannot feed, shelter, and clothe so many. And they're a dangerous liability, since most have no woodcraft and could lead the sheriff or the king's foresters right to our camp. I give most of them a few coins and try to find a safe place for them to hide in villages far from Sherwood Forest. The rest, I try to train to survive here in Sherwood. A few—John Little, Will Scarlet, and the strange newcomer, Cecil—have actually become quite good at it.

And what about Marian? I love her so much that I quarrel with her every time she comes into Sherwood Forest to visit. She and Much are the real leaders. They're the ones who have the dream of providing a haven for Saxons and bringing confusion and distress to the Normans. I would just as soon they all left me alone to take care of myself. I hate the responsibility for all these lives entrusted to my care. Sooner or later the sheriff will have had enough of our minor robberies and poaching and come after us seriously. And when that happens, how will I protect all these people? I am no warrior. What am I to do? If I give myself up, will the sheriff spare the others? Or is it too late for us all?

—*Abbie V. Landry*

The Outside Child
By Nina Bawden
(Notables 1989)

Have you ever seen a picture of children peering through a steamy window into a warm kitchen where someone is cooking and family members are enjoying each other's company? A real Norman Rockwell picture, except the children in this scene are dressed in rags and standing out in the cold. They are "outside children," and that's what Jane feels she is—an outside child. Her mother is dead, and she lives with her Aunt Sophie and Aunt Bill (whose real name is Wilhelmina). Her father is a merchant engineer, so he's away at sea most of the time.

One day, during one of her father's brief visits, Jane makes an astonishing discovery: she's not her father's only child. She has a half sister, a half brother, and a brand new baby brother. Somewhere, there's a real family: a mom, three children, and a dad—her dad—and she's on the outside, just like her friend Plato always said. Jane is determined to find out about her half family and spends hours tracking them down. During one of her scouting missions she actually talks to her sister and brother. This victory just makes her want to find out more. Jane has a lot of questions about her other family—and she may not like the answers!

—*Cynthia L. Lopuszynski*

Paradise Cafe, and Other Stories
By Martha Brooks
(SLJ/C 1990)

Love come in lots of shapes and styles, but it is never perfect. And in these stories you'll see all kinds of love. You'll meet a boy who loves his dog, but dogs don't live forever. You'll meet Karl, who comes to the skating rink and seems so perfect that all the girls giggle and dream. He's always with Sheila, also perfect—perfectly formed, perfectly pretty—until one night she has a spot on her white sweater. Meanwhile, Deirdre is trying a bit of matchmaking on her single dad, and maybe it will work. Get to know these people and others all looking for love wherever they can find it.

—*Cecilia Swanson*

The Pennywhistle Tree
By Doris Buchanan Smith
(Notables 1991, SLJ/C 1991)

The four boys watched from their perch in the tree as the strangers began to unload furniture and boxes from the topless, dilapidated school bus. They had never seen anything like this scene—noisy screaming kids, piles of stuff, and the monstrous bus that looked as if someone had hacked off the top with kitchen shears. Alex called it "the incubus," an evil creature from a horror movie.

The family that emerged from the bus was pretty horrible too. The kids were brats, and they were everywhere, into everything. And sure enough, the oldest boy—Sanders—was in the sixth grade, in the same class with the four friends, although he didn't seem to be able to get along with anyone.

Yet Jonathon found himself drawn to this strange, wild boy, helping him without actually meaning to, even giving him his special penny-whistle. His friends couldn't understand his changed attitude toward Sanders and his family. Jonathon wasn't sure he understood it himself. But suddenly, inexplicably, he knew he would help them in any way he could.

—*Carol Kappelmann*

The People Could Fly: American Black Folktales
Retold by Virginia Hamilton
(Notables 1985, SLJ/C 1985)

They say that long ago in Africa, some of the people knew magic and could fly. When they were captured for slavery, however, they shed their wings and they stopped flying. But they kept their power, their secret magic, even in the land of slavery, and there were times when the people who could fly, did fly away, when the suffering became too great. And this is only one of the black folktales you'll find in this book, born of sorrow and passed on in hope.

—Janet Loebel

Philip Hall Likes Me, I Reckon Maybe
By Bette Greene
(Newbery Honor 1975)

Can you blame me for liking Philip Hall? After all, he's the smartest, best-looking boy in class. And he's got this way about him that makes me glad he likes me. OK, so he beats me at just about everything: homework, tests, spelling bees, you name it. But lately I've got to thinking a little bit more about the situation—how Philip Hall is always first, and I'm always second. I've started to wonder something that I never wondered before: Could it be that Philip Hall is number one because *I let him be?* Is it possible that I'm afraid he wouldn't like me, Beth Lambert, if *I* came in first and *he* came in second? Well, I sure don't think so, and I certainly don't hope so, because I'm about to find out if it's true. You see, I've decided to become a veterinarian, and my teacher says that if that's my goal, then I'd better do my very best in school. No more settling for second place. Will Philip Hall still like me? I reckon maybe!

—Sister M. Anna Falbo, CSSF

Phoenix Rising: or How to Survive Your Life
By Cynthia D. Grant
(SLJ/C 1989)

How to survive your life—Tip #1: Don't Get Cancer.

Helen found the first tumor when she was fourteen. From the beginning, she refused to let the cancer change her. Some days she felt better than others, but no matter what, she never told anyone at school that she was sick. She didn't want to be treated differently from the others, or have people feeling sorry for her. When she had to go to the hospital for chemotherapy, everyone thought she was just home with cramps or something. For years only her family and her best friend knew the truth.

Her family never allowed themselves to think that Helen could die from her disease. She couldn't die—she had too many plans for her life and too many things she wanted to do. Helen's dream was to become an author. Almost from the time she could write, she had kept a diary. She wrote down everything she was feeling and experiencing and bared her soul in its pages. For her creative writing class she worked on poems and short stories, tales of other lives.

Then, when she was eighteen, Helen went into the hospital for a routine transfusion. She'd been feeling pretty bad, but her family thought it was a cold or the flu, and that the transfusion would make her feel better, as it always had before. But this time she died. Just like that.

And without Helen, what's left of her family is falling apart. Jessie, her younger sister, never believed that 5 minus 1 could equal 0, but for their family, the equation seems to be true. Jessie doesn't think she can live with this much pain. Helen was the golden one—everyone loved her best. If someone had to die, it should have been Jessie, not her sister.

Then Jessie finds Helen's final diary, and as she reads about her sister's last year of life, she realizes that she has no choice: she must go on. But how can she, without Helen?

—Susan Dunn

Pick-up Sticks
By Sarah Ellis
(Canadian Governor General's 1991)

Polly's life is perfect, or as near perfect as she can imagine. She lives with her Mum in the upstairs apartment of an old house. Polly's bedroom is small, but it has a glowing stained-glass window that Mum made for her at the studio. The window is a rainbow, and just looking at it makes Polly feel happy all over.

The Protheros own the house. They live downstairs. Polly is friends with Ernie Prothero. He collects postmarks, and sometimes she can bring him a new one from her job in the library.

But one day, when Polly comes home from the library, she finds Mum going through the newspaper with a highlighter, looking for apartments to rent. The Protheros have sold the house, and now Polly and Mum will have to move somewhere else. Finding a nice apartment they can afford on the little money Mum makes as a artist is extremely difficult, and two months isn't much time. In the end they have to move out of their wonderful old apartment before they've found any place to move into. Mum decides to camp out at her studio for the time being, but Polly chooses to go and live with her uncle and his family in their big, comfortable house. It's quite a change for Polly—she's not used to being rich, or to her cousin's little ways. Why did things have to change? Why couldn't they have stayed the way they were, the way they'd always be in a stained-glass window?

—Colleen Stinson

A Place Apart
By Paula Fox
(ABA 1983)

"Birdie" he calls her. She knows where he got the name. Victoria's last name is Finch, a type of bird. It doesn't seem to matter much to Hugh whether she likes being called "Birdie" or not. He goes on calling her that because *he* likes it. But Hugh is so special, so rich, so brilliant that Victoria doesn't really mind. He can change her name, because at last she is someone special, Hugh's special friend. And Hugh has great plans for her, for turning her writing into a play for senior graduation. It doesn't matter much what Victoria wants. But that's okay, because Hugh is bigger, better than the rest. It's enough just to be Hugh's special friend—until, that is, someone else comes along to take Victoria's place. Someone else Hugh can manipulate and have do his bidding. Someone else to be special. Instead of her.

—Colleen Stinson

The Place Where Nobody Stopped
By Jerry Segal
(Notables 1991)

Halfway between the Russian cities of Smolensk and Vitebsk is a small, nameless village known as "the place where nobody stops." Folks traveling between the two cities spur their horses on and look neither right nor left. If they're on foot, they quicken their steps as they pass by this pitiful group of wretched huts half hidden in the woods. They cross themselves and hurry onward, thinking, "Surely this place is haunted! Only ghosts or demons could stay in these rickety shacks in the forest's shadow."

I've been through here many times without seeing a living soul, and I too have wondered about ghosts. But in fact the village is inhabited by real people—poor woodchoppers and their families, and also Yosip the Baker. After meeting him, you might wonder, "What brings an educated man like Yosip to this desolate spot? Why does he, a man who so obviously likes people, shut himself away in his forest hut? What is the dark secret that he holds within his heart, and for which he punishes himself every day of his life?" For although the village may not be haunted, I think that Yosip is!

—*Kathy Ann Miller*

The Planet of Junior Brown
By Virginia Hamilton
(Newbery Honor 1972)

Three social outcasts spend their days in a secret basement room in a school in New York City. Junior Brown is an extremely talented pianist and artist, but he feels ugly and alone because he weighs almost 300 pounds. Buddy Clark is a street-wise kid who has lived on his own since he was nine years old, all the time making up stories about his family. The third outcast is Mr. Pool, who was once a teacher but is now the school's custodian. He feels that young black children have not been given the opportunity to learn and to live up to their potential, and that's why he's retreated to the secret basement room.

But in the basement Mr. Pool has created a new world for Junior and Buddy. A model solar system hanging from the ceiling of the basement room symbolizes Junior's and Buddy's worlds. Junior Brown's planet is the most attractive planet of the solar system, an artistic creation that reflects Junior's own talents. Buddy Clark's planet actually embodies two worlds—one where he is the friend and protector of kids like Junior and another where he could use some protection himself, trying to survive on his own in the inner city.

As the children in the school above go about their day, the three outcasts build their secret world, create their planets, and begin their friendship. But what will happen when their hideaway, their world, is discovered?

—*Anne Liebst*

Playing Beatie Bow
By Ruth Park
(BGHB 1982, Notables 1982, SLJ/C 1982)

Until that late, wintry evening, Beatie Bow was only a game, a scary game that children played in the park in Sydney, Australia. It was a game of hide-and-seek, with the ghost of Beatie Bow rising up from the grave to catch those who couldn't get away. That evening, the game became a terrifying reality for fourteen-year-old Abigail Kirk.

Abigail only wanted to speak to the strange little girl who stood in the shadows watching the other children play. She seemed so alone, and so frightened. But when Abigail reached out to touch her, the little girl ran away up the old cobblestone lane. Abigail followed. There was a muffled cry of terror, and then out of the gathering dusk came a high, old-fashioned, horse-drawn cab. Abigail was stunned—where was she? She stood right in the middle of the street until she could see the very breath from the horse's nostrils in the cold air, and the alarm on the face of the tall-hatted cabbie. It wasn't a dream—it was true! The year was 1873, and Abigail was trapped in the past—about to meet the *real* Beatie Bow.

—Marianne Tait Pridemore

Poems of A. Nonny Mouse
Compiled by Jack Prelutsky
(Notables 1989)

When we don't know the name of an author or poet, we say the poem or book was written by Anonymous. There are lots of poems signed Anonymous, and now someone has stepped forward to admit that she was the real author. Her name is Ms. A. Nonny Mouse, and she claims that because of an unfortunate misspelling of her name long ago, she never received the proper credit for all those poems. This book, *Poems of A. Nonny Mouse*, is the very first collection of her verses. And you can find Ms. Mouse herself, wearing a straw hat and carrying an umbrella, on every page.

Ms. Mouse has a very off-beat sense of humor. Consider this poem about a goat:

There was a man—now please take note—
There was a man who had a goat.
He loved that goat—indeed he did—

He loved that goat just like a kid.

One day that goat felt frisk and fine,
Ate three red shirts from off the line.
The man, he grabbed him by the back
And tied him to a railroad track.

But when the train drove into sight,
That goat grew pale and green with fright.
He heaved a sigh as if in pain,
Coughed up those shirts, and flagged the train.

Then there is her version of a familiar nursery rhyme:

Mary had a little lamb,
A lobster, and some prunes.
A glass of milk, a piece of pie,
And then some macaroons.

It made the busy waiters grin
To see her order so,
And when they carried Mary out,
Her face was white as snow.

A. Nonny Mouse's work includes limericks like those of the famous Edward Lear and tongue-twisters worse than the one about the woodchuck chucking wood. At last this hard-working author is getting the recognition she deserves!

—*Diane L. Deuel*

Poetspeak: In Their Work, About Their Work
Selected by Paul B. Janeczko
(SLJ/C 1983)

A father and his four sons
run down a slope toward
a deer they just killed.
The father and two sons carry
rifles. They laugh, jostle,
and chatter together.
A gun goes off,

and the youngest brother
falls to the ground.
A boy with a rifle
stands behind him, screaming.

Gregory Orr *is* the boy with the rifle, screaming. The poem, called "Gathering the Bones Together," is the story of the day he accidentally shot and killed his younger brother. Writing the poem, Orr says, helped him come to terms with his personal anguish. He thinks people are often unable to talk about the events that affect their lives most deeply, and sometimes poetry can do the talking for them.

But not all the poems you'll find here are as sorrowful as Orr's. Ed Ochester's "The Gift" is about the joy of a "sweet-faced cat" jumping over your fence and allowing you to stroke him, all the while humming "like a furry dynamo" and brightening your day.

Or maybe you'll identify with David Allen Evans, who spent summers when he was a boy catching bullfrogs. Craftily hiding in the muck, the frogs sit motionless, safe until the boys lure them out with a tiny piece of worm or even a scrap of cloth. They deleg them, pack the legs in ice, and throw the remains back in the pond for the turtles to eat. But what Evans remembers after so many years are the "quiet-bulging eyes nudging along / the moss's edge, looking up at us, / asking for their legs."

Where do poems come from, and why do people write them? *Poetspeak* will tell you.

—*Vicki Reutter*

Polar Express
By Chris Van Allsburg
(BGHB 1986, Caldecott 1986)

I remember a very special Christmas long ago when I was about your age. My friends started saying that there was no Santa Claus, but I didn't believe them. On Christmas Eve, very late, a wonderful train pulled up in front of my house. It was the Polar Express, and on board were other children my age. We ate candy, drank hot chocolate, and sang Christmas carols, and all the while the train carried us through the dark forests and over mountains covered with snow toward the North Pole. We learned that we were on our way to pick the first Christmas gift of the year. At the North Pole the train dropped us off, and we made our way through the crowds of elves.

Soon we found ourselves at the edge of a large circle. In the center stood Santa Claus, next to a sleigh filled with Christmas presents. Suddenly Santa's finger was pointing at me—*I* was going to choose the first Christmas present! I knew just what I wanted—something to show me that Santa Claus and this special night were real.

What would you have chosen if you'd been on the Polar Express?

—*Linda Olson*

Prairie Songs
By Pam Conrad
(IRA 1986)

What's it like to live in a house made of dirt? Well, it's cool in the summer and warm in the winter, just the opposite of the prairie outside.

My name is Louisa Downing. I think the prairie is like a big plate and me and my brother Lester are two tiny peas, left over from dinner. I love the prairie wind and the beautiful stars in the night sky, but Lester and I know a secret—a terrible secret. If you're not strong, the prairie can kill you. It killed our baby sister, who died because she was weak.

We got a new doctor from New York. His wife is pretty, and she smells good. Her name is Mrs. Emmeline Berryman. She's lonely here, so she teaches reading and numbers. She misses trees—only grass grows here on the prairie. Her hands shake. She's going to have a baby. Its cradle arrives by wagon, all broken up because the journey was rough. Mrs. Berryman seems broken up too: she tells Doc he's destroying her and the baby. Doc says it's just her nerves, and she ought to rest.

Momma stays with Mrs. Berryman when she has her baby. It's born dead. I help Poppa dig a grave to bury it. I don't want to have children, ever! I think Mrs. Berryman is a hot-house flower, like Doc says. She's acting strange, packing away all her books somewhere. She looks funny, too, like she's drying up, and she doesn't talk much anymore, just sits and stares.

Indians walked right in our door yesterday. Poppa was gone with Doc to help people hurt in a train wreck. Lester screamed and hid, but Momma fed the Indians and they left.

Poppa didn't come home. We worried about him all night. Momma woke up this morning and remembered something terrible. Mrs. Berryman is in her sod house all alone! What if the Indians found her?

—*Suzanne Bruney*

Princess Ashley
By Richard Peck
(SLJ/C 1987)

There's one in every class: the perfect girl. Everyone knows who she is and everyone wants her approval. You probably know who she is at your school, but at Crestwood High her name is Ashley Packard. And even though Chelsea is a new student and is seeing all these kids for the first time, she can tell right away that Ashley Packard is different from the rest of the sophomores—somehow she's "in charge" of everything that's important and exciting at Crestwood High. And of course she's dating the most gorgeous boy in the tenth grade, Craig Kettering.

Chelsea and Ashley have a couple of classes together. And in those classes, Chelsea spends most of her time watching Ashley instead of the teacher, and wishing she could be like her. She even cuts her hair like Ashley's and starts dressing in the same style. Chelsea has told herself over and over not to expect too much in the beginning—this sophomore year won't be a lot of fun at first because she's new. But now, watching Ashley, she wishes things could be different. Weeks have gone by since school opened and she still feels alone in the crowd. And to make matters worse, she has a terrible secret: her mom is the new school counselor. Chelsea doesn't want anyone to know this because she doesn't want to be singled out by the teachers or the other students. She even insists that her mom use her maiden name at work so that no one will suspect they're related—she's totally paranoid about this.

Then, out of the blue one day, Ashley invites her to come over after school. Chelsea is in shock: Ashley Packard showing interest in being her friend? It's too good to be true, but it *is* true!

Unfortunately, Ashley has more in mind than simple friendship, but Chelsea's going to find that out the hard way.

—*Susan Dunn*

Pyramid
By David Macaulay
(Christopher 1976)

Long ago, before cranes, dump trucks, and cement mixers, some of the biggest and strongest buildings in the world were made—the great pyramids of Ancient Egypt. Every massive piece of stone was cut by hand and dragged to the pyramid site. Precise measurements and plans were made without calculators or computers. Hundreds of people worked for thirty years or more to build each one, and today, over four thousand years later, the great pyramids are still among the wonders of the world.

And now you can follow the story of one pyramid as it is constructed in 2400 B.C. Discover how the giant pieces of stone were moved, why the pyramids faced a special direction, and what each room was built for. This is as close as you can get to designing and building an Ancient Egyptian pyramid yourself.

—Collen Stinson

Quest for a Maid
By Frances Mary Hendry
(Notables 1990)

I know it's my own fault. I know I should never have gone into my sister Inge's storeroom. *No* one is allowed in there without her permission; it's where she works her spells, they say.

But my toothache was hurting fiercely, and I had accidently swallowed the clove she'd given me to ease the pain. I know how precious they are, the cloves—worth their weight in gold, so my sister Birget says. I didn't dare tell Inge how foolish I had been. But I could not bear the pain a minute longer!

So I slipped into her storeroom and took a clove from the bag. No sooner was it in my mouth than I saw a light approaching the door. I dreaded to think what Inge would do to me if she caught me, so I hid under the table, and that's where I heard Inge cast the spell that killed King Alexander.

Inge is now a lady-in-waiting for Lady Marjory de Brus, whose son Robert would be next in line for the Scottish throne were it not for the dead king's granddaughter, a child living in Norway. I don't think Inge or Lady Marjory want her to be crowned, but they wouldn't go so far as to harm a wee bit of a princess, would they?

Or would they?

—Donna L. Scanlon

The Rabbi's Girls
By Johanna Hurwitz
(Notables 1982)

Carrie's father once told her that life was both "bitter and good," and Carrie is beginning to see the truth of that during her family's first year in Lorain, Ohio. The first good thing to happen after they move in is the birth of a new baby sister, but then that meddling Mrs. Fromberg hints that maybe Papa would have rather have had a son—he has five daughters already. Their new house is bigger than any they have ever lived in, but the girl next door is not allowed to play with Carrie because Carrie's Jewish. The Levin family has moved six times that Carrie can remember, but this small Jewish congregation seems to like Rabbi Levin a lot so Carrie hopes they will be able to stay put for a while. As a rabbi's daughter Carrie is used to always being on her best behavior, but she worries about her older sister, who breaks the Sabbath laws. A gentile doctor is able to save the life of her sister, but the Jewish doctor is so angry with the rabbi that he won't speak to him again.

Life is indeed both bitter and good. Will Carrie and her family be able to deal with the bitter, so they can enjoy the good?

—*Maureen Whalen*

Rabbit Hill
By Robert Lawson
(Newbery 1945)

Times have been tough on the Hill. Lots of animals live there—families of rabbits, moles, deer, skunks, mice, and other creatures. Back in the good days, when folks were living in the old farmhouse, life was easy for the animals. The fields and gardens were full of delicious food, the grass was well-tended, and the house was neat. But the last family who lived in the house didn't take care of it. And they didn't plant a garden, either, so food became scarce for the animals. And when that family moved away, the animals had nothing. It was a long, hard winter for them.

Now there's a rumor that new folks are coming to the farm. Workers have been out there, looking at the roof and fixing up the bricks. All the animals are talking about the new folks and the wonderful garden they'll have. All the animals are looking forward to watching things grow and having plenty to eat. If only the new folks really come! And if only they grow a garden that the animals can share!

—*Colleen Stinson*

Rabble Starkey
By Lois Lowry
(BGHB 1987, Golden Kite 1988)

When my grandmother first saw me she predicted trouble, on account of my green eyes and ginger hair, you see. So to keep that trouble away, she gave me a name from the Bible: Parable. But everyone calls me Rabble, so maybe the name didn't work. Oh, not that I've caused much trouble myself, but it does seem like there's always some sort of trouble nearby. I mean, look what happened to poor Mrs. Bigelow. Sure, we knew something was wrong with her. After all, that's why my mother and I came to live with the Bigelow family. Mrs. Bigelow just couldn't seem to cope with her children, Veronica and Gunther, so Mr. Bigelow asked Sweet Ho (that's my mom's name, short for Sweet Hosanna) to come and help. It worked really well for everyone except Mrs. Bigelow, who got worse instead of better. In fact, she started acting so strange that we all got scared, and now she's in a hospital for the mentally ill. See what I mean by trouble? But that's only part of it. Now that Mrs. Bigelow is away, Sweet Ho and I seem like a part of the Bigelow family. We were close to them before, but now we even eat our meals together, and spend our evenings together too. It feels wonderful! If only Mrs. Bigelow would stay away forever, so I could have a real family instead of just a mother. Right now it feels like forever. But how long will forever last?

—Sister M. Anna Falbo, CSSF

Rachel Chance
By Jean Thesman
(Notables 1990)

Rachel knows that not too many people in Rider's Dock have much good to say about the Chance family. Grandpa can be downright cantankerous, and he isn't afraid to let folks know just how little he values their opinions—at least, if they differ from his own. Some people in town don't appreciate that, and they don't think Grandpa is a proper influence on young children, either.

And the climate has been getting even frostier now that Rachel's widowed mother has given birth to Rider, Rachel's adorable—and illegitimate—baby brother. It's no secret that half the people in town feel that such scandalous behavior disqualifies adults from raising children at all.

Rachel is convinced that that's why Rider has disappeared. She's convinced that he's been kidnapped by a religious group that believes Mama and Grandpa have no right to be raising children. And since the police don't seem to be interested in helping her family search for Rider, Rachel decides that it's going to be up to her—she takes things into her own hands, determined to find her brother and bring him back home. It's a big job for a fifteen-year-old girl. Can she succeed?

—*Helen Schlichting*

Rain of Fire
By Marion Dane Bauer
(Addams 1984)

"It just gets started. You don't really know how, but it does. And there you are . . . doing things. Terrible things . . . it's like there's no way to stop."

It had started with little white lies, a bit of bragging, trying to impress people, and suddenly Steve was in a mess and he didn't know how to get out of it.

Now Celestino was threatening to send information to the FBI about Matthew, Steve's brother, information that would prove Matthew was a coward and a Jap-lover. Celestino was using the information as blackmail, to get Steve to steal some dynamite for him.

It seemed as if everything Steve did just got him into more trouble. What was he going to do now?

—*Carol Kappelmann*

Ralph S. Mouse
By Beverly Cleary
(Golden Kite 1983, SLJ/C 1982)

Ralph the mouse is beginning to think he'll have to leave his pleasant home at Mountain View Inn. It just isn't safe anymore. His relatives are multiplying like rabbits, and they all want to ride on his motorcycle—they're wearing out his bike! The whole situation is getting out of control.

So he talks his friend Ryan into taking him to school. Tucked down in Ryan's shirt pocket, Ralph feels snug and secure—so secure that he decides to peek out and see what this thing called school is all about. (It's getting too hot in this pocket, anyway.) But just as he raises his head above the edge for a look around, Melissa turns—and stares right at him!

School may be more of an adventure than Ralph was expecting.

—Carol Kappelmann

Ramona and Her Father
By Beverly Cleary
(BGHB 1978, Newbery Honor 1978)

Ramona's grandmother must have had a saying for everything. Her dad was always coming up with another one, like "A smack at the table is worth a smack on the bottom," whenever Ramona smacked her lips, or "It will never be noticed from a trotting horse," when Ramona thought something looked awful.

But the sayings Ramona put up all over the house had even more of an impact than Grandmother's words of wisdom—signs like, "No smoking," "Stop air pollution!" "Smoking is bad for your health," "Cigarettes start forest fires," and "Smoking stinks!"

Poor Mr. Quimby was getting it from all sides. He had lost his job. The bills were piling up. And now Ramona and Beezus had decided that he had to quit smoking. The timing really wasn't right, but Ramona's campaign was going full speed ahead anyway.

Her poor father didn't have a chance!

—Carol Kappelmann

Ramona and Her Mother
By Beverly Cleary
(ABA 1981)

Ramona Quimby is trying to be very grown up. Daddy has started his new job at the supermarket and Mommy is working full-time at the doctor's office, so it is Ramona's job to go to school and then over to Howie's house, to play nicely until Mommy or Daddy gets home. It's a very hard job, especially the playing nicely part.

And the time Ramona has at home with her family can be hard too—when she tries to make slacks for Ella Funt, her stuffed elephant, for instance, or squirts all the toothpaste out of the tube to make a toothpaste cake. It's not that Ramona means to get into trouble, it's just that somehow she does! And now all the adults are saying how much Willa Jean, Howie's pesky little sister, reminds them of Ramona at that age.

Ramona can't imagine what they mean. She's never been anything like Willa Jean! But how can she convince everyone else?

—*Colleen Stinson*

Ramona Quimby, Age 8
By Beverly Cleary
(Newbery Honor 1982)

Ramona Quimby is in the third grade now, and she really likes her new teacher, Mrs. Whaley. Daddy's going to school too, to learn how to be a teacher; on Saturdays he works in the big freezer at Shop-Rite Markets, to help pay the family bills. Mommy is still tired from working all the time at the doctor's office, but she's usually happy. Even Ramona's big sister has stopped being crabby all the time. Everything is looking pretty good to Ramona, except that she still has to go to Howie's house after school and play nicely with his pesky little sister, Willa Jean.

But on the day she takes a hardboiled egg to school for lunch like everyone else, cracks it on her head, and ends up with raw egg running down her face and hair, things start going bad for Ramona. Next she throws up in class, and then she finds out that Mrs. Whaley, the teacher she likes so much, thinks she's a nuisance! How will Ramona ever become a good girl like Beezus, when such bad, bad things keep happening to her?

—*Colleen Stinson*

Ratha's Creature
By Clare Bell
(IRA 1984)

Millions and millions of years ago, intelligent cats evolved from the sabertooth tiger. They are the Named, and they have their own language, society, laws, and leaders. But they are not the only intelligent beasts—there are also predatory cats who raid the herds of the Named for food. They cannot speak, and so they are called the Un-Named.

Ratha is a young female of the Named who is learning to hunt and to guard the herds. After a huge fire sweeps through their lands, Ratha dares to learn something about it. She discovers that fire can keep her warm and cook her food. She learns how to feed it twigs so it won't die out, and how to keep it small, so she can control it. But when she takes fire back to her clan, they exile her. They are afraid of fire and of her power over it.

Ratha is on her own, alone. She calls the fire Red Tongue, her creature. Will her creature enable her to survive on her own in the wilderness?

—*Mary Hedge and J. R. B.*

Rats on the Roof, and Other Stories
By James Marshall
(Notables 1991)

What do you do when you can't sleep at night because there are rats dancing the mambo on your roof? Who do you call when a stubborn brontosaurus begins to eat the tree in which you make your home? Where do you turn for help when a couple of sneaky, hungry wolves decide to cook *you* for their Christmas dinner?

For the answer to these and other tricky questions, read *Rats on the Roof, and Other Stories*. Satisfactory solutions guaranteed!

—*Sister M. Anna Falbo, CSSF*

Redwall
By Brian Jacques
(SLJ/C 1987)

It was the Summer of the Late Rose, and all seemed well with the world. Within the cloistered walls of the ancient stone abbey of Redwall, the Monastic Order of mice lived in peace with one another and with their neighbors throughout the countryside. The Order was well-established and well respected, for all its members took a solemn vow never to harm another living creature—unless that creature was an enemy who sought to harm the Order. Because they cared for the sick and the injured and helped the poor and unfortunate, the mice of the Order were loved by all who knew them. And so for countless years they had lived in security, untouched by the violence of the world without.

But now it was the Summer of the Late Rose, and Cluny the Scourge was on his way! He was the biggest, toughest rat that had ever lived, an evil, one-eyed rodent who feared no living thing. Now he was on his way with a army five hundred strong, and he had vowed to conquer the abbey.

Beautiful, peaceful Redwall Abbey: can it possibly be saved? Are its days of glory over, or have they only just begun?

—*Sister M. Anna Falbo, CSSF*

Reluctantly Alice
By Phyllis Reynolds Naylor
(SLJ/C 1991)

Alice McKinley is starting seventh grade. At first she's sure she'll hate junior high, but after a week she decides it won't be too bad. If only she can achieve her goal for the year: to be liked by absolutely everybody! That's going to be a lot harder than she thought. Even her best friends don't always like her, or at least not everything she does. And once she's had a run-in with Denise "Mack-Truck" Whitlock, forget about being universally beloved. Denise can hold a grudge forever, and Alice just embarrassed her in front of the entire gym class. Now Alice has an outright enemy. And that's not her only problem. Sometimes disasters seem to come in dozens, and from all directions. Will Alice be able to survive the seventh grade—and accomplish her goal as well?

—*Cynthia L. Lopuszynski*

The Remarkable Journey of Prince Jen
By Lloyd Alexander
(SLJ/C 1991)

Prince Jen—I really like this guy. I admire the way he feels responsible for people. It's nice to see him fall in love. And I like the way he handles bad situations. Jen's story is definitely a journey, and he has a long way to go and a few lessons to learn. (I'm with him all the way.)

Jen's goal is to visit the governor of a far-off land and to learn from him the secrets of wise rule. Someday Jen will be king himself, and he wants to bring peace to his people and promote harmony and prosperity in his lands.

He starts out with a collection of gifts for the governor. Many of the gifts are everyday objects, and this worries Jen—he's not at all sure that the governor will appreciate a simple flute, a saddle, or a bowl made of bronze. But perhaps Jen's learning process has already begun—one must know how to value simple things.

On a narrow mountain road, he faces more tests—lots of them. Can he trust the advice he's been given, or the word of that annoying old fellow who has cadged a ride with his party? A general and his army offer to protect Jen—should he go along with them? Then his carts get stuck in the mud, and one of the gifts is stolen! But at least one thing goes right: Jen meets the most beautiful girl in the world, Voyaging Moon. They fall in love, and Jen and his friends find a nice town where they can rest for a while. Maybe all the mistakes, the struggles, have been worth it. (He's learning.)

But too many people know about Jen by now. Continuing the journey has become more difficult. Suddenly there's a second army, marching toward the first, and where will they meet in battle? Right across Jen's path, of course.

Well, Jen can take battles and thieves and liars, but nothing has prepared him for the worst—to love someone and then lose her. In the floods that follow the storm of the century, Voyaging Moon is swept away.

But there are still lessons to be learned, so don't give up on Voyaging Moon, and don't give up on Jen, either. Do you think they can survive apart, alone and lonely, making their separate ways toward each other? There will be obstacles between them, but wonderful people will help out Jen and Voyaging Moon. A painter, a cook, and the crew of a traveling circus will all recognize the goodness in these young lovers' hearts.

All that remains is to find out what lies at the end of the trail, in the land where all good things happen. The governor is there. Let's hope that true love is there too. And don't forget the lessons, for in order to become a great king, Jen must not forget the simple things.

—*Mark Anderson*

Remembering the Good Times
By Richard Peck
(Notables 1985, SLJ/C 1985)

Sometimes you have to let go of everything else and concentrate on remembering the good times. There were lots of good times, at least till things began to change.

Trav, Buck, and Kate first became friends the year they were all eighth-graders at Slocum Township Junior High. The school was divided along distinct lines. The "Slos" were the kids who'd always lived in Slocum Township; the "Subs" were the kids from the new subdivision—the suburbanites. Trav was clearly a "Sub" and Kate undeniable a "Slo." Buck, a transfer student, didn't fit into either group. They made an unlikely trio, but that made their friendship very special. They were together a lot—mostly at Kate's since she had to look after her great-grandmother, Polly Prior. After a while, Polly just became one of the group. They would spend the afternoons talking or playing cards. At times they worried that Trav was getting too serious, too intense, but none of them could have asked for a better friend.

Then things began to change, and everything seemed to slide out of sync. Maybe they should have seen what was happening, maybe they should have realized that you never know even your best friend as well as you may think. Can friendship change as friends change, or will the survivors find themselves left with only their memories of good times?

—*Helen Schlichting*

The Return
By Sonia Levitin
(National Jewish 1988, Notables 1987)

I dream of my village, high in the mountains, my home that I left so long ago, and when I wake up my face is wet with tears. My eyes can still see the blue-green of the misty mountains, the homes and the schools, and the synagogue, with its tin roof and star on top. But all that is gone now, and I have only my memories left.

My name is Desta. I am a Jew, and I am also an Ethiopian. This is the story of how I left my home to travel back to Israel, which is also my home. It was a long journey, and dangerous, because while the government did not want us in Ethiopia, it didn't want us to leave, either—that was strictly forbidden. When my brother and I started on our secret journey, we had to leave the rest of our family behind. Had we known what dangers lay ahead, how many of our friends would die along the way, we might have stayed behind ourselves as well. Sometimes not knowing the future make it easier to live through it.

Come and travel with us as we search for a new home in a new country, as we try to create new lives for ourselves, as we do what all Jews' long someday to do—return to Israel, and to Jerusalem.

—*J. R. B.*

Return to Bitter Creek
By Doris Buchanan Smith
(Notables 1986, SLJ/C 1986)

Yes, they were returning to Bitter Creek—Lacey, her mother Campbell, and David, who was the closest thing to a real father Lacey had ever known. Ten years ago, when Lacey was just a toddler, Campbell had run away with her, escaping from Bitter Creek and from her own parents, who had been determined to take custody of the child.

Now Lacey and Campbell and David were coming back, to start a business and perhaps to reestablish family ties.

Would it work? Could it work?

Would the family accept David for who and what he was? Could Grandmother keep "hands off" now and give her daughter and granddaughter the love and respect they needed?

Bitter Creek could prove to be just as hurtful as its name. Only time would tell.

—*Carol Kappelmann*

Rhythm Road: Poems to Move To
Selected by Lillian Morrison
(Notables 1988)

Tired of sitting still? Then prepare yourself for a workout! How about starting off with a dance?

> all you children gather round
> we will dance and we will whorl
> we will dance to our own song
> we must spin to our own world
> (from "Dance Poem," by Nikki Giovanni)

Need a break? Let's go for a drive!

> The cars in Caracas
> create a ruckukus,
> a four-wheeled fracacas,
> taxaxis and truckes,
>
> Cacaphono-comic,
> the tracaffic is farcic;
> its weave leads the stomach
> to turn Caracarsick.
> ("The Cars in Caracas," by John Updike)

Well, for a smoother course let's hit the slopes:

> Away she flies and he follows,
> Their out-thrust profiles glow,
> Already their speed is fused with the frisson

That expert skiers know;
Their hearts beat fast, beat faster,
Where she leads he will go
With a sibilant, swift and sugary hiss
Over the perfect snow.
   (from "Anglo-Swiss, or a Day Among the Alps," by William Plomer)

Not afraid of exercising your mind? Then try *Rhythm Road: Poems to Move To* for a great poetry workout!
—*Sister M. Anna Falbo, CSSF*

Rifles for Watie
By Harold Keith
(Newbery 1958)

My name is Jefferson Davis Bussey, and I am from Kansas. My father took me to hear Abraham Lincoln speak, and I never forgot his words about preserving the Union. In Kansas we were always in danger from proslavery bushwhackers who would ride in from Missouri. They had raided farms in our area, stolen our only two horses, and nearly killed my father. I was sick and tired of being a sitting duck and never striking back, so I persuaded my father to write out permission for me to join the Kansas Volunteers at Fort Leavenworth. Two of my friends went with me—they ran away from home to do it.

I was excited when I first arrived at the fort, but things weren't easy there. Captain Asa Clardy took a real dislike to me. Our uniforms were not regulation, and there was hardly any decent food. But I tolerated all this because I wanted to fight the people who had terrorized my family. I was also making some new friends.

Finally our training was over, and we went marching towards Missouri for our first action. I wasn't scared at all; I was eager to engage the enemy. During the long march I was startled by a shot and even more surprised to learn that a boy from my company had been wounded. Clardy accused the boy of shooting off his own finger to get a discharge. How could anyone want to leave the army, when we were finally heading into battle?

Just as we were getting ready to engage the enemy, a mounted staff officer ordered me to go find the quartermaster. I didn't want to leave my company, but the officer insisted. I was going to miss my first battle!

The war would probably be over before I got my chance to fight the enemy! How would I face my friends, after they had earned all the honor and glory?

—*Abbie V. Landry*

A Ring of Endless Light
By Madeleine L'Engle
(Newbery Honor 1981)

Grandfather is dying.

That would be hard enough for Vicky to accept, as the Austin family spends a last summer with him on his beloved island, but then, unexpectedly, their friend Commander Rodney dies after rescuing a teenager whose sailboat capsized. When charming troublemaker Zachary Gray shows up after the commander's funeral, Vicky has a feeling that he's involved. It turns out that she's right—and that the sailboat incident was *not* an accident.

Still, Zachary intrigues Vicky, and she'd like to see more of him. At the same time, Commander Rodney's son Leo wants more than friendship from Vicky. Then there's Adam Eddington, who works at the Marine Biology Station with her brother John and who has a special interest in dolphins—and in Vicky.

But Vicky can't figure Adam out. She can't decide if his interest in her is personal or professional—or both. One minute she's his peer, the next minute she's just John Austin's kid sister. That doesn't surprise Vicky—she's not too sure herself who she is from one day to the next.

Whoever Vicky is, she has a special talent when it comes to dolphins. Maybe they can help her discover who she is and which way to go.

—*Donna L. Scanlon*

River Runners: A Tale of Hardship and Bravery
By James Houston
(CLA 1980)

Andrew looked strong and capable. Strangers saw him as a confident young man of twenty or so. Actually he was shy, somewhat awkward, and only fifteen.

Andrew went to northern Canada to serve as an apprentice clerk at Fort Chimo, a trading post. Unfortunately, the captain of the ship he was on was afraid of the ice-blocked river, and decided to leave Andrew and the shipment of supplies at its mouth. Someone from Fort Chimo would have to come downriver to pick them up. Before Andrew understood what was happening, he found himself standing on a block of drifting ice at the mouth of the river.

The air was extremely cold. Andrew could no longer even imagine how warm his parents might be in their New England summer home. Somehow it didn't feel like summer here, pacing back and forth to keep his blood circulating, at 6:07 in the morning on a drifting chunk of ice.

Luckily, the first mate had warned Andrew to bundle up in all his warmest clothing. But when a chill breeze arose, he sensibly arranged the crates into a shelter. He mounted the signal flag at the highest point of the cargo and settled in to wait.

As the hours passed, he remembered that the captain had suggested he eat from the shipment and tried to pry open a case of sea biscuits, but the metal straps made it impossible. Andrew fought down his hunger, curled up in his little shelter, and fell asleep.

He woke suddenly with the eerie feeling that he was not alone. A bony hand crept around one of the nearby crates. In horror Andrew screamed and thrashed out to defend himself.

Suddenly, being alone didn't seem quite so bad.

—Bernice D. Crouse

The Road from Home: The Story of an Armenian Girl
By David Kherdian
(Addams 1980, Newbery Honor 1980)

I remember growing up in our stucco house in the Armenian section of Azizya, in Turkey. At that time, around 1910, Father was a prosperous businessman, well-respected in the community. Mother was happy and friendly, a wonderful cook and a hard worker. Our family—Grandma, aunts, uncles and cousins—was a close one. At Easter, we would share a feast at Grandma's. I loved our church and the choir's joyful songs. How my life has changed since those days!

There had always been problems with the Turks, partly because they were Moslems and we were Armenian Christians. In 1895 some of our people had been massacred by the Turks, and more had been killed in 1909. Then on a Sunday in 1915, we were told that we had to leave immediately. We were given just three days to gather our belongings. As we bumped along in our wagon towards the Tarsus Mountains, we wondered what lay ahead. The winds of war were swirling about—Turkey and the Germans fighting on one side, and England and France on the other.

This was but the beginning of the destruction suffered by my family and many of our fellow Armenians. I dreamed of many things in those days: of continuing my schooling, being reunited with my family, and maybe someday going to America. But even as I dreamed, I wondered if any of my hopes could ever come true.

—*Nancy Bardole Hanaman*

The Road to Memphis
By Mildred D. Taylor
(King 1991)

It all started with my brother Stacey's new car. It was beautiful—a 1938 Ford with gray upholstery, a wooden dashboard, and carpets that looked like new. It was wine-colored, with shiny chrome and whitewall tires. There wasn't a dent or a scratch on it anywhere. Stacey was as proud of it as he could be. He'd put every cent he had into it, and he had a year to pay off the balance.

We talked about going to Jackson, but things just started happening too fast. Charlie Simms ran his truck into the ditch, and we had to help him get it out—he was white, and there was no way we were gonna be able to just walk away. Then we all went on a coon hunt, and about the time we had a big coon treed, Jeremy Simms came along with a bunch of his friends and decided that Harris should be the coon—and they treed him and sicced the dogs on him. When a branch broke, Harris fell out of the tree and busted up his head, his leg, and a bunch of his ribs.

That was the night it all changed—the night that Stacey and Jeremy both realized that childhood was over. The gap between black and white was too big to be crossed. What Jeremy had done to Harris would stand between them now forever. When Stacey drove home in that new car, some things were just beginning, but others were coming to an end.

—*J. R. B.*

Roll of Thunder, Hear My Cry
By Mildred D. Taylor
(BGHB 1977, Newbery 1977)

Cassie and her family were the only black landowners in Spokane, Mississippi, in 1933. Sometimes it seemed as if their life was just one long fight, whether it was the big struggle against the white plantation owner who had sworn to take that land away from them or the little everyday struggles—like Cassie and her brother's fight with the school bus. You see, in those days black children in Mississippi couldn't ride the several miles to school—they had to walk, while the white children, whose school was much closer than the black school, got to ride in a brand new shiny bus. And every day that bus would catch Cassie and her brother on the long, cold, muddy patch through the forest—no matter how early or late they left—and when the driver saw them he always did the same thing—step on the accelerator and roar through the deepest puddle while Cassie and Little Man scrambled up the muddy banks for safety. And every morning they got to school wet and filthy. But Cassie knew how to fight back—she'd fix that school bus some day—and her Papa too would stand up to the nightriders and the burnings and hang on to their land, even if it, and they, were destroyed in the process.

—Elizabeth Overmyer

Ronia, the Robber's Daughter
By Astrid Lindgren
(Batchelder 1984, Notables 1983)

On the night Ronia was born, a thunderstorm raged on Matt's mountain. In the great stone hall, twelve robbers eagerly waited for word of the child's birth. Suddenly Matt, the robber chieftain, burst through the door beaming with good news. A new daughter had been added to the clan at Matt's fort.

As Ronia grew up, she explored every inch of the fort. She learned the robbers' songs and listened to their stories. When she had explored all the fort, she started on the forest. She learned to find her way through the woods so she wouldn't get lost. She learned to watch out for the wild harpies and the grey dwarfs. She was very careful not to fall into Hell's Gap, the chasm that split Matt's territory in two. But most of all she learned to watch out for the enemy—the Borka robber clan.

Then Ronia befriended Birk, the son of the enemy. Could their friendship survive the bitter quarrels between their warring families? Could Ronia and Birk bring peace to the rival robber bands?

—Linda Olson

The Root Cellar
By Janet Lunn
(Notables 1983, SLJ/C 1983)

Until Rose Larkin was twelve she had a life almost anyone would envy. She lived with her grandmother and traveled all over the world, staying in luxurious hotels and apartments. Her grandmother didn't believe in public schools, so Rose had tutors instead; she was far more comfortable with adults than with kids her own age. But when her grandmother died, all that changed.

Rose was sent to stay with her aunt and uncle, who lived with their four noisy boys in a house that was 160 years old. Rose knew that someday, when the house was all fixed up, it'd be nice, but now it was just a mess—especially her bedroom, with its fading, shredded wallpaper.

Then one day, when Rose was hiding out in the overgrown garden, she found the door to an old root cellar. The door was stuck fast, but after pulling and straining, Rose got it open. She crept down the stairs to investigate and found a room lined with shelves of preserves. When she turned around, she met a girl in an old-fashioned dress, apron, and boots. And not only was Susan dressed strangely, she talked strangely too. Rose had stepped from the present into the past, and now she was in Susan's world and time. But why had it happened, and however would she get back home again?

—Colleen Stinson and J. R. B.

Rosemary's Witch
By Ann Turner
(SLJ/C 1991)

Rosemary likes her family's new house; it's much bigger and nicer than their old house in the city, and the country town is pretty and peaceful. Still, she has an eerie sense that something is not-quite-right about this house—and now she has proof.

First, things mysteriously disappear: a bicycle, a teacup, a bag of clothes. Then Rosemary finds a picture of a sad, pinched-faced girl drawn in one of the roses on the wallpaper of her room. Even though it's July, the weather is cold and foggy, making Rosemary's mother's joints swell up—bad news for a dancer. Then the school playground equipment is vandalized, and the whole town is overrun with toads. Rosemary's parents begin to talk about giving up the house and moving back to the city.

Then Rosemary learns about Mathilda, the sad little girl who once lived in the house and whose face appeared on Rosemary's wallpaper. And, incredibly, Mathilda's still around: she's 149 years old, and she's the one who's causing all the trouble. Even though she's now a powerful witch, she's still sad and lonely, and all the power in the world can't give her what she wants—a home.

But Rosemary thinks she knows how to help. She just has to find the courage to face Mathilda—Rosemary's witch!

—*Donna L. Scanlon*

The Sandman's Eyes
By Patricia Windsor
(Poe 1986)

I'm back home, back with Grandpop and Rosie in the only home I've ever known. After two years in that institution (actually, they call it a school), I feel like a complete stranger. But everyone in town recognizes me—I'm the murderer. Even Rosie acts as if it might be true.

I know I should leave town. No one's going to give me a job. They don't even want me around.

But I have to find out what really happened that night in Monrovia Park, the night that man pushed the woman over the edge. How can I get on with my life until I find the answers to my past?

—*Carol Kappelmann*

Sarah, Plain and Tall
By Patricia MacLachlan
(Christopher 1985, Golden Kite 1986, Newbery 1986, Notables 1985, O'Dell 1986, SLJ/C 1985)

Talk 1

Sarah brought something from the sea for each of us. For Caleb she had a shell, a moon snail which curled and smelled of salt. She gave me the smoothest and whitest stone I had ever seen. Sarah had a faraway look on her face. Papa didn't see it, I know, but Caleb did, and so did I. I wished that Papa and Caleb and I could all be perfect for her. But what if Sarah didn't like us, or what if she was too lonely for the sea, or what if she thought we were too pesty—would she go back to the sea before the preacher came to marry them at the end of the week?

Papa began to sing again. Sarah learned how to plow the fields. We made dunes of haystacks and rode them to the ground. One morning Sarah got up early, put on her blue dress and yellow bonnet, climbed up into the wagon, and drove off to town. Papa and Caleb and I watched Sarah leave for town. It was sunny and warm—a day just like the one when our Mama went away and didn't come back.

"What has Sarah gone to do?" "I don't know." said Papa. "Ask if she's coming back," whispered Caleb. But I would not ask the question. I was afraid to hear the answer.

—*Barbara K. Foster*

Talk 2

"What did I look like when I was born?" Caleb asked.

"Well, you didn't have any clothes on. Mama handed you to me in a yellow blanket and said, 'Isn't he beautiful, Anna?'"

I remember what I thought. You were homely and plain, you had a terrible holler and a horrid smell. But that was not the worst of you. Mama died the next morning.

It was hard to think of you as beautiful. It took three whole days for me to love you, sitting by the fire, Papa washing up the supper dishes, your tiny hand brushing my cheek.

"Did Mama sing every day?" Caleb asked. "Every single day," I said, "and Papa sang too."

Papa leaned back in his chair and said, "I've placed an advertisement in the newspaper. For help."

"A housekeeper?" asked Caleb.

"No, not a housekeeper," said Papa slowly. "A wife."

Caleb stared at Papa. "A wife? You mean a mother!"

Papa reached in his pocket and unfolded a letter written on white paper. It was an answer to his ad.

Dear Mr. Jacob Whitting,

I am Sarah Wheaton. I am answering your advertisement. I have never been married, though I have been asked. I am strong and I work hard. I would be interested in your children and where you live. And about you.

Very truly yours,
Sarah Elizabeth

When Papa finished reading, no one said a word. Then I said, "Ask her if she sings."

Caleb, Papa, and I wrote letters to Sarah. We all received answers.

Dear Anna,
    Yes, I c

Dear Cale
    I hav

Dear Ja
    I w wear a yellow bonnet. I am
plain g.

                                Sarah

  Sarah a drove off along the dirt road to fetch
her. Pap ur new mother? Maybe. Find out when
you rea l.

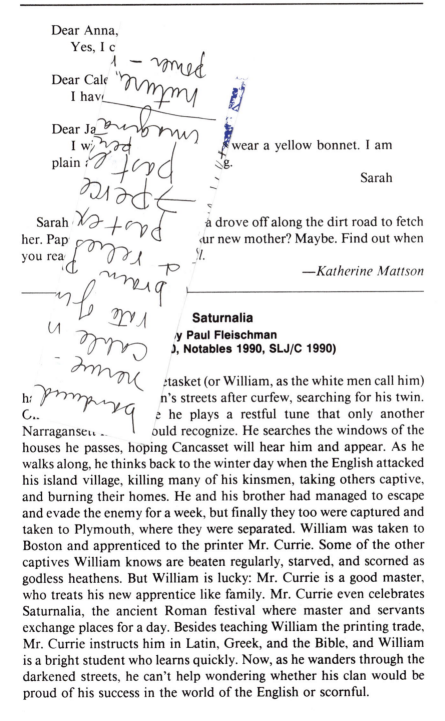

                           —Katherine Mattson

Saturnalia
y Paul Fleischman
), Notables 1990, SLJ/C 1990)

tasket (or William, as the white men call him)
h n's streets after curfew, searching for his twin.
C. e he plays a restful tune that only another
Narragansett ould recognize. He searches the windows of the
houses he passes, hoping Cancasset will hear him and appear. As he
walks along, he thinks back to the winter day when the English attacked
his island village, killing many of his kinsmen, taking others captive,
and burning their homes. He and his brother had managed to escape
and evade the enemy for a week, but finally they too were captured and
taken to Plymouth, where they were separated. William was taken to
Boston and apprenticed to the printer Mr. Currie. Some of the other
captives William knows are beaten regularly, starved, and scorned as
godless heathens. But William is lucky: Mr. Currie is a good master,
who treats his new apprentice like family. Mr. Currie even celebrates
Saturnalia, the ancient Roman festival where master and servants
exchange places for a day. Besides teaching William the printing trade,
Mr. Currie instructs him in Latin, Greek, and the Bible, and William
is a bright student who learns quickly. Now, as he wanders through the
darkened streets, he can't help wondering whether his clan would be
proud of his success in the world of the English or scornful.

There is one Englishman, though, who despises William's intelligence. It's Mr. Baggot, the tithingman, who drills William and the Currie children on their knowledge of the Bible. Mr. Baggot vows that one day he will see the dark-skinned scholar suffer. "I want you to know that my eye is upon you. Like the spider's eye upon the fly," he tells William. "And that one day soon—I'll snare you!" Mr. Baggot has the power to have William publicly whipped, put in the stocks, or branded. All he has to do is catch William with one foot outside the law. Though breaking curfew is risky, William can't give up his search, and after he finds his cousin and uncle, he begins to sneak out every night. He smuggles food to them from the Currie kitchen, and in exchange his uncle teaches him how to heal the sick, bring rain, and see into the future. But then his uncle's master is murdered, and William is accused of the crime. Not only must he defend himself against this false accusation, but he must also decide whether to remain among the English or escape with his uncle back to his own people.

—*Kathy Ann Miller*

Save Queen of Sheba!
By Louise Moeri
(Notables 1981)

When King David woke up, the first thing he saw was a huge, greenish-black fly crawling along his hand, just in front of his face. He took a breath, felt pain, sat up and looked around. An overturned wagon and a man underneath, a smashed water keg, and more bodies— horses, women, children, with arrows in them.

King David stood up and felt his head, which hurt—he seemed to be half scalped, but he could walk. The Sioux raiding party was gone, and he was the only person left alive. The only one, that is, until he looked under a feather bed thrown out of the farthest wagon—and found his six-year-old sister, Queen of Sheba.

There were twelve bodies, and two live children—King David was only twelve. But it was up to him to see that he and his little sister caught up with the rest of the wagon train—and their parents. They were on their own—with only a small amount of water, in two canteens, a small pack of cornmeal, one little piece of bacon, some apples, and a gun.

King David was almost delirious from the infection in the wound on his head. Queen of Sheba was a stubborn, spoiled brat who would refuse to help or do anything King David asked her to—and they were alone in the middle of the prairie.

But before they'd gone too far, they found one of the horses from the wagon train caught in some bushes. Now at least they had a chance, King David thought—if only he could put up with Queen of Sheba till they found the rest of the wagon train.

—*J. R. B.*

The Seance
By Joan Lowery Nixon
(Poe 1981)

Lauren had a very comfortable life with Aunt Mel until a few months ago. Then Sara moved in. Poor Sara needed a foster home, and Aunt Mel couldn't say no, not when the preacher himself had asked. And since Lauren and Sara were about the same age—seventeen—Aunt Mel thought they'd become friends.

That hasn't happened. They don't get along at all, and Sara baits Lauren at every opportunity. Lauren tries not to respond.

One day Sara asks her—almost dares her—to come to a seance after school. Some other girls will be there too, but Sara wants Lauren. It all sounds too creepy for words, but Lauren agrees—and immediately knows that she's made a bad move.

Inexplicable things happen during the course of the seance. Mysterious hints are dropped. Then, suddenly, the lights go out, and when they come back on, Sara's gone—she's no longer in the room, or in the house. Days later her body is found in the swamp.

Lauren is just beginning to wonder if there could be a connection between Sara's murder and the strange goings-on at the seance when a second girl disappears, another girl who was there that night. Now the police are asking a lot of questions, and some of the townspeople are up in arms, looking for someone to blame. And the murderer is still out there. With a cold chill Lauren realizes that she is one of the last links to that fatal scene. She may be the next victim.

—*Colleen Stinson*

The Secret World of Polly Flint
By Helen Cresswell
(Notables 1984)

Have you ever thought about time? Oh, I don't mean just about clocks and watches, but about whether time is real or not. Is it always straightforwardly the same, or could it somewhere, somehow or other, be stopped or frozen? Well, to tell you the truth, this is not a subject I think about often myself. But then, neither did Polly Flint—until the day she saw that angel. She was quite alone, picking flowers in a field, when she saw him. He was so beautiful, so brilliant, that she knew his appearance must have some special meaning for her. And the more she thought about that shining angel, the more she began to feel that she was on the fringes of another world, a world locked in another time. Soon she was living in two separate worlds. One was the world of everyday, with clocks ticking away and her family and friends close by. And the other was her own secret world, where time stood still—the world of the lost village of Grimstone, whose inhabitants had slipped through the nets of time centuries ago.

Enter the secret world of Polly Flint: you never know what may happen when you meddle with time.   —*Sister M. Anna Falbo, CSSF*

Seventeen Against the Dealer
By Cynthia Voigt
(SLJ/C 1989)

Cautiously, Dicey approached her boat-building shop. The window had been broken and the door stood ajar. Her tools! Sure enough, the worktable was bare. All her saws, hammers, nails, planes—gone. Even the adze was gone. Dicey would have to replace everything out of the money she had gotten just that morning, up-front money to begin building a dinghy for a rich man's cruiser. Doing without insurance had been a gamble, and now she had lost.

Mina, her best friend, came over to help Dicey clean up the broken glass and the spilled paint. Dicey was beginning to wonder if passing up a college scholarship to start this business was another gamble she shouldn't have taken, but Mina assured her that someday she'd be "the Sara Lee of boat-building." Becoming a professional boat-builder had always been Dicey's dream, and she was determined to make it happen.

For such a young woman, Dicey Tillerman was no stranger to hard work, or to hard luck, either. Only eight years before, she had been abandoned at a shopping mall by her mother. Leading her three younger siblings, she had walked all the way to Maryland to find relatives who would take them in. That's how the Tillermans had ended up living with Gram in her big old house by the ocean. Gram didn't have much money, so they all pitched in. Dicey worked nights at MacDonald's, Sammy chopped wood and kept the old truck running, and Maybeth grew herbs and sold them at the market. James and Dicey had both won scholarships to college, but Dicey had turned hers down to start her own business.

Now she didn't want to burden the others with her troubles. She would just have to work harder and faster, and take on more jobs to keep up with the bills. She could use some help. And one morning, as that thought was running through her mind, a stranger appeared, standing quietly in the doorway of the shop, watching her paint. "Who are you?" Dicey said. "What do you want?" Little did she know then that he would lead her to take the biggest gamble of her life.

—Vicki Reutter

Shabanu: Daughter of the Wind
By Suzanne Fisher Staples
(Notables 1989)

In Pakistan, a girl becomes engaged when she is eleven or twelve years old. As soon as her monthly periods begin, her parents quickly find a good man for her to marry and then set a date. It doesn't matter whether their daughter agrees with their choice or not; that's the way it's done. For countless generations, that has been the law of the people. So the girls grow up knowing that their childhood homes are only temporary. Their real homes are the ones they will go to when they marry.

Shabanu and her sister have been raised in the desert. Their father is a camel herder, and the family moves wherever the water is. The girls love the wide, open landscapes and the brilliant stars and the way the entire desert blossoms immediately after a rain—they don't ever want to live anywhere else. But unfortunately both of them are betrothed to men—brothers—who live outside the desert. These men come from a good family, and that's the most important thing to Shabanu's parents. Marriage will be a step up in status for both girls.

Phulan, Shabanu's sister, is to be married this summer to the older of the two brothers. Then next summer it will be Shabanu's turn. She's known her future husband all her life, but still the thought of marriage and of being separated from her parents is scary. Shabanu is glad she has another year to wait.

When summer arrives, the family load up all their belongings on their camels and head into the city. Phulan is beside herself with excitement. But almost as soon as they arrive at the wedding site, Phulan's husband-to-be is killed in a fight. The only thing her father can think to do is to allow Phulan to marry the second brother, the man who was supposed to be for Shabanu. This saves Phulan's honor but it leaves Shabanu without a husband. Then a wealthy landowner steps in and asks for Shabanu. He seems nice, but he's old enough to be her grandfather; he already has three wives, which basically means that Shabanu will be little more than a slave for them and their children. Shabanu doesn't want to have anything to do with him, but she has no choice. Her father has made the decision for her—that's just the way things are. Can Shabanu find the strength to rebel against generations of tradition and defy her family's wishes?

—Susan Dunn

Shades of Gray
By Carolyn Reeder
(Notables 1989, O'Dell 1989)

As he left, Doc Martin told Will, "You'll do fine here—it's a lot different from what you're used to, but you'll do fine."

Very quickly, Will learned just *how* different life in rural Virginia would be. Even though the war was over, food and money were still scarce. There would be no school in the fall because there was no money to pay a teacher. His aunt's house was small but comfortable, but Will remembered the spacious, well-furnished rooms of his mother's house in Winchester.

Also, back in Winchester, Will's family had had three slaves to work and wait on them, but no one waited on anyone here, and everyone was expected to work all day, every day!

And without big brother Charlie around, Hank and the other boys bullied Will. But hardest of all to take, Will had to live with his uncle—a man whom Will considered a *traitor*, a coward who had refused to fight the Yankees.

This is Will's story: how he learned farm work from his uncle, including running trap lines, getting the animals from the traps, hoeing the garden, and replacing the fence posts. It's the story of how Will handled the bullies (did he *really* have to fight Hank?), and it's the story of what he did when the Yankee soldier came, needing a place to spend the night.

But, most of all, it's the story of what Will learned about his uncle, and how he learned what a coward is, and what courage is, too.

—Dorothy Davidson

Shiloh
By Phyllis Reynolds Naylor
(Newbery 1992, Notables 1991)

Shiloh is a beagle puppy who's abused by his owner.

Mr. Judd is a mean man. "Never name any of my dogs. Dogs one, two, three, and four, is all. When I want 'em, I whistle; when I don't, I give 'em a kick. 'Git,' 'Scram,' 'Out,' and 'Dammit'—that's my dogs' names."

Shiloh is the beagle puppy who runs away from Mr. Judd. Eleven-year-old Marty Preston finds him and falls in love, but his parents tell him that he must return the dog to its rightful owner. It almost kills Marty to take Shiloh back to his cruel master, but he obeys his parents—the first time.

But when the dog runs away again, Marty decides that he'll defy his parents, lie to the world, and do anything else necessary to save Shiloh. Will he be successful, or will Shiloh have to go back to Mr. Judd's yet again?

—Jo Berkman

The Shining Company
By Rosemary Sutcliff
(Notables 1990, SLJ/C 1990)

I am Prosper, second son of Gerontius, and I am a shieldbearer to one of the Three Hundred, the Shining Company. We were assembled by the king in 600 A.D., to ride against the Saxons who have invaded our land. I am accompanied by my servant and friend, Conn, now also a shieldbearer.

Who knew, on that autumn day so long ago, when Conn, my kins-woman Luned [Linn´ed], and I went into the woods to search for a lost hound, that our simple task would lead to our present path! For that was when we saw the white hart, and although we never told anyone, others also spotted the magnificent beast, and word soon spread.

Soon after that, Prince Gorthyn and his companions rode into our valley seeking to hunt the white hart. I went with them, intending to kill it before the dogs pulled it down, but when my chance came, *I could not do it!*

Neither could Prince Gorthyn.

A bond was forged between us that day, a bond that the prince never forgot. When the time came for him to choose his shieldbearers, he called upon me, and upon Conn. We followed him to Dyn Eidin [Dun ee´din], to the castle of the Golden King, and there all of us, warriors and shieldbearers alike, pledged the Great Oath.

Now we ride to face the Saxons. I do not know if I will ever see my home or my family again. But for now, it is enough for me to follow and serve the Shining Company!

—*Donna L. Scanlon*

Shoebag
By Mary James
(SLJ/C 1990)

Life gets *very* complicated for Shoebag, a young cockroach, when he suddenly turns into a boy. Now he has to wear clothes, go to school, and be in bed by 10 pm. No more late-night scavenging parties with his large and lively family, whom he misses terribly. He can still see them, of course, and he talks to them when no one else is around and even leaves out food for them to eat, but it's just not the same. Humans hate cockroaches—how can he possibly be a human? To make matters worse, his relatives (the roachy ones) have decided to move to a nicer place. If they do that, Shoebag may lose track of his family altogether!

Is there any way he can turn back into a cockroach and live happily ever after, or is he doomed to be a human being forever?

—*J. R. B.*

The Sign of the Beaver
By Elizabeth George Speare
(Newbery Honor 1984, Notables 1983, SJL/C 1983)

My father and I moved into the Maine wilderness to build a cabin and start a few crops on our new land. After we'd fnished the cabin and planted corn and pumpkins, Father had to go back to Massachusetts to get my mother, sister, and the baby, who was just born. He said he should be back in about seven weeks with the whole family in tow, and he helped me prepare tally sticks to count off the days. He swapped guns with me, too, so that I could have the good rifle, and last of all he told me to be respectful, should I run into any Indians. I swallowed, and hoped I wouldn't see any.

As soon as Father disappeared down the trail, the loneliness set in. I did chores to keep busy and wondered if my food would hold out. My days soon fell into a pattern of chores and hunting. From time to time, I had the feeling that I was being watched, but I could never see anyone around.

One evening a man approached the cabin. I didn't know whether he was friend or foe, so I greeted him cautiously. But he seemed friendly, and it had been a while since I'd seen another person. He said his name was Ben. He told me stories about trapping and Indians as I cooked our supper; then he fell asleep on the floor, and I went to bed. In the morning Ben was gone, and so was Father's rifle.

Not being able to hunt made things more difficult, but I could still fish. Then one day, when I came home from fishing, I found the cabin ransacked, the flour spilled, and the molasses gone. A hungry bear had raided my supplies. There was a bee tree not far away, I remembered, and I thought I would replace the molasses with honey. Father had always said to leave the bees alone, but I was desperate. I climbed up the tree, tore off a piece of bark, and suddenly bees were all over me, stinging! I fell out of the tree and ran for the pond. As I hid underwater, holding my breath, the bees circled, waiting for me to surface. I must have passed out—I dreamed my father came and picked me up. And then I woke up, back inside the cabin—with two Indians looking at me! My whole body was shaking. What did they want? What were they going to do?

—Abbie V. Landry

The Silent Voice
By Julia Cunningham
(Notables 1981)

Ice covered the littered streets and sidewalks of Paris in that early winter dawn, and the wind stirred a ragged scrap of material atop a bony mound huddled against the wall. Suddenly a girl rounded the corner and stopped short. "Mon Dieu! There's been a murder!" she screamed. Her fellow street urchins—Jerome, Francois and Thomas— came quickly, ready to rob the corpse until Astair stopped them—the boy was in fact alive. She insisted that they bring him to that cellar room in an abandoned hovel that Astair called home, although the boys were convinced that the stranger could not live. Even so, they pitied the poor form as they laid him on Astair's ragged mattress, for they too had experienced starvation and misery in times not too long past. They soon left to sing for their supper in front of the factory gate. Astair stayed behind to care for her new charge. As she removed his coat, she discovered a small box of red velvet. Maybe she could sell whatever was inside for enough to buy herself a new pair of shoes to replace the newspaper-stuffed ones that she now wore. Imagine her surprise and joy when she found that the box contained a gold medallion with a sapphire in its center! What a find! How could such a boy possess such a treasure? Maybe the boy could tell her. He stirred at her touch. Astair quickly closed the box as the boy spoke to her with his eyes. She placed the box in his hands and closed his fingers around it. In response to his faint smile, Astair told him how she and her friends had found him nearly frozen to death, and she asked him who he was and where he had gotten the box that had been pinned to his shirt. Only silence met her questions at first. Then the boy moved his hand over his mouth to indicate that he could not talk. Astair gave him a bit of soup warmed over a can of Sterno and explained how she and the three others managed to live by performing on street corners, pilfering from markets, and running errands to keep their stomachs at least half-filled. Finishing the last drop of his soup, the boy pulled an imaginary pen from the air and began to write on paper that wasn't there. Astair laughed at his cleverness and brought him a stub of chalk to write on the floor, explaining that she could read—a little. He spelled out his name in seven round letters: AUGUSTE. Astair told Auguste that he didn't have to tell her where he had gotten the box but that he'd better keep it hidden. She too had to go out and help perform for their supper. As she left the cellar, she gazed back at someone so frail that he was close to being no person at all, and yet she sensed in him a power unlike any she had ever known.

How did Auguste get that medal to which he clung as to life itself? Was he more than he appeared to be? Would that strange power that Astair sensed in him make itself known? Find out, in *The Silent Voice.*

—*E. Lynn Porter*

Sing Down the Moon
By Scott O'Dell
(Newbery Honor 1971)

Bright Morning had everything a young Navajo woman could ever ask for—a beautiful home, a loving family, good friends, her own herd of sheep, and soon, if she was lucky, a wonderful husband. All of this changed the morning she and Running Bird were captured by Spanish slavers and taken far from their home. It would be many weeks before they would see their friends and families again. When Tall Boy, Bright Morning's intended husband, tried to rescue them, he was shot in the shoulder. Even Bitter Water, the tribe's medicine man, could not heal him, and without the use of his right arm, Tall Boy could no longer be a warrior and protect his people from danger.

And danger was coming. One day United States soldiers arrived and told Bright Morning's people that they had to leave their canyon home and go with them. When the tribe refused, the soldiers destroyed their homes, their crops, and their orchard. After that, they had no choice but to leave; they followed the soldiers, not knowing what lay ahead.

What will happen to Bright Morning's dreams? Will any of them ever come true? Will she ever see her canyon and her sheep again, or hear her children's laughter echo off the tall canyon walls? Find out as you follow her and her fellow Navajos on the Long Walk.

—*J. R. B.*

Sixteen: Short Stories by Outstanding Writers for Young Adults
Compiled by Donald R. Gallo
(SLJ/C 1984)

There's nothing like a good short story. A quick hit. Now you can read your favorite authors in that form: Cormier, Kerr, the Mazers, Peck, Sebestyen, Sharmat. Sixteen of them, crampacked into one concentrated volume. Take M. E. Kerr's story, "Do You Want My Opinion?", for instance. . . .

"I've heard you're getting serious about Eleanor Rossi," John's father accused. "Spending all night talking with her."

John kept silent, waiting for the inevitable lecture.

"You've got lots of time to get intimate with a girl," his father started. "Don't let one get a-hold of you."

"Don't worry, Dad. I think about a lot of them."

"That's your problem. You think too much. Just stick to lovemaking and keep your ideas to yourself. OK, son?"

John knew he was going through a phase. But it was hard to escape the temptation. On the bathroom walls were scribblings: "Josephine Merril is a brain! I'd like to know her opinion." Leering things like that. If only he could stick to hugs and kissing, not this confiding business. . . .

Then there was Lauren, who nearly caused a scandal imagining a world where people openly shared their thoughts but kept lovemaking private. Where would that end?

Sound thought-provoking? Wait until you read the other stories in this great collection!

—Lesley S. J. Farmer

The Sky Is Falling
By Kit Pearson
(CLA 1990)

Over England the sky was falling. Not the way Chicken Little thought, but all the same pieces of things kept falling from the sky. Pieces of shrapnel, a boot, and one day a whole plane—a German war plane. There was war going on. But it wasn't really scary; in fact, it was kind of fun. Norah and her friends even had a secret club where they watched for German planes and for spies. The war didn't seem quite real—until the day Grandfather's house was bombed. It's a good thing he wasn't home, because his house was flattened. Everyone had heard stories, but this was first time anything like this happened to someone Norah actually knew. Maybe the war was more dangerous than she'd thought.

Then, when Mum and Dad told Norah about leaving England, she knew things must be getting very dangerous indeed, even in their small village. Because now Norah and her little brother Gavin were going to be sent to Canada, not for vacation but for a long time—until the war was over. And they would have to go alone. Mum, Dad, and Grandfather were staying behind.

It wasn't fair! Norah wanted to stay and do her part to help fight the war. She wanted to watch for enemy planes and collect money for the war effort. She didn't want to look like a coward, like the other children who had been evacuated. She didn't want to go to Canada. And she certainly didn't want to live with a bunch of strangers!

—*Colleen Stinson*

The Slave Dancer
By Paula Fox
(Newbery 1974)

Before he was kidnapped, Jessie loved to play the fife. He liked to see people enjoying his music, and he loved to watch them dance. But things are different now. Everything changed the night he was attacked on his way home. Almost before he knew what was happening, he was bundled into a canvas and carried aboard a ship. By the time he was released, the ship was far out to sea.

To his horror, Jessie discovered that he had been kidnapped to serve aboard a slave ship. Now he must be the slave dancer—he must play his fife so the slaves will dance. They spend most of their time below deck, crowded into the dark, smelly hold of the ship. Each day, however, they are brought up on deck in groups for fresh air and exercise. Slavers know that if the men get not exercise, they will no be in prime condition when they put up for sale at the end of the voyage. So each day Jessie is ordered to play his fife, and the slaves are ordered to dance—music and dancing that will keep them fit for a life of bondage. Every day Jessie watches as the slaves move around the deck, their legs weighted down by the shackles that bite into their skin. Jessie doesn't enjoy playing the fife anymore. He hates what he sees, but he's helpless to change it. Is there any hope of a brighter future for the captive Africans—and for Jessie?

—*Helen Schlichting*

So Much to Tell You
By John Marsden
(Australian CBY 1988, Christoper 1990)

Fourteen-year-old Marina has not spoken for a year. Her face is permanently disfigured. Her father is in jail.

What happened to her that was so horrible that it took away her voice? Will she ever be able to trust again? To talk again? To share what she remembers, what she thinks, what she feels?

This is Marina's diary, and in it, she has so much to tell you.
—*Dara Finkelstein and J. R. B.*

A Solitary Blue
By Cynthia Voigt
(BGHB 1984, Newbery Honor 1984, Notables 1983)

I was in the second grade when my mom left. I found her note when I came home from school. It said she wasn't ever coming back, because other people in the world needed her more than we did. That really hurt, but I knew my father wouldn't want his life disrupted, even if she was gone, so I never said anything about it. I just made dinner when my homework was done. We went on that way for years, the Professor (that's what I called my father) working at the college, then coming home to work some more, closed in his office, and me going to school and coming home to do homework and make dinner. Some years we had a student who lived with us and did the cooking and housecleaning, but when I reached sixth grade the Professor decided I could do both after school. I never questioned it.

I never questioned anything. I just did it. It didn't matter. I was afraid that if I did anything wrong, or upset him or anything, he'd leave too. And then I'd be all alone.

But the summer after sixth grade I went to South Carolina to stay with my mother. It was the first time I'd seen her since she left. She and the Aunts lived in a big house in Charleston. That summer was great; that summer I got to know my mother. That summer changed my life.
—*Colleen Stinson and Susan Dunn*

Something Big Has Been Here
By Jack Prelutsky
(Notables 1990, SLJ/C 1990)

Something big has been here,
What it was, I do not know,
Captain Conniption, the woolly wurble,
Or tigers on tiptoe.

Something big has been here,
What it was, I cannot see,
Flying hotdogs, wumpaloons,
Or a big fat bumblebee.

Something big has been here,
What it was, I cannot say,
An elephant or brontosaur,
I really shouldn't stay.

Something big has been here,
What it was—just take a look!
You'll meet them all and more besides,
When you read this funny book.

—*Cecilia Swanson*

Stepping on the Cracks
By Mary Downing Hahn
(Notables 1991, SLJ/C 1991)

If there's anyone in Chapel Hill worse than Gordy Smith, Margaret doesn't know who it could be. Gordy is the meanest boy in the sixth grade, and Margaret and her best friend Elizabeth seem to be his favorite targets. Way back in kindergarten, the first time he ever saw Elizabeth, Gordy walked right up to her and pulled her hair—hard!— for no reason at all. Elizabeth (being Elizabeth) turned around and punched him in the stomach, and they've been sworn enemies ever since. Just a few days ago, Gordy grabbed Elizabeth's bookbag, tore up her homework, and threw the rest of her stuff all over the street. Two boys from their class saw the attack, but they were so scared of Gordy they wouldn't tell the teacher what had happened, so Elizabeth had to stay in at recess that day and do her homework over.

The only person who could be worse than Gordy Smith is Hitler, Margaret thinks. America is right in the middle of World War II, and Hitler and his Nazis are on everyone's mind. Both Elizabeth and Margaret have older brothers fighting overseas, and so does Gordy. Almost every house in town has a star hanging in the front window. A blue star means someone from that house is fighting in the war; a gold star means someone has been killed. On any day, at any hour, the girls know, a telegram could arrive with bad news, and then the blue stars in their families' windows would be replaced by gold ones, the signs of honor—and of grief. The girls are fiercely loyal to their brothers and don't want to let them down.

After the homework incident, Elizabeth swears she'll get even with Gordy Smith. She and Margaret shadow him for days, until they come up with the perfect plan: they'll trash his secret hideout, that tumbledown shack in the woods where he goes when he's not bullying other kids. But as the girls sneak up on their target, they make a shocking discovery: someone's living in Gordy's hideout. And it's not Gordy.

—*Susan Dunn*

Stonewords: A Ghost Story
By Pam Conrad
(BGHB 1990, Poe 1991)

My name is Zoe, and I live with my grandfather and Zoe Louise. Zoe Louise is a ghost. She died in a fire in 1870, when she was eleven years old. I was only four when I met Zoe Louise.

"What's that, Pop Pop?" I asked.

He turned and looked, then broke into a smile. "Why, that's a little playhouse I built for your mother a long time ago. . . . I can fix it up for you."

"And will it be mine?" I asked. Suddenly something hit lightly against my shin, and I looked under the table. A little brown shoe was tapping impatiently. When I raised my head, I saw a girl, older than I was, frowning. I had never seen anyone so pretty before—or so translucent. She was like a block of ice that I could see and yet see through at the same time.

And that was just the beginning!

—*Deb Kelly*

A String in the Harp
By Nancy Bond
(IRA 1977, Newbery Honor 1977)

Wales is cold and wet in the winter, and today, for the millionth time, Peter Morgan, age twelve, wonders whatever possessed his father to bring him and his ten-year-old sister Becky to the tiny village of Borth on Cardigan Bay. Peter knows that it was partly to get away from memories of their mother, killed in an automobile accident the December before, but did his father have to go all the way to *Wales*?

Becky seems happy, but Peter hates everything about their new home. He hates the eternal cold rain and having to learn Welsh at school. He hates it that his older sister Jen got to stay behind in the United States, coming to Wales only for her Christmas vacation. Most of all, he hates how his father hasn't really seemed to see or hear him since Mom died.

Then Peter finds a peculiar-looking, Y-shaped object, which turns out to be the tuning key for the harp of the legendary bard Taliesin. The key draws Peter and the others back to the time of Taliesin, weaving together past and present. Can it bring harmony to Peter and his family?

—Donna L. Scanlon

Summer of My German Soldier
By Bette Greene
(Golden Kite 1974)

Patty tried so hard. She tried to be good and polite and neat, to please her mother. She tried to be smart and interesting and obedient, to please her father. But it never worked. Her mother always found something to complain about, usually Patty's hair, and how terrible it looked. And her father—well, Patty's father didn't complain. He hit instead, leaving bruises and marks that didn't go away.

That summer, during the war, Patty tried again to please her parents. She helped out at their store, she kept out of their way, she tried to fill them in on the latest war news. She was especially hopeful on the day the prisoners-of-war arrived on the train. Now, this would be something to tell her parents. How could they help but be impressed?

Then one day the prisoners came into the store! And Patty got to wait one of them! He was interesting and nice. His English was very good, and he really seemed to like Patty. And Patty liked him. Finally, a true friendship.

But Patty couldn't know how that friendship would change her life. Because a German POW and a Jewish girl weren't supposed to become friends during the Second World War. And a Jewish girl certainly shouldn't help an escaped prisoner hide, no matter what kind of friend he might be.

—Colleen Stinson

Summer of the Swans
By Betsy Byars
(Newbery 1971)

When she went to call Charlie for breakfast and realized that he was gone, Sara was panic-stricken. Where could he have gotten to? He was *never* supposed to leave the yard! Even though he was retarded, Charlie knew the rules.

Sara had taken him down to the lake the day before, to see the swans. Charlie hadn't wanted to go home. He loved to watch the beautiful birds and to throw pieces of bread in the water. But when it started getting late, Sara had insisted they go home.

Where could Charlie be? Everyone panicked. He couldn't swim— suppose he had slipped and fallen into the water! He never spoke—how were they going find him when he couldn't call out for help?

Was the summer of the swans about to become a summer of tragedy?

—*Carol Kappelmann*

A Summer to Die
By Lois Lowry
(IRA 1978)

Fifteen-year-old Molly is blonde and popular, a happy, out-going girl who plans someday to be Molly Something Else, Mrs. Somebody, and have lots of children. Thirteen-year-old Meg is smart, restless, and dissatisfied, impatient to realize her driving but still unfocused ambitions. She wants to *do* something, *be* something, even though she isn't sure what. Although Meg loves her older sister, sometimes she envies Molly's calm certainty about the future and her easy confidence.

When their father takes a sabbatical to finish his book, the girls have to leave their familiar lives and move to the country for several months. They have to attend a new school, make new friends, and worst of all, share a room for the first time in their lives. Meg can't believe how hard it is to room with Molly.

But except for her sister's moods and complaints, Meg is enjoying her time in the country. She has made friends with Will, their landlord, and with Ben and Maria, the young couple who live across the field. Her father has built her a darkroom, and she's teaching Will how to develop photographs. But Molly's erratic behavior and her frequent illnesses are not just reactions to the new scene and the freezing winter.

Soon it becomes obvious, even to Meg, that she is very seriously ill.

—Evette Pearson

Sweet Whispers, Brother Rush
By Virginia Hamilton
(King 1983, Newbery Honor 1983, Notables 1982, SLJ/C 1982)

For most of her thirteen years, it seemed like, Tree had been taking care of her older brother Dab. Dab may have been older, but he wasn't wiser. He was retarded. Although he went to school most days, he had really done all of the learning he was ever going to do.

So when he wasn't in school, Tree had to make sure he washed, ate the meals she cooked, and stayed where she could keep an eye on him. Her mom worked away from home, often for weeks at a time, as a practical nurse. When she came home it wasn't a break for Tree, but a whirlwind of buying groceries and supplies to be ready for her next few weeks away. It wasn't fun. Tree's whole world seemed to revolve around school and Dab.

Then came the day when she saw the strange man out on the street, though no one else seemed to notice him. She saw him again in the back room. This time he was almost transparent—he seemed to be coming right out of the table.

It means something when you see a ghost. Tree's life was about to change . . . perhaps not for the better. She didn't know which way to turn. She didn't know where to find help.

—Carol Kappelmann

Sweetgrass
By Jan Hudson
(Canadian Governor General's 1985, CLA 1984,
Notables 1989, SLJ/C 1989)

Sweetgrass lived with her tribe on the prairie, moving from one place to another as the seasons changed and the game moved on. Her greatest dream was to convince her father that she was grown-up enough to marry. After all, at fifteen she was probably the oldest unmarried girl in the entire Blackfoot nation. And here she was helping Pretty Girl, who was only thirteen, prepare for her wedding!

Sweetgrass worked hard: she cooked, sewed, and followed the ways of her people, but her days were filled with dreams of marriage, and not to just anyone but to Eagle-Sun, a young hunter and warrior. She watched for him, and on the night of the Sun Dance she had a chance to walk with him. Someday it would happen—her father would give his consent, and she would marry Eagle-Sun. It had to be!

But soon after the Sun Dance, Eagle-Sun and other men of the tribe went to visit the Piegans' camp, to trade and barter. And there they got more than they bargained for, because the Piegans were dying—of smallpox, the white man's sickness, the disease that could travel through the air on a look, so swiftly it flew. Many men from Sweetgrass's tribe had gone to the Piegan camp. Now they brought the sickness home to their own village. Would anyone survive the epidemic?

—*Cara A. Waits*

A Swiftly Tilting Planet
By Madeleine L'Engle
(ABA 1980)

The phone call from the White House shatters the Murry family's peaceful Thanksgiving dinner. Mad Dog Branzillo, president of the small South American country of Vespugia, has threatened the Western world with nuclear war in twenty-four hours.

The Murrys are all together again for the holiday—Mr. and Mrs. Murry, still working on their scientific projects that mystify the townspeople; fifteen-year-old Charles Wallace, with his extraordinary intelligence and unusual sensitivity; the twins, Sandy and Dennys, still cheerful extroverts, home from law and medical school; and Meg, now married to Calvin O'Keefe and expecting their first child. Although frightened by the news, the family makes an effort to have a normal Thanksgiving. Except for Calvin, who's in London, the family is together, and tonight Calvin's mother has joined them for dinner, something she has never done before.

An uneducated, bitter woman, old before her time, Mrs. O'Keefe cares little about anyone, even her children. And yet she turns to Charles Wallace and gives him a rune that she says will stop Branzillo. Despite his misgivings, Charles Wallace accepts the seemingly impossible challenge, and begins a dangerous journey through time to alter the future—and to save his world.

—*Evette Pearson*

Sydney, Herself
By Colby Rodowsky
(SLJ/C 1989)

My junior year in high school was the year I decided that the father I never knew was a member of the famous Australian rock group, the Boomerangs. My mother had always said that my father was a student at the University of Sydney when she met and married him. He had been killed, she said, in a car accident a month before I was born. But why did she have only one small, dog-eared snapshot of my supposed father, Arthur Downie? I just *knew* that my father was a Boomerang— after all, my name was the same as the title of one of their albums, *Sydney Downie Down Down.*

Only a few of my best friends would have known of my Boomerang blood if we hadn't had this class assignment to write a letter to the editor of the local paper, the *Sun.* In my letter I told how my mother had met and married one of the famous Boomerangs. I wanted to be an author, so it was really exciting to see my letter in print with every word just the way I'd written it.

Unfortunately, my mother wasn't as excited as I was. She was so upset she wouldn't even let the reporter from the *Sun* interview me. And that was only the beginning!

I kept a record of that year in my diary, and you can read the whole story for yourself.

—Marianne Tait Pridemore

Taking Terri Mueller
By Norma Fox Mazer
(Poe 1982)

For as long as she can remember, it's been just the two of them: Terri and Daddy, Daddy and Terri. There isn't a mommy: she died when Terri was four. Terri doesn't remember her at all, and Daddy doesn't like to talk about her—it makes him sad. So it's just Terri and Daddy. They move around a lot—Daddy says he has restless feet—but they are always together, they always have each other.

Now Terri is thirteen. She can remember all the different cities and towns they have lived in, all the apartments, all the landlords, all the neighbors and the schools and the best friends. But even when she tries hard, she can't remember her mother.

This year they're living in Ann Arbor, Michigan. Terri has a new best friend with a huge family of aunts and uncles and grandparents and cousins. Besides Dad, Terri has only his sister, Aunt Vivian, who comes to visit once a year or so. This time, when Aunt Vivian comes to visit, Terri keeps feeling that something is wrong. There are things she doesn't know—things she *almost* knows. Why hasn't her father ever let her have Aunt Vivian's home address? What is this blurry memory she has, about orange soda and a car ride? What is this other memory about yellow sunglasses? Why won't Aunt Vivian tell her anything about her mother?

And then, late one night, Terri overhears Aunt Vivian and Dad talking. "You *have* to tell her," Aunt Vivian is saying. "She has to know. Tell her the truth." And Dad is saying, "No, I can't. Don't tell her, Vivian; don't betray me now."

What is it all about? What secret is her father keeping from her?

—*Sarah Flowers*

Tales of the Early World
By Ted Hughes
(Notables 1991)

Did you ever stop to think just how or why earthworms came to be? I mean, what purpose do they really serve, except as bait for fishing? Well, Ted Hughes has his own story about that.

It was back at the dawn of creation, and God had been making an elephant out of great hunks of elephant clay. It was such a big job that He was very tired when He finally got finished. He threw himself down in His chair with a sigh and poured a cup of tea. Absentmindedly, He began to scrape the last of the elephant clay out from under His fingernails, and when He finished He had a little ball. He began to play with it, rolling it back and forth on His palm. He was thinking of the elephant He had just made, particularly its trunk. He was very proud of that trunk because He'd never made one before—it was a brand new invention. So just as an experiment, He began to make a miniature trunk out of the tiny piece of clay. He put it up to His lips to blow nostrils into it and without thinking accidentally blew life into it instead. The little trunk squirmed in His hand and yelled at Him in a tiny little voice. And what it said was, "Finish me! Where's the rest of me? Finish me!"

And now God was in a predicament, because He had no more elephant clay. He'd used it all up—that's why the elephant had turned out so big. And to make matters worse, elephant clay was rare and precious stuff, very difficult to find. The tiny trunk was most upset to hear this and began to cry. It was meant to be an elephant, it said; it had elephant thoughts and feelings, and it felt horrible wiggling around with no elephant body or head or legs. It wanted God to start looking for some clay immediately! But God was tired. So He gently laid the little trunk down on the ground and told it to start digging. As soon as it came up with the right sort of clay, He would finish it. The tiny trunk began to dig, And dig. And dig. But none of the clay it brought back was right, and God sent it out again to keep looking. So the days passed. And the weeks, and the months, years, centuries . . . and the little trunk is still digging today, looking for the elephant clay that will finally make it whole.

And that is the story of how the earthworm was created. Except now we know the earthworm isn't really an earthworm, is it? And if that's how the elephant and the earthworm came to be, what about the horse, the parrot, and the cat? Discover their stories in *Tales of the Early World*.

—Susan Dunn

Tancy
By Belinda Hurmence
(Golden Kite 1985, SLJ/C 1984)

Tancy was a slave, but a slave with special privileges. She didn't have to sleep where the field hands slept—she slept on the floor of her mistress's bedroom. The food she ate was better than anything the field hands got. And Tancy knew how to read.

But there were things Tancy wanted that she didn't have. She wanted to know who her father was. She wanted to know where her mother was. Her mother had been sold right after giving birth to Tancy.

At the end of the Civil War, when the slaves were freed, Tancy was tempted to leave the plantation too and go in search of her mother. But Miss Puddin had been so kind to her all the time she was growing up that she felt a certain amount of guilt in just walking away.

Then Billy assaulted her in the lumber room, and Tancy knew she couldn't go on living under the same roof with him. It was now or never . . . and never could be a long, long time.

—Carol Kappelmann

A Telling of the Tales: Five Stories
By William J. Brooke
(Notables 1990)

Sometimes, in the telling of tales, unexpected things can happen. Take "Jack in the Beanstalk," for example. What would have happened if the giant had caught Jack before he could get away down the beanstalk with the golden harp?

Let's suppose the giant catches him. He ties him down on the chopping block and prepares chop off his head and grind his bones. Poor Jack! *What* is he going to do? Whip out a machine-gun? a bow and arrow? a magic bean? How about appealing to the giant's humanitarian instincts: "I'm a poor misguided youth, my mother's a widow," etc? Of course, a bone-grinding giant might not *have* many humanitarian instincts. Is there *any* chance here for "happily ever after"?

—*Carol Kappelmann*

The Third-Story Cat
By Leslie Baker
(IRA 1988)

Alice liked to lie in the sunshine and stare out the window. She liked to watch the birds. She liked to daydream about visiting the park across the street. Alice lived in a third-story apartment with her friend Annie. She liked Annie quite a lot. Annie fed her and played with her and stroked her fur. But Alice longed to visit the park across the street.

One day when she was exploring the apartment, Alice found a window that had been left open just a crack. She poked her nose through, she poked her head through, she wiggled and jumped and squeezed her whole self out the window.

Alice was free! Now for the adventure in the park!

—*Colleen Stinson*

Time Train
By Paul Fleischman
(SLJ/C 1991)

Are you tired of taking the same old field trips year after year? Feel like you just can't handle one more visit to the local zoo, or another trip to the nature preserve? How about an excursion to Dinosaur National

Monument in Utah? Better yet, how about a trip back in time, to the days when dinosaurs roamed the earth! Think it can't be done? Well, then, I challenge you to join Miss Pym and her class aboard the Rocky Mountain Un-limited for an unforgettable train ride back into the prehistoric past. All aboard!

—Sister M. Anna Falbo, CSSF

Time's Up
By Florence Parry Heide
(Notables 1982)

Can you imagine living with an efficiency expert? With someone who plans everything right down to the very last second, or the very last inch? Noah's dad is like that. He takes a different route to work each day, so he can record the different times and mileages and determine the best and most efficient way to go. He's calculated the most efficient way to mow the lawn, so now Noah has to push the mower around in a very specific pattern.

Life with such a scheduled person can get pretty tense. Mom just puts in her earplugs and vanishes into her room, where she's writing her thesis, but Noah has no place to run. They're new to the neighborhood, and it's summer vacation—he doesn't have friends to visit yet, and he can't even escape to school. Much as he loves his dad, Noah's beginning to wonder if he can survive this summer of efficiency without blowing his top!

—Carol Kappelmann

The Tombs of Atuan
By Ursula K. Le Guin
(Newbery Honor 1972)

Arha is only five when she is brought to the Place of the Tombs of Atuan. The other women tell her that she is "the nameless one, the Priestess Reborn." She spends her days in common labor, surrounded by other women, but she also learns the Rites of the Nameless Ones.

Ten years pass, and Arha comes into her full powers as the One Priestess of the Tombs. All must defer to her, but as the days pass in the same endless way, Arha realizes that she is bored.

She learns her way around the Labyrinth that sprawls beneath the Tombs; it is her domain, and hers alone. But one day she finds that someone has entered the Labyrinth—a man, and a sorcerer at that. He calls himself Sparrowhawk, and he has come to find the other half of the amulet of the sorcerer Erreth-Akbe, which is supposed to lie hidden in the Great Treasury under the Tombs.

At first he is Arha's prisoner. But a great and burning curiosity persuades her to keep him alive, and before long he is the closest thing to a friend she has ever known.

Meanwhile, Kossil, Priestess to the Godking, has begun to challenge Arha's authority and her worthiness to rule. Soon Arha is no longer simply trying to keep Sparrowhawk alive but herself struggling to survive. Is there a way out, a way to escape from the Tombs of Atuan?

—*Donna L. Scanlon*

Touch Wood: A Girlhood in Occupied France
By Renee Roth-Hano
(Notables 1988)

Renee's world changed with the announcement on the radio—the announcement that Germany and France were at war. The war wasn't going well for France, and soon the news came to their town in Alsace that the Germans would be occupying the area, and that all Jews would have to leave. Renee's parents weren't really surprised—they knew how much the Nazis hated the Jews. Thinking ahead, they had decided that they would be safest in Paris, where Maman had friends, where Papa could find work, and where, so far at least, the German authorities had left the Jews alone. Soon they were crammed into a tiny Paris apartment, but, though Papa was content with his job, all was not well. Renee noticed the little things, the new rules and regulations—Jews were forbidden to have a radio, they were ordered to register with police, and their identity cards were stamped "Jew." Slogans began appearing on the sides of buildings—slogans like "Kill the Jews." Maman assured her that things wouldn't get any worse, touch wood. But things did get worse. Friends and neighbors were taken away, and the Roths realized that would have to disguise their identity to survive. Could Renee and her family survive the dangers of occupied France?

—*Helen Schlichting*

Traitor: The Case of Benedict Arnold
By Jean Fritz
(Notables 1981, SLJ/C 1981)

There is a monument of the battlefield of Saratoga that is inscribed, "In memory of the most brilliant soldier in the Continental Army, who was desperately wounded on this spot . . . 7th October, 1777, winning for his countrymen the decisive battle of the American Revolution." But the monument bears no name, only the carving of a military boot and a major general's epaulet. Likewise, in a small chapel at the United States Military Academy at West Point where plaques are dedicated to the generals of the American Revolution, there is one plaque that has only a set of dates, 1741-1801, and no name. Both the monument and the plaque are for Benedict Arnold, perhaps the most infamous traitor in American history. No one wanted to honor his name.

All his life, Benedict Arnold was a man who hungered for attention and wealth. He longed for action and for the best of everything. He was bold and bright and undeniably courageous. But he was also greedy, pig-headed, and careless, and beneath his bravado was a secret fear that he might be laughed at or under-appreciated. Even though his actions secured the American victory at Saratoga, the battle during which he lost his leg, the Continental Congress did not give Arnold the promotion he thought he deserved. His resentment over this and his hunger for cash led him to plot against his own side. He made secret plans to let the British capture the American fort West Point, which guarded the Hudson River. If his plan had succeeded, England might well have squashed the colonial bid for independence.

Benedict Arnold: today his name is synonymous with "traitor." But who was he, and why did he take the road he did?

—Maureen Whalen

Travelers by Night
By Vivien Alcock
(Notables 1985)

Murder, that's what Belle called it. Oh, the adults said it was "a necessity," "the kindest thing to do," or "the best possible solution." After all, the circus was going out of business. Everyone was looking for another job. The animals were being transferred to other circuses or zoos. But no one wanted Tessie, the circus's oldest elephant, so she was marked for the slaughterhouse.

Marked for murder was the way Belle saw it. Wasn't Tessie the kindest of creatures? And she, Belle, ought to know. Why, life in the small traveling circus was all she'd ever known. And Tessie had been an important part of that life. The slaughterhouse? No way! Not if Belle could help it, and she thought that she could—thought she'd hatched the perfect plan to save poor Tessie. Belle and her brother would "kidnap" the elephant when the coast was clear and lead her on foot to a safari park a hundred miles away. It wouldn't be easy hiding an elephant, and the journey promised to be long and dangerous. So what? Tessie was worth every bit of it!

Travelers by Night: it's the *biggest* kidnapping case on record!

—*Sister M. Anna Falbo, CSSF*

The Trial of Anna Cotman
By Vivien Alcock
(SLJ/C 1990)

Anna was new in the neighborhood and starved for friendship—a perfect target for someone like Lindy. Lindy was starved for friendship too, because no one really liked her, or at least not for long—she was one of those people who enjoy manipulating others. Lindy deliberately lured Anna into an unequal friendship and a strange, secret club, run by her big brother and his friends. The Society of Masks, it was called. To become a Companion, Anna pledged to do the bidding of the Lords and Lady of the Masks.

That's why she was up on the roof of the clubhouse when the ceremony began. The Yellow Lord had seen her and banished her to skylight-cleaning duty for as long as he pleased, and Lindy had gone back inside for the ceremony, leaving Anna stranded on the roof. Well, she could either start yelling for a ladder or wait it out. Since she wasn't in any danger, waiting seemed like the best choice. Anna cleaned the window, ate her apple, and read a whole book. She wasn't going to start yelling; she could stay here all night if she had to. Then the screaming started. The sound was desperate, piercing, like nothing Anna had ever heard before. The word "No!" rang out in real terror. What was going on down there? She couldn't bear to sit quietly listening. "Lindy!" she called, over and over again. The sounds below ceased abruptly. At last Lindy came out of the clubhouse door. The Red Lord came too, holding a ladder. "It wasn't my fault," he was saying. "How was I to know he'd have hysterics? They can't blame me!"

What had happened? Anna still didn't know. But she suspected something awful. For a while now she'd been aware of an evil glowing in the eyes of some of the members of the Society of Masks. But Anna had been sworn to secrecy. Breaking her oath would leave her friendless and alone—to face the anger of the Masks.

—Bernice D. Crouse

The Tricksters
By Margaret Mahy
(SLJ/C 1987)

It's Christmastime, and since this is New Zealand, the Hamiltons are off to their beach house, Carnival's Hide, for a summer vacation. Harry Hamilton is right in the middle of her large, complicated family and their friends. Her names's really Ariadne, but at seventeen, nearsighted and just dieted and exercised out of her baby fat, she doesn't feel quite up to assuming her full name—plenty of time for that when her romantic novel is published, her secret project for the summer.

The run-down Victorian house where the Hamiltons vacation was once the scene of a tragedy. Teddy Carnival, the son of the family who used to own the house, was drowned right here at the beach in mysterious circumstances. Now mysterious things are happening to the Hamiltons—a hand clutches at Harry while she's swimming underwater, and later three identical young men materialize upon the beach; they call themselves the Carnival Brothers.

Who are these men? Are they really real? Or are they the projections of Harry's romantic imagination? Perhaps they're ghosts—but then why are there three of them, when there was only one Teddy Carnival?

There are more secrets at Carnival's Hide than even Harry could have imagined.

—Rene Mandel

The True Confessions of Charlotte Doyle
By Avi
(Golden Kite 1991, Notables 1990, SLJ/C 1990)

"Miss Doyle, the facts have spoken otherwise . . . the penalty for such a crime is to be hanged by the neck from the yardarm. Within twenty-four hours, you shall be hanged until you are dead."

Thus spoke the captain. My fate was sealed. I, Charlotte Doyle, daughter of one of the owners of the ship, had been sentenced to death, for the murder of Mr. Hollybrass.

I looked around the deck of the ship. We were alone in the middle of the Atlantic Ocean, and there wasn't a friendly, or even a sympathetic face among the crew. I have never, in all my thirteen years, felt so alone.

How could this have happened to me? Was there any hope, any way the truth could come out?

—*Carol Kappelmann*

The True Story of the Three Little Pigs, by A. Wolf
By Jon Scieszka
(Notables 1989)

I was framed! My name is Alexander T. Wolf (you can call me Al). I don't know why wolves have such a bad reputation—maybe it was that thing with Red Riding Hood and her granny—but I'm really a good guy. I was only trying to borrow a cup of sugar from those rude porker brothers when their houses collapsed, just like that, all by themselves. Oh, I admit, I did have a cold that day, and my sneezes have always been pretty powerful. But they just don't make houses the way they used to!

The whole thing was an accident, a tragic misunderstanding. Read my side of the story and I'm sure you'll agree. Trust me, I'm a wolf, and I'll tell you the true story of the Three Little Pigs.

—*Cecilia Swanson*

The Truth about Unicorns
By James Cross Giblin
(Notables 1991, SLJ/C 1991)

When I say the world "unicorn," a certain image probably comes to your mind: a pretty white horse with a gleaming horn—an imaginary creature. But if unicorns are imaginary, why do we have such a clear picture of them?

Actually, our image of the unicorn is only about 500 years old. It is based mainly on a set of Belgian tapestries now hanging in the Cloisters museum in New York [show pictures of tapestries from book]. But that's only one version of the unicorn.

About 2,500 years ago, a Greek writer went to Persia, where he heard stories about a wild donkey with a white body, red head, and bright blue eyes [show picture]. It had a horn on its forehead that was white at the base, black in the middle, and gleaming red at the sharp point.

Another unicorn, this one from India, was described as being the size of a horse, with reddish hair, a mane like a lion's, feet like an elephant's, and a goat's tail [show picture]. On its forehead it had a black horn.

People from many different cultures and times have told stories about a rare and sometimes magical creature with a single horn. Often, according to the stories, the horn has magical or healing powers. If unicorns are imaginary, where did all these stories come from? Is there any basis for them in nature? Could unicorns have been real after all?

—*Sarah Flowers*

Tuck Everlasting
By Natalie Babbitt
(Christopher 1976)

"One day . . . not so very long ago, three things happened and at first there appeared to be no connection between them."

At dawn that day, Mae Tuck woke up and excitedly remembered her boys were coming home tomorrow. It had been ten years since she had last seen her boys. She decided to go to Treegap and wait for them. Her husband warned her not to go into the village, and Mae agreed, although it had been ten years and she doubted that anyone would recognize her. Still, it was best to be cautious. She would wait for the boys in the woods.

At noon that day, Winnie Foster sat by the fence and stared at the woods and made plans to run away from home. She was very angry. As an only child, she had both her mother and her grandmother watching over her every minute, nagging and correcting. She was tired of being supervised. She wanted to be alone for once. She would just have to run away, she decided.

At sunset that day, a stranger wearing a yellow suit came to the village of Treegap. He stopped at the Fosters' front gate and began asking Winnie and her grandmother all kinds of questions. He seemed to be looking for someone. Suddenly a faint wisp of music coming from the wood reached their ears. It was the same elf-music Grandmother had heard years ago.

Three different events that all happened on the one August day in and around the village of Treegap. No connection among them—wouldn't you agree? But things can come together in strange ways. By the end of this story there will have been a kidnapping, a murder, and jailbreak—all starting with the things I just told you. What's the connection? You'll see!

—*Linda Olson*

The 25¢ Miracle
By Theresa Nelson
(SLJ/C 1986)

Elvira never complains. Her father goes off and leaves her alone all day, but she never complains. There is almost no food in the house, but she never complains. They don't even live in a real house—they live in a dingy old trailer in a run-down trailer park. But Elvira never complains. In fact, she tries to make the best of things. That's why she bought the rosebush.

One day, when her father gave her a little money for groceries, Elvira used twenty-five cents to buy a rosebush. It would grow large and beautiful, and it would help make their old trailer beautiful too.

But the rosebush isn't doing very well; in fact, it looks half dead. That's why Elvira is so glad to find the public library. They'll have books there about how to make a rosebush grow.

Inside the library Elvira meets Miss Ivy, who helps her find the books she needs. But Miss Ivy helps Elvira with a lot more than that. She becomes a true friend. And though Miss Ivy may not know it yet, she holds the key to Elvira's future—because Elvira is going to make sure that her father marries Miss Ivy!

Can you really buy a miracle for a quarter?

—Colleen Stinson

Two Short and One Long
By Nina Ring Aamundsen
(Notables 1990)

Best friends always have a special secret between them—like a certain expression that always makes them laugh, or a signal that no one else can read. Jonas and Einar have that kind of friendship. Their special signal is "two short and one long," and it punctuates their ongoing friendship. Jonas knows a lot about Einar and his quirks, like the way he always leaves something behind at your house, so you know he'll always be back.

But there's something Jonas can't figure out about Einar, something he's keeping secret about his past. And when a new boy comes to their school—a boy from Afghanistan—Einar becomes even more distant and aloof.

Jonas realizes he has to find out what his friend is hiding, before they lose their connection forever.

—Judy McElwain

The Two-Thousand-Pound Goldfish
By Betsy Byars
(Notables 1982)

The police and soldiers were going to destroy his goldfish! They were going to annihilate him, blast him off the face of the earth, just because he weighed two thousand pounds and looked like a menace.

"It's not my fault," said Warren. "So I flushed my pet goldfish down the toilet—how was I to know he'd be changed into a gigantic mutant by XX-109?"

Then he came up with the perfect solution. If everyone flushed the toilet at the same time, the water running through the sewers would swell into a humongous wave and sweep the fish out to sea. The town would be saved, the police could go home, and the two-thousand-pound goldfish would swim peacefully off into the sunset.

This was the perfect ending for Warren's latest daydream disaster movie. And he even had a sequel in mind.

Now, if he could just stick some perfect endings onto his own, real-life disasters, he might be able to forget about "The Return of the Two-Thousand-Pound Goldfish." But is that likely?

—Carol Kappelmann

Unclaimed Treasures
By Patricia MacLachlan
(Notables 1984)

It was a summer that began and almost ended with a death, a summer that Willa hoped would be important and extraordinary, a summer that changed all their lives. Eleven-year-old twins Willa and Nicky and their parents had just moved into a new house, one with plenty of room for them and the new baby. Horace Morris and his father and his three unmarried aunts, the "unclaimed treasures" as they were affectionately called, lived in the big house next door. When one of the aunts died, the two families met at the funeral, and that's also where Willa met her "true love."

Willa was always on the lookout for her true love, scanning every line outside the movie theater or the ice rink or inside the bank, watching the people stopped at a red light. She knew exactly what he'd look like, her true love: he'd be tall and solemn.

Horace's father, tall and solemn with a sweet sad smile, is an artist. His wife—Horace's mother—has left him; she's out in the world looking for something that needs her. Willa readily agrees when Mr. Morris asks her to pose for a painting he is working on. She knows he asked because she so resembles his wife, but she also knows this will give her the chance to be near him every day. Will she be able to convince Horace's father that he is her true love? Will she have a chance to do something really important and extraordinary?

—Maureen Whalen

Up a Road Slowly
By Irene Hunt
(Newbery 1967)

I guess you could call it my night of triumph . . . the night I graduated from high school. Would I be able to deliver my valedictory speech without a flaw? Of course I would. Hadn't I had the best teacher I could have had? The best upbringing? Thinking back to the year when I was seven, motherless, brought to live with Aunt Cordelia who was to be my guardian as well as my teacher for the next ten years, I marveled at the changes in my life.

At first it was awful not being in my old familiar home with my father and beloved sister. But Aunt Cordelia was kind, and she was a wonderful teacher.

As I looked out over the audience of parents and friends who had come to see us graduate, to listen to the often dull speeches, I knew that the road I had taken was the right one. The bumps and swerves along the way had only enabled me to become a better person, one who could meet life's challenges head-on and find a lifetime of peace. It had taken every one of those ten years to change myself from a miserable little girl to the person I was today—and the road hadn't ever been easy. Discover why I decided to travel it, in *Up a Road Slowly.*

—Carol Kappelmann

Up from Jericho Tel
By E. L. Konigsburg
(BGHB 1989, Notables 1986)

Jeanmarie and Malcolm are both bossy, both twelve, both latchkey kids, and both fully determined to be famous someday, but other than that, they don't have a lot in common. But when Jeanmarie finds a dead bird and Malcolm helps her bury it, an unlikely friendship develops. They meet regularly in a clearing they call Jericho Tel, and one day they are suddenly pulled underground by an ancient actress named Tallulah, who happens to be dead (that's d-e-a-d, dahlings).

Tallulah's got something to tell them. It takes three qualities to make a star, she says, talent, timing, and . . . . Well, if they really want to know the third, all-important ingredient of stardom, they'll have to do something for her. And to help them do it, she'll even make them invisible.

It seems that back when Tallulah was still a living legend, she befriended some young street performers. They were having dinner together at her home the night she died. As Tallulah left her body, she realized that someone in the room had taken her most cherished possession, a truly beautiful and valuable diamond known as the Regina Stone, from around her neck. It had to be one of the three young performers. Jeanmarie and Malcolm must find out who.

Was it Nicolai Ion Simonescu, the ventriloquist? Now a married man with two children, he's made a small fortune dealing in puppets. Where did he get the money to start his business? What about Patrick Henry Mermelman, the really bad magician? He too is doing well these days; he owns his own record store. Or was it Emmagene Krebs, the lovely folk singer with the repertoire of 18,000 songs? Unlike the others, she seems to have dropped out of sight—and she always admired the necklace.

Can Jeanmarie and Malcolm identify the thief after all these years? Can they learn the third ingredient of stardom? And what will Tallulah do to them if they fail?

—Evette Pearson

The Upstairs Room
By Johanna Reiss
(Addams 1973, Newbery Honor 1973)

I thought at first that we were safe. I thought that Hitler would only persecute the German Jews—that because we lived in Holland, no one would hurt us. That even though our village was only a few miles from the German border, we wouldn't be affected. But I was only a child when World War II began. How could I have guessed that soon the Nazis would invade Holland, bringing with them their leader's hatred of all Jews? And with that hatred would come all sorts of suffering for the Jews of Holland: restrictions, punishments, arrests, exile, and death. My family and I were Jewish, which meant we were suddenly undesirable and in very great danger. We had no choice but to go into hiding, my father to one place, my oldest sister to another. As for my sister Sini and I, we hid together during the last few years of the war, sheltered by a kindly family in their tiny farmhouse.

It's still painful to recall those frightening, endless days. But if you're willing to listen, and if you have the courage to hear the truth, then join Sini and me in our hiding place, the upstairs room.

—*Sister M. Anna Falbo, CSSF*

The Village by the Sea
By Paula Fox
(BGHB 1989, Notables 1988, SLJ/C 1988)

I'm sure these are going to be the worst two weeks of my life. My dad is having open-heart surgery, and since Mom will need to stay with him almost the whole time, I'll have to stay with Aunt Bea and Uncle Crispin in their big cottage by the sea. I'm not only worried sick about my dad, I'm also nervous about having to live with Aunt Bea for two weeks. She's my dad's sister, but she's older than he is and not easy to get along with. My uncle tries to make me feel at home, but still, it's very strange here.

One morning I decide to explore the beach. It's a whole different world down there, away from Aunt Bea. I make friends with a girl named Bertie, who is staying at her grandmother's place. Together we create our own world, far from the troubles we have at home. With stones, shells, sea-glass, and driftwood, we build a village by the sea, complete to the smallest detail. It's ours. No one else even knows about it. It's the place I can go to escape from the strange, unpleasant house of my aunt and uncle, as I wait for these two weeks to be over so I can live with my parents again.

—Colleen Stinson

A Visit to William Blake's Inn:
Poems for Innocent and Experienced Travelers
By Nancy Willard
(BGHB 1982, Caldecott Honor 1982, Newbery 1982, Notables 1981)

At William Blake's inn, dragons do the cooking and angels make the beds. A man in a "tender green" mackintosh transports you to the inn, and a rabbit will show you to your room. Once there, you may find that your bed is really a bear.

You'll meet the other guests, including the Man in the Marmalade Hat, the Wise Cow, and the King of Cats. And of course you will make the acquaintance of your host, Mr. William Blake, who is as comfortable walking the Milky Way as he is finding the right room for a group of sunflowers or composing a tale for the Tiger.

Of course, in the end, you'll have to go home again. But for now, wonders await you, so pack your bags (remember to travel light), grab your hat (with or without marmalade), and make a visit to William Blake's inn!

—Donna L. Scanlon

Voices from the Civil War:
A Documentary History of the Great American Conflict
Edited by Milton Meltzer
(SLJ/C 1989)

Short booktalk

Another boring history report to write? Want to know how to impress your teacher? While everyone else writes a bunch of facts and figures, strategies and statistics (bor-ing), you can dazzle Mr. Marvel with personal letters and diaries from everyday people who lived through the Civil War. And where do you find these great letters? In this book, *Voices from the Civil War*, by Milton Meltzer. These men and women were there—Gettysburg, Andersonville, Richmond; listen to them. These are the *Voices from the Civil War*.

Long booktalk

I don't read war books.

A bunch of names, dates, and places. Who cares?

I don't read war books, but I read this one. *Voices from the Civil War* isn't a textbook crammed with facts and figures, statistics and strategies. It doesn't talk about battles and troop maneuvers as if they were moves on a chessboard. Sacrificing some to save others. Acceptable losses. Cold. Emotionless.

Voices from the Civil War is a collection of the letters and diaries of soldiers and of prisoners and nurses and civilians. They were not observers; they were participants. They don't try to present the "big picture"; they didn't see it. What they saw and lived was war on a personal level.

Any book about the Civil War tells of Sherman's march through Georgia. The number of men. The number of miles. The number of bridges blown up. The number of houses burned. But have you ever wondered about the humanity behind the statistics? Samuel T. Foster marched through Georgia. His voice rises from the page to describe the hell that was the battlefield: "Dead men meet the eye in every direction. . . . It seems like they have nearly all been shot in the head, and a great number of them have their skulls bursted open and their brains running out. . . . "

Andersonville. Quantrill's Raiders. Draft riots. History books tell us the facts, but *Voices from the Civil War* tells us more. It tells us the hopes and fears, triumphs and tragedies of the men and women who lived one day at a time through each of the one thousand, four hundred, and sixty days that were the Civil War. Let them speak to you. Hear them. Theirs are *Voices from the Civil War.*

—*Tracy Chesonis Revel*

The Voyage of the *Frog*
By Gary Paulsen
(Notables 1989, SLJ/C 1989)

He was fourteen years old and the *Frog* was his—his own sailboat, complete with equipment and provisions. It was just what David had always wanted, and right now he'd give anything not to have it. Uncle Owen was dead. They'd sailed together on the *Frog,* but now Uncle Owen was gone, and David had inherited his boat.

He remembered his uncle's words: "I want you to take my ashes out alone on the *Frog,* out to the sea alone, and leave me there. Take me where you can't see land, and scatter my ashes there on the water."

So here he was, doing what Uncle Owen had asked. It wasn't till after he'd spread the ashes on the water that he noticed the storm approaching and realized that he was many miles from shore, with no radio and very little food.

Could he survive a storm at sea, alone, in a small boat, or would he be joining his Uncle Owen far sooner than he'd expected?

—*Deb Kelly and J. R. B.*

Waiting for the Rain: A Novel of South Africa
By Sheila Gordon
(Notables 1987)

PROTEST IN TOWNSHIP TONIGHT! Signs are going up on every wall and window. Fliers are being handed out on every street corner. The place is South Africa and the time is years ago, when the hated apartheid policy was in effect.

Tonight Johannesburg will be a dangerous place, but Tengo will be there. He's a young black student from the country, come to the city to go to school. He knows first-hand the injustice that the protest is about.

Frickie will be there too. He's also from the country, and now he's a soldier. He will put on riot gear because his unit has been called out to keep order in the streets.

The protest begins, but things are going badly. People have scattered. Frickie is chasing a man down a dark street.

A blow to the head, and Frickie is down. A black man stands over him, waiting, but he doesn't strike again. Tengo recognizes Frickie. They were friends once. They grew up together. Now they must talk—about those times when they were boys. Things that were never said then must be said now. Back then they were great friends—playing soccer, walking in the fields, working together in the garden.

But Frickie's family owned the farm, and Tengo's family worked for them, without privileges or hope for advancement. Things that were normal for Frickie's family were seen as insulting by Tengo's.

Questioning a whole culture, an entire way of life, is hard, but Tengo and thousands of others were doing just that. The questions had to start somewhere, and now, finally, two men are talking—a white man who has been hurt in an instant, and a black man who has been feeling pain all his life.

You will live their story, from the golden fields of the Transvaal to that dark street in Johannesburg, and you will know that somehow, a solution had to come.

—Mark Anderson

War Boy: A Country Childhood
By Michael Foreman
(Greenaway 1990)

What would it be like to grow up in the middle of a war, with soldiers stationed all around and enemy bombers making nightly raids? Michael Foreman, an English artist and illustrator, grew up in Pakefield, on the Suffolk coast near a large naval base, during World War II. His town was a regular target for the German air force.

Michael doesn't consider the bomb that lands on his home one night a disaster: it's an adventure. Can you imagine any good coming out of an air raid? "One result of the bombing," Michael says, "was that millions of seeds would be blown out of gardens and showered around the district. The following spring and summer, piles of rubble burst into bloom. Marigolds, irises, and, best of all, potatoes sprouted everywhere."

When school starts, classes are frequently interrupted by wailing sirens and retreats to the bomb shelter, to the detriment of old-fashioned discipline. The United States enters the war on Britain's side, and suddenly the town is full of American soldiers. Michael quickly decides to give up his dream of moving to Hollywood; instead, he fantasizes about becoming a trumpeter in a jazz band. The new soldiers like to visit the shop on the corner for their sweets, cigs, a coffee, and a wee motherly chat, all provided by Michael's mom and his aunt.

When the war is over and normal life has resumed, this extraordinary time seems very far away. But Michael's memories allow him, and us, to return whenever we want, to a world that combined the terror of war with the open-eyed wonder of childhood.

—Susan Trimby

A Wave in Her Pocket: Stories from Trinidad
Retold by Lynn Joseph
(Notables 1991)

Almost every family in Trinidad has a Tantie. A Tantie is usually a great-aunt, and she always has a story—a story to teach her nieces and nephews a lesson, or to make them laugh, or to give them a good shiver. Amber and her four cousins love and respect their Tantie because no matter what, Tantie can tell a story. Tantie has stories about strange creatures like the soucouyant and the ligahoo, and scary creatures like the jumbies. As a matter of fact, the jumbies are practically her neighbors. Tantie lives on a lonesome street. At one end of the street is a forgotten graveyard, at the other is Tantie's house, and in between there's nothing except grass and left-over pieces of houses that used to be there. Many years ago, the jumbies, the spirits of the graveyard, forced the people to move out of their homes and broke the houses to pieces.

When Tantie invites Amber and her cousins to her house for a sleepover party, the children are frightened about spending the night so close to the haunted graveyard. They're afraid that the jumbies will come into Tantie's house when it's dark. But Tantie tells them not to worry, the jumbies won't come into *her* home. Then, in the middle of their party, the lights go out! Is it the jumbies? Yes, it is! But Tantie makes the children feel better by telling them a story that explains why the jumbies will never come inside—and also why they knock the lights out from time to time. This story is one of six that will captivate you just as surely as they captivated Amber and her cousins.

—Maureen Whalen

The Way Things Work
By David Macaulay
(BGHB 1989, Notables 1988, SLJ/C 1988)

How does a key open a lock, or a can-opener open a can? Why do airplanes fly and boats float? What makes a video recorder work? Where does the picture in your television come from?

All these questions and many more are answered for you in *The Way Things Work*. Did you know that the cooling system that keeps your car's engine from boiling over works basically the same way as the air conditioner in your house? Did you know increasing the number of pulleys allows you to lift a bigger load? Did you know your TV remote is built like a calculator? Find out how all these things work, and why, in *The Way Things Work.*   —*Colleen Stinson*

The Way to Sattin Shore
By Philippa Pearce
(Notables 1984, SLJ/C 1984)

Secrets, secrets, secrets. Lies and secrets. Kate's family life had been built on lies. No wonder she had strange feelings about coming home to her dark house after school. Her best friend, Syrup, the golden cat, greeted her when she came into the house and followed her upstairs, to curl up on the bed in her attic room.

Gradually the house began to stir with life. Granny had been downstairs in her room all along. She wasn't real company, but soon Kate heard Lenny and Brian whispering as they came through the front door and went up the stairs to Lenny's room.

Kate tickled Syrup and was comforted by his purr. She heard the door open and close again. From the sounds in the kitchen, Kate knew that her mother was home. Syrup stopped purring and listened, then dropped to the floor and headed for the kitchen. Suddenly Kate was cold and very, very lonely.

Strange things were happening to Kate's family. Granny had received an upsetting letter which no one dared to discuss. Then the tombstone disappeared from the churchyard. No one else seemed disturbed, but to Kate this was a devastating loss. That stone was very precious to her, because the date on it was her birthday—she had been born on the day her father died.

Maybe that was the missing piece of her life. No one would talk to Kate about her father. His entire life was a complete mystery. And mentioning the morning of his death on Sattin Shore was strictly forbidden. Kate was sure that Sattin Shore held the key.

                                                              —*Bernice D. Crouse*

Weasel
By Cynthia DeFelice
(Notables 1990, SLJ/C 1990)

I'll bet you think "weasel" is just the name of a sneaky animal that pillages chicken coops. Well, you are wrong, dead wrong.

Weasel is a man—I won't demean the human race by calling him a human being. He has the conniving, bloodthirsty personality of a four-legged weasel, but he hunts real human beings. The tales the adults weave about Weasel sound like nightmares. The truth goes something like this:

Weasel and Ezra were sent to Ohio Territory about fifteen years ago by the United States Army. Their mission was to remove the Shawnee and make the land safe for civilized white folks. They went about their task by fair means and foul, terrorizing the Indians until most died or moved away. When the mission was almost complete, Ezra became sickened by his own actions and began to sympathize with the Indians. In the end, he married a Shawnee squaw who had stayed behind. They made a cozy home not far from our cabin.

But Weasel couldn't stop. He went crazy for blood and began terrorizing the white settlers he had been sent to protect. When he heard that his old friend, Ezra, had married a squaw, he went on the rampage. He took revenge on Ezra with an act so savage that I will always have nightmares about it. He deserves to die for his bloodthirsty crimes, but there are no lawmen in Ohio Territory. To think that as a God-fearing boy I once passed up my chance to kill this animal! I won't be so charitable again. Since Weasel has now raised his cruel hand against my family, I feel a strong kinship with Ezra. I have a burning desire for revenge myself. Maybe pulling the trigger on Weasel will take away my nightmares.

What I don't knew is just how far I will go in the name of justice—or in the name of revenge!

—*Bernice D. Crouse*

The Westing Game
By Ellen Raskin
(BGHB 1978, Newbery 1979)

Who killed Samuel W. Westing? That's the question asked of sixteen people who are his heirs and invited to the reading of his will. The right answer could make them millionaires. All sixteen are residents of the Sunset Towers apartment building, owned by Samuel Westing and visible from his mansion. Who killed Samuel Westing? Was it, one Tabitha-Ruth-Alice Wexler, otherwise known as TURTLE? She was in the mansion the night of the murder and it was she who found the corpse. Or was it her mother, GRACE W. WEXLER, who fancies herself an, interior decorator, or her father, JAKE WEXLER, a podiatrist with a bookmaking operation on the side? It might even have been Turtle's perfect sister ANGELA, who spends most of her time embroidering, or Angela's fiancé DR. DENTON DEERE, an intern in plastic surgery. Surely no one would suspect HER HONOR JUDGE J.J. FORD of murder! We might be more likely to choose JAMES SHIN HOO, a restaurant owner who once sued Mr. Westing over a patent for disposable diapers, or SANDY, the doorman at the Sunset Towers—he was fired from the Westing Paper Products Plant. Could we suspect Hoo's wife, MADAME SUN-LIN HOO, who doesn't speak English, or his son DOUGLAS, a jogger getting ready for his big race? What about THEO THEODARAKIS, the writer and chess player, or his crippled brother CHRIS? Chris spends a lot of his time bird-watching and saw someone limping across the lawn of the mansion the night Mr. Westing was killed. How was Samuel Westing connected to the Towers cleaning woman, BERTHA, or to OTIS, the delivery man; to FLORA BAUMBACK, dressmaker, or SYDELLE PULASKI, secretary?

When the will was read, the sixteen were paired off and each pair was given $10,000 and a set of clues—none of them alike. The players were snowbound for several days and spent their time trying to figure out what all the other clues were. The Westing game was tricky and dangerous, but the heirs played on in spite of blizzards, burglaries, and bombs bursting in air.

But who *did* kill Samuel Westing? Only Turtle knows and she isn't telling. You'll have to read *The Westing Game* by Ellen Raskin to find out.

—*Claranell Murray*

The Whipping Boy
By Sid Fleischman
(Newbery 1987, Notables 1986, SLJ/C 1986)

"Fetch the whipping boy!" The words echoed throughout the castle. Prince Brat had been up to his old pranks again. This time he had tied the lords' and ladies' powdered wigs to the backs of their chairs. When they rose to toast the king off came their wigs. They turned purple with embarrassment, and the king looked mad enough to spit ink. But Prince Brat, laughing behind his hands, knew he had nothing to fear. He had never been spanked in his life. He was a prince! By law it was forbidden to spank, thrash, cuff, smack, or whip a prince. So Jemmy the whipping boy was brought from his small tower bedroom to take the twenty whacks the Prince had earned.

For more than a year now, Jemmy, the son of a rat-catcher, had been the official whipping boy. When the Prince made mischief, Jemmy took the punishment. When the Prince didn't know his lessons, Jemmy got a beating. So it went, day after day: the Prince would pull pranks and refuse to learn, and Jemmy would be whipped—but he did learn to read, write, and do sums.

Then Prince Brat got bored and decided to run away. He took Jemmy with him as his servant. Now, Prince Brat knew nothing of life beyond the royal castle, so it wasn't too long before the runaways found themselves in serious trouble—caught and held for ransom by cutthroat robbers!

How could they escape? And which one of them would lead the way? Remember, they're in Jemmy's world now, and things are *very* different.

—*Linda Olson*

White Peak Farm
By Berlie Doherty
(Notables 1990, SLJ/C 1990)

They were a family, and, as in every family, they were also individuals. White Peak Farm was a sheep farm, a family sheep farm. They had grown up being part of that enterprise, everyone doing his or her part, working together.

Then Kathleen married the son of her father's worst enemy. Martin decided he wanted to go to art school—he wasn't ready for farming. Jeannie was so bright she *had* to go on with her education. Marion had her music.

With Dad disabled after the tractor accident, it looked as if there might not be a future for the farm. Yet, deep down, Jeannie knew they'd "always make their way back—to White Peak Farm."

—*Carol Kappelmann*

Willie Bea and the Time the Martians Landed
By Virginia Hamilton
(Notables 1983)

It was October 31st, Halloween, in 1938, and Willie Bea was looking forward to taking Bay and Bay Sister out "begging for treats."

But Aunt Leah's dramatic arrival changed everything. She announced that she had just heard on the radio that the world was coming to an end—New Jersey had been invaded by men from Mars!

Willie Bea and Toughy decided to venture out and see what, if anything, they could see. And see they did! There in the night was a rolling, ear-splitting, outlandish alien—huge! It had one big evil white eye, blindingly bright. Its neck came out of its side, and its head was shaped like a V.

Willie Bea was overwhelmed with terror. Was this really the end of the world?

—Carol Kappelmann

Window
By Jeannie Baker
(Notables 1991)

Once there was a baby boy named Sam, who looked out his window with his mother. All around he could see trees and other green growing plants. When Sam turned four years old, he could see another house from his window, and when he was eight, there were more houses and people, and not so many trees or green growing plants. By the time Sam was a teenager, the houses outside his window had become a village. At night he could see their lights. When Sam got married, in his twenties, the village outside his window had become a city. Sam moved to a new house, where he now stands at a new window with his new baby. Once again there are trees and green growing plants to enjoy. But for how long?

Outside all our windows, the world is changing rapidly—and not always for the better. But if we can understand how we affect the natural world and change some of our ways, we can make a difference.

—Linda Olson

The Winter Room
By Gary Paulsen
(Notables 1989)

Farm life in Minnesota changes with the season. Spring is full of soft, sticky, and stinky surprises. Summer is long days of hard work. Fall is killing time. Winter is frozen outside, but warm inside the winter room. The winter room is the special place where the whole family gathers on winter evenings to sit around the wood stove—Mother, Father, Eldon, and his older brother Wayne. Nels and Uncle David are there too. They are the old men who live on the farm and help Eldon's father. In the winter room, while Father whittles, Mother knits, and Eldon and

Wayne watch the flames through the isinglass of the stove window, Uncle David tells stories about the old country, Norway. His first story is always about his long-dead wife, Alida. Then he tells stories about Viking conquerors and heroes like Crazy Alen. Uncle David tells stories that are "not so much for believing as for believing in". One night Uncle David tells a new story. It's about the Woodcutter, and this story makes things happen.

—Sue Padilla

Wise Child
By Monica Furlong
(SLJ/C 1987)

Euny came the same day Juniper and I made the disgusting, smelly ointment from the henbane leaves we had picked earlier. That evening there was no supper. I went to bed angry and hungry. In the middle of the night, Euny woke me and told me to come downstairs. Juniper was waiting beside a tub of water. She asked me to take off my clothes; then she bathed me in the water. I saw Euny come into the room with a bowl full of that awful ointment we had made before, and then she and Juniper started spreading that horrible stuff all over me. Every inch of me got covered, even my hair and my face! The stench was nauseating. My eyes smarted and watered. I couldn't understand why they were doing this to me.

Suddenly the roof peeled off of Juniper's house. I could see the stars, and I began to move upwards towards the sky. Juniper grabbed my hand and gave me her broomstick. I jumped on, Pearl the cat joined me, Juniper let go, and I was flying—up and up. I saw the village below me; then the broom headed out over the sea. After awhile the broom started to descend towards some islands that I'd never seen before. On one of them there was a great circle of huge stones. As I landed, Pearl jumped off and led me into the circle. In the very center was a flat stone like an altar. "What do you want of me?" I asked the altar stone at last. (I was not very surprised when it didn't reply.) Then I saw Juniper's broom approaching. Pearl and I jumped back on, and suddenly I was back in Juniper's house, sitting in my little green chair.

I found out later from Juniper that everything I'd experienced was a test—a test that I had passed. I, Wise Child, could become a *doran*, a witch like Juniper.

—Linda Olson

The Wish Giver: Three Tales of Coven Tree
By Bill Brittain
(Newbery Honor 1984, Notables 1983, SLJ/C 1983)

Coven Tree, our small town in Maine, is named for the old twisted tree at the crossroads. The story goes that groups of witches, called covens, used to gather there as far back as colonial times. Every family in town has its share of stories of the supernatural, but none beats mine.

It began on the morning of the Coven Tree Church Social, with the arrival of Thaddeus Blinn, the Wish Giver. By the time he left town, at the end of the day, he had let loose forces that threatened to destroy us all.

Within a matter of days, young Polly couldn't speak. She could only croak like a frog, "jug-a-rum, jug-a-rum." A salesman had mysteriously disappeared, a huge tree had grown, almost overnight, at the edge of the woods, and it wouldn't stop raining (raining up!) on Adam Fiske's farm.

What *else* was going to happen? And how were we going to stop it?

—*Carol Kappelmann*

Witch Baby
By Francesca Lia Block
(SLJ/C 1991)

Witch Baby lives with the most slinkster-cool family. They aren't all related, even though Weetzie, Cherokee, My Secret Agent Lover Man, Dirk, and Duck love each other as much as any family can. But Witch Baby has always been different. They found her on the doorstep, abandoned when she was baby. She had purple tilted eyes, black hair, and a fierce temper—she was obviously a Witch Baby.

Witch Baby's dark anger hides her need to know who she is and where she belongs. Will her boyfriend, Angel Juan, come back to her? Is My Secret Agent Lover Man her real father? And who is her mother? Witch Baby is going to find the answers.

—*Cecilia Swanson*

The Witch of Blackbird Pond
By Elizabeth George Speare
(Newbery 1959)

It is 1687, and Kit Tyler has been forced to leave the island of Barbados, where she has lived all her life surrounded by her grandfather's wealth and his love. She's a free spirit, used to having her own way and making her own decisions. But now that her grandfather is dead, Kit must live with her aunt and uncle in a bare Connecticut village governed by strict Puritan rules.

Kit makes her first mistake even before she gets to the village. She jumps from the longboat into the river to save a little girl's doll. She's known how to swim for years and doesn't think twice about plunging into the water. But the Puritans don't know how to swim: to them this is close to magic, and many believe that only a witch can float in water.

Things get worse when Kit arrives at her new home. Although her aunt and cousins are willing to accept her, her uncle is deeply suspicious of this happy, carefree girl with a wardrobe of silk dresses and embroidered gloves. Life in the village is hard, and there are chores to do from morning till night. And when the chores are done, there are church services to attend.

Then one day Kit discovers a huge green field, the Great Meadow, that reminds her of Barbados. She goes there whenever she has any free time. Hannah, a Quaker woman who's been banished from the village, lives in a small cottage near the meadow, and the two of them become friends.

But even this is a mistake, because Hannah is rumored to be a witch, and soon Kit is accused of witchcraft too. In the New England of the 1600s, witches are put to death. Is that the fate that awaits Kit and Hannah?   —*Bernice D. Crouse and J. R. B.*

Witch Week
By Diana Wynne Jones
(SLJ/C 1982)

"Someone in 6B is a witch," reads the note Mr. Crossley finds among the tests he's correcting. A joke, he thinks, but not a very funny one. For Mr. Crossley teaches in Larwood House, a boarding school where many of the pupils are witch orphans—children of men and women who were burned as witches. It is quite possible that some of the children have inherited magic powers, and of course if they have—and if they're discovered—they too will be burned. That's just the way things are nowadays in England, where the Emergency Witchcraft Act permits anyone to be arrested on the merest suspicion of witchcraft.

Mr. Crossley decides to ignore the note at first, but it's not so easy to ignore the flock of birds that comes swooping into Room 6B—just after the music teacher has made the class sing three bird songs in a row. And nobody can ignore the night when every shoe in the entire school vanishes—and then reappears in the hall. What with six hundred pupils and all the school staff, there are hundreds and hundreds of shoes—far too many to have been moved around by human hands.

Then there's Simon, the kid who has all the best friends and the best grades and never gets into trouble. Suddenly everything he says comes true, just like the game Simon Says, only it isn't so funny in real life. "I've got the golden touch," he jokes, and from then on, everything he touches turns to gold—including Theresa's hand. When he tries to make it better by saying, "You haven't got a golden hand," her hand disappears altogether!

Is Simon a witch? What about Nan, who was named after the most famous witch of all time? What about Charles, who finds himself becoming invisible one night, or Nirvipam, whose brother, a student at the school last year, was actually burned as a witch?

Before the week is over, the witches in 6B are out in full force, a portal between two worlds has been opened, and only a desperate trick can save the witches—and the world.

—*Elizabeth Overmyer*

The Witches
By Roald Dahl
(Notables 1983)

As children, it's vitally important that you learn how to recognize witches. Forget that pointy-hat, wart-on-the-nose, broomstick-riding image. That's nowhere near the real thing. *Real* witches dress in ordinary clothes, have ordinary jobs, and look as much like ordinary women as possible. They *do* like to destroy children, though, in more ways than you can imagine.

If you value your life, then, learn to recognize witches by these tell-tale signs:

1) They always wear gloves (to hide their long, sharp claws).

2) They are totally bald. Of course they disguise that fact with first-class wigs, but any wig, no matter how expensive, will be very itchy on a bald head.

3) Their nostrils are larger than normal, with a pink and curvy rim. These nostrils aid their incredible sense of smell. Clean children smell exactly like dog droppings to witches (all the more reason not to bathe this evening).

4) Their eyes keep changing color.

5) They have no toes. Their feet have square ends, which makes wearing shoes very uncomfortable.

6) Their spit is blue.

Now that you are in on the secret, let me tell you what happened to a young boy whose grandmother had carefully instructed him in these danger signs. The two of them were on holiday at a grand hotel in England. He had found a nice quiet place to get away and play for awhile behind a screen in a ballroom, when a large group of ladies came in for a meeting.

He thought nothing about it until he noticed they were all scratching their heads furiously. And they all wore gloves. Imagine his terror when they all whipped off their wigs, stripped off the gloves, kicked off their shoes, and began to plot the end of every child in England!

He was secure in his hiding place until, with horror, he remembered he had just taken a bath! Soon waves of dog-dropping odor would reach all those oversized nostrils!

—Jeff Blair

The Witches of Worm
By Zilpha Keatley Snyder
(Newbery Honor 1973)

Jessica had never really liked cats. When she found the abandoned kitten, she didn't intend to keep it, just find it a good home. But somehow she found herself raising the little orphan. He wasn't a very appealing cat, even when he began to grow. Ugly, without much fur, he reminded Jessica's mother Joy of a blind, gray worm. Worm quickly grew into a very serious and intent animal, without any of the endearing cat traits that people love.

Nevertheless, he became Jessica's companion, her only companion. Jessica had lost her best friend Brandon the year before to other boys, and when her mother wasn't off at work, she was out with her boyfriend. When Worm entered her life, Jessica was spending most of her time alone, reading.

Jessica didn't really think much about Worm's intensity or his unusual behavior at first. But gradually the cat became almost menacing, and then Jessica began hearing his voice in her mind. His voice kept suggesting that she do dreadful things, and Jessica found herself doing them against her will.

When she got caught, she pretended to be disoriented and forgetful, but that wasn't going to work for long. Could Worm be a demon, a witch's cat? But if he is a witch's cat, who is his witch? What is the source of the irresistible power he has over Jessica? Jessica must find out what makes Worm the cat he is, and break the hold he has over her—before it's too late.

—*Evette Pearson*

Wolf
By Gillian Cross
(Carnegie 1991)

On good days, life is almost normal for Cassy, who lives with her grandmother, Nan. But once in a while, straight out of the blue, Nan pulls out the old brown suitcase and pushes Cassy out the door to visit her mother, the irresponsible and flighty Goldie. Why does Cassy have to leave? And why this time does Nan rush her out the door with a dozen postcards and a bag that feels like it's stuffed with rocks?

Goldie is now living with Lyall and Robert, who go around to schools doing presentations on different subjects. Cassy gets involved in the new one on wolves, which shows the difference between the "big bad wolf" of folklore and real wolves in nature. She and the others do research at the zoo, spending hours watching the wolves and studying their social customs. They practice the play until each of them responds naturally, interweaving the truth and the fables about these beautiful animals.

Then one day Cassy discovers that all that heavy stuff at the bottom of her bag is plastic explosives. How did it get there? Did Nan put it in Cassy's bag? Where did she get it? Is she all right? Is there some connection between the explosives and her shoving Cassy out the door that morning?

Cassy needs to get back home to discover the truth—and to meet the mysterious stranger who is living in the back room. Will he want the explosives back? Will he trade Nan for a bag of death?

—*Susan Trimby*

Wolf of Shadows
By Whitley Strieber
(SLJ/C 1985)

The big black wolf has always been a loner, standing aside from the pack. It's not because he wants it that way—he longs to be part of the pack, to feel their closeness and share in their camaraderie; but he's always been different—all black, and much bigger than the others. From his cub days on, the pack hasn't been willing to accept him because of his color and size, and so he stays away from them—but never too far away—in the shadows. He is called "Wolf of Shadows."

Because he longs so for companionship, he has at times traveled many miles and seen the camps of men. He has learned to fear men, with their firesticks and killing ways. There is one human he does not fear, though, and that is a female, with two little female cubs. Sometimes she comes on a big bird in the summer and lives near one of the northern lakes. She carries no firestick and doesn't seem to fear him. They have learned to tolerate each other's presence.

One day Wolf of Shadows feels something rumbling in the earth that he's never felt before, he smells something in the air he's never smelled before, and he knows it means danger and even death for his pack. The time has come when he must fight to become their leader, so he can take them to a safe place. But not only will he have to fight the old leader, he will also have to gain the confidence and loyalty of the pack.

Before he can do this, however, the large bird lands on the lake, and the female and her cubs fall out of the bird and start swimming to shore. He can tell they are badly hurt, and he can actually smell the life going out of one of the cubs. Now the air is filled with a burnt smell he can't identify, and a black mist is beginning to fall.

Minneapolis has been the target of a nuclear bomb, and now a nuclear winter is beginning. The human female knows this—that's why she has tried to escape. Wolf of Shadows knows only that something terrible has happened, and his pack must travel south to warmth and, maybe, safety.

So begins the story of Wolf of Shadows and his pack as they and their adopted humans begin the journey south, struggling together for life and warmth in an increasingly hostile environment.

—Barbara Flottmeier

Woodsong
By Gary Paulsen
(Notables 1990, SLJ/C 1990)

Gary Paulsen started running sled dogs when he was in his forties. He thought he knew all there was to know about the woods and about dogs, but his lessons were just beginning, and the dogs became his teachers.

Meet Columbia: he taught Gary about humor. Columbia's doghouse was next to Olaf's. Olaf was a big and none-too-bright bully. One day Columbia pushed his bone towards Olaf, stopping when the bone was just out of Olaf's reach. Then Columbia sat back and laughed (yes, dogs laugh) as Olaf strained and generally went crazy trying to reach that bone.

Cookie taught Gary to trust the dogs. On a day when stormy weather made seeing anything beyond the sled impossible, Cookie fought Gary over every change in direction. Whenever Gary won, they would end up in trouble, but when they went the way Cookie wanted to go, everything would be fine. But Gary was stubborn; all day they fought, and still he didn't learn. Finally, after a bad spill into a deep gully (following Gary's lead), the team went on strike. They wouldn't move at all until Gary learned his lesson!

Finally, meet Storm. Storm taught Gary many lessons. The first was about the intense need some dogs had to pull a sled. The last was about death.

Gary first used his dog teams to run his trapline. He soon gave up trapping but continued to run the dogs and to learn from them. After a few years, he began preparing for the Iditarod, an 1100-mile dog-sled race through the frozen Alaskan wilderness, where temperatures frequently fall to 50 degrees below zero. During the race, Gary would encounter moose who hated just about everything. He would suffer hallucinations caused by sleep deprivation. And he would have to find a way to deal with Willie, his lead dog. Willie would get so bored running across the featureless tundra he would fall asleep as he ran.

Meet Gary's canine teachers and learn about the great Iditarod race in *Woodsong* by Gary Paulsen.

—Linda Olson

Words by Heart
By Ouida Sebestyen
(ABA 1982, IRA 1980)

Lena wants to do something to make her papa proud, something special, so she enters a Bible recitation contest. It's sort of like a spelling bee—the contestants stand in front of an audience and take turns reciting Bible verses they've learned by heart. Anyone who misses a turn or makes a mistake is out, until, in the end, there's only one person left—the winner! And that's who Lena wants to be.

She's studied hard, and it's soon clear that she has a real chance. Only one of the other kids is a match for her—Winslow Starnes, last year's champion and the son of a minister. When they're tied at fifty-four verses apiece, the Reverend Starnes suggests they call it a draw, but Lena's determined to finish the game. She wants to win, and she does, when the Starnes boy finally admits he's stumped.

As the contest organizer presents her with the prize, he stumbles over his words. He seems oddly embarrassed—and when Lena opens the package, she sees why. Nestled inside the box is a brand-new bow tie. She wasn't expected to win. She wasn't *supposed* to win. A black girl doesn't beat a white boy.

All Lena's relatives are very proud of her, but they're also very uneasy. And when they get home, they find their fresh loaf of bread pinned to the kitchen table—with a knife!

—Mary Hedge and J. R. B.

A Wrinkle in Time
By Madeleine L'Engle
(Newbery 1963)

Laid out before them, as far as their eyes could see, was a housing project of identical houses with identical yards, with identical kids all playing in the yards with balls and jump-ropes. There was something wrong, though. A chill went through Meg when she realized what it was. The balls all hit the ground at the same time. The ropes all slapped the ground simultaneously. How did they do that? she wondered. Then identical mothers appeared at the identical doors and clapped twice. The children turned as one and marched into the houses, the doors clicking shut in unison behind them.

Welcome to the planet Camazotz, the home of ιτ, the thing that has their father captive.

Meg, her brother Charles Wallace, and their friend Calvin had gotten their first glimpse of IT just a wrinkle ago. The strange creatures who were their guides in this trip across the universe had shown them a vast view of known space, and in the heart of it was the blackness that was IT, reaching tendrils out to wink out the stars.

Surrounding the total darkness of the areas IT controlled was a gray area where the star systems were fighting back. Earth was in such a gray area. Meg's father had been pulled into the fight over a year ago and was now a captive. Silently Meg resolved that she would not leave Camazotz without him, regardless of what dangers she and the others had to face.

But what can the three of them do against the all-consuming power of IT?

—*Jeff Blair*

Year of Impossible Goodbyes
By Sook Nyul Choi
(Notables 1991)

For years they have lived under the domination of the Japanese. Sookan's family keeps hoping for a spring that will bring them peace and freedom, but that seems very far away. Even though they hear rumors that the tide of war has turned, Japanese control over the Korean people just seems to get tighter and tighter. Sookan's family has been ordered to give up all metal tools and objects, to be melted down for the Japanese war effort, and commanded to run a factory in their back yard. There's never enough food, and Korean families must survive on the shortest of rations. In secret, Sookan's family preserve their love of freedom, and of their country. Although it's forbidden, her grandfather teaches Sookan to read and write the Korean language. Danger is always a footstep away. The Japanese police keep watch on their activities and can search their home at any time. Sookan's father is in Manchuria, fighting with the resistance. Her older brothers have been seized and taken to Japanese labor camps. Sookan fears that the little they have left may also be taken from them, and that she may never see her family together again. It is a Year of Impossible Goodbyes, a time, in the midst of war, when hope must be kept alive.

—*Helen Schlichting*

The Year without Michael
By Susan Beth Pfeffer
(SLJ/C 1987)

Jody knew Michael had been worried—worried about what was happening between their parents, worried they were headed for divorce. Still, he'd seemed like himself when he left to play softball with his friends. He'd even promised not to be late for supper. But he *was* late—so late that after a while they stopped being mad and started to worry. When they began calling his friends, they discovered that nobody had seen Michael. He hadn't turned up for softball. Now everybody was frightened. They called the police and started organizing people into search parties. But it was hopeless. They couldn't find a clue.

Thus began their year without Michael. The questions never seemed to go away. Had Michael run away? Had he been kidnapped? Was he even alive?

What do you do when someone you love doesn't come home? How do you survive the year without Michael?

—Helen Schlichting

The Young Landlords
By Walter Dean Myers
(King 1980, Notables 1979)

Everybody in our group is fifteen, but I'm the oldest, 'cause I was born in March. That's how I got to be the owner of this apartment building. See, we all went down there to complain to the owner about the condition of the place. He got real mad and demanded a name and address for the leader of our group. That's when we figured out I was the oldest. He asked me for a dollar. A couple of days later, his lawyer sends papers saying that dollar just bought the building and I'm the new owner. What we didn't know then was that slumlords were walking away from buildings like ours; hey, they were running away.

But we're not. We're going to use the rent money to fix up the place and make it nice. Trouble is, no one is paying any rent, they're all demanding we fix stuff, and that crazy karate guy keeps busting things. Being a landlord is a tough job, even for a kid!

—Cecilia Swanson

Z for Zachariah
By Robert C. O'Brien
(Poe 1976)

Ann is alone in the valley. Everyone else is dead. There was a brief nuclear war, and after that the fallout killed everyone who was left. Ann's parents and brothers had gone to look for survivors. They never returned. But the valley where Ann's family had their farm seems to be safe, protected from radioactive fallout by a fluke of weather and water patterns. And so Ann is alive—alive and alone. For a year now, she has managed by herself.

But now there's a man in a radiation suit coming toward the valley. Ann hides and watches him as he approaches. She wants company—of course she does! She envisions companionship, a family, a future. But . . . being alone is surely better than being with someone who is . . . what? Crazy? Violent? Domineering? How can she know who this person is? How can she tell from a distance? How can she prepare herself for whatever is about to happen?

A is for Adam, the first man on earth. Is the man in the radiation suit the last?

—Sarah Flowers

LIST OF AWARDS AND
AWARD-WINNING TITLES

Award-winning titles represented in this book are listed after the description of the award. Titles that received more than one of these awards are marked with an asterisk (*).

Addams

Jane Addams Children's Book Award
Jane Addams Peace Association,
    777 United Nations Plaza, New York,
    NY 10017. 212-682-8830

This award was established in 1953 by Marta Teale of Ithaca, NY, and is sponsored by the Jane Addams Peace Association and the Women's International League for Peace and Freedom. Its goal is to promote the cause of peace, social justice, world community and equality for all races and sexes. It is awarded annually to a children's book published in English during the preceding year, and consists of a certificate presented to the winning author in September of each year.

Anthony Burns (Hamilton) '89
**Big Book for Peace* (Alexander et al.) '91
**Hiroshima No Pika* (Maruki) '83
**Never to Forget* (Meltzer) '77
Nilda (Mohr) '74
Rain of Fire (Bauer) '84
**Road from Home* (Kherdian) '80
**Upstairs Room* (Reiss) '73

ABA

American Book Awards
Association of American Publishers, Inc.,
    71 Fifth Avenue, New York, NY
    10003. 212-255-0200

First presented in 1980, these awards were established to honor books of distinction written, translated, or designed by U.S. citizens and published by American publishers. Children's books were a category until 1984, when the scope of the awards was scaled back.

**Gathering of Days* (Blos) '80
**Night Swimmers* (Byars) '81
Place Apart (Fox) '83
Ramona and Her Mother (Cleary) '81
Swiftly Tilting Planet (L'Engle) '80
**Words by Heart* (Sebestyen) '82

Australian CBY

Children's Book of the Year Awards
Children's Book Council of Australia,
    PO Box 387, Croydon, Victoria 3136,
    Australia. (03) 725-2206

Annually the Children's Book Council selects the Book of the Year, the Junior Book of the Year, and the Picture Book of the Year from among Australian publications. Prize money amounting to $30,000 is distributed among winners and runners-up.

**So Much to Tell You* (Marsden) '88

Batchelder

Mildred L. Batchelder Award
Association of Librarians in Service to
    Children, American Library Association, 50 E Huron St., Chicago, IL
    60611. 800-545-2433

This award was established in 1968 to honor the first executive secretary of ALSC, formerly the Children's Services

Division. It is awarded annually to the publisher of the most outstanding book for children first published in a foreign language or in a foreign country and subsequently published in the United States. The recipient is chosen by a committee of ALSC, and the winner is announced at the ALA Midwinter Conference, and the award is given at the following ALA Annual Conference. The award consists of a citation.

Battle Horse (Kullman) '82
Buster's World (Reuter) '90
Crutches (Hartling) '89
Hiroshima No Pika (Maruki) '83
Island on Bird Street (Orlev) '85
Konrad (Nostlinger) '79
Ronia, the Robber's Daughter (Lindgren) '84

BGHB

The Boston Globe—Horn Book Award
The Boston Globe & Horn Book, Inc.,
11 Beacon St., Suite 1000, Boston,
MA 02108. 617-227-1555; 800-325-1170

This award is intended to honor the best trade books for children published in the United States each year, in the categories of fiction, nonfiction, and poetry. The award consists of $500. Winners are announced at the fall meeting of the New England Library Association.

All Together Now (Bridgers) '79
Dark Is Rising (Cooper) '73
Dicey's Song (Voigt) '83
Eva (Dickinson) '89
Friendship (Taylor) '88
Great Little Madison (Fritz) '90
Hiroshima No Pika (Maruki) '82
Howl's Moving Castle (Jones) '86
Joyful Noise (Fleischman) '88
Jumanji (Van Allsburg) '81
Like Jake and Me (Jukes) '85
Little by Little (Little) '88
Lon Po Po (Young) '90
M. C. Higgins, the Great (Hamilton) '74
Machine Gunners (Westall) '77
Maniac Magee (Spinelli) '90
Moves Make the Man (Brooks) '85

Mrs. Frisby and the Rats of NIMH (O'Brien) '71
Never to Forget (Meltzer) '76
Night Swimmers (Byars) '80
Playing Beatie Bow (Park) '82
Polar Express (Van Allsburg) '86
Rabble Starkey (Lowry) '87
Ramona and Her Father (Cleary) '78
Roll of Thunder, Hear My Cry (Taylor) '77
Saturnalia (Fleischman) '90
Solitary Blue (Voigt) '84
Stonewords (Conrad) '90
String in the Harp (Bond) '76
Village by the Sea (Fox) '89
Visit to William Blake's Inn (Willard) '82
Way Things Work (Macaulay) '89
Westing Game (Raskin) '78

Caldecott

Randolph Caldecott Medal
Association of Librarians in Service to
Children, American Library Association, 50 E Huron St., Chicago, IL
60611. 800-545-2433

The Randolph Caldecott Medal was established in 1937, and is awarded annually to the illustrator of the best children's picture book published during the previous year. The winner and possible Honor Books are selected by a committee of the association and announced at the ALA Midwinter Conference. The award is presented at the following ALA Annual Conference. United States citizens and residents are eligible for the award, which was established by Frederic C. Melcher, publisher, who donated the original medal, and honors Ralph Caldecott, noted nineteenth century illustrator. The award consists of a bronze medal and a citation.

Black and White (Macaulay) '91
Jumanji (Van Allsburg) '82
Lon Po Po (Young) '90
Polar Express (Van Allsburg) '86

Caldecott Honor

Visit to William Blake's Inn (Willard) '82

Canadian Governor General's

Governor General's Literary Awards, Canada Council, Box 1047, 99 Metcalfe St., Ottawa, ON K1P 5V8, Canada. 613-598-4376

These awards are presented annually to Canadian authors of the best books in English and French in seven categories. The two categories relevant here are: Children's literature (text) and Children's literature (illustration). The winning author and illustrator each receive $10,000 (Canadian). The awards were established in 1936.

Bad Boy (Wieler) '90
Days of Terror (Smucker) '80
Pick-up Sticks (Ellis) '91
*Sweetgrass (Hudson) '85

CLA

Children's Book of the Year Canadian Library Association, 200 Elgin St., Ottawa, ON K2P 1L5, Canada. 613-232-9625

An annual award for the best Canadian children's book.

Garbage Delight (Lee) '78
Hold Fast (Major) '79
River Runners (Houston) '80
Sky Is Falling (Pearson) '90
*Sweetgrass (Hudson) '84

Carnegie

Carnegie Medal
The Library Association, 7 Ridgemount St., London WC1E 7AE, England. 71-636-7543

This annual award honors the author of an outstanding fiction or nonfiction children's book written in English and published during the previous year. Books published simultaneously in the UK and abroad are also eligible. The Carnegie Medal was first awarded in 1936 in honor of Andrew Carnegie, and is sponsored by Peters Library Service, Ltd. The award is a medal.

*Boys' War (Murphy) '91
*Haunting (Mahy) '83
*Machine Gunners (Westall) '76
*My War with Goggle-Eyes (Fine) '90
Wolf (Cross) '91

Christopher

The Christophers
12 East 48th St., New York, NY 10017. 212-759-4050

These annual awards honor adult and juvenile books (fiction and nonfiction) that affirm human values. The Christopher Awards were established in 1949. The prize is a bronze medallion.

*All Together Now (Bridgers) '80
*Class Dismissed II (Glenn) '86
Come to the Edge (Cunningham) '78
Dear Bill, Remember Me? (Mazer) '77
*Formal Feeling (Oneal) '83
Gentlehands (Kerr) '79
Gold Cadillac (Taylor) '87
*Great Gilly Hopkins (Paterson) '79
*Into a Strange Land (Ashabranner & Ashabranner) '87
Mississippi Bridge (Taylor) '91
*One-Eyed Cat (Fox) '84
Pyramid (Macaulay) '76
*Sarah, Plain and Tall (MacLachlan) '85
*So Much to Tell You (Marsden) '90
Tuck Everlasting (Babbitt) '76

Golden Kite

Golden Kite Award
Society of Children's Book Writers, Box 662966, Mar Vista Station, Los Angeles, CA 90066. 818-347-2849

This annual award recognizes excellence in the writing and illustrating of children's books. It was established in 1973, and awards are given for fiction, nonfiction, and illustration. Members of the Society are eligible, and books are submitted between February and December of the year of their publication. The award consists of a golden kite statuette and an acknowledgment certificate.

*After the Dancing Days (Rostkowski) '87

Borrowed Children (Lyon) '89
Boys' War (Murphy) '91
Girl Who Cried Flowers (Yolen) '75
Jenny of the Tetons (Gregory) '90
One More Flight (Bunting) '77
Rabble Starkey (Lowry) '88
Ralph S. Mouse (Cleary) '83
Sarah, Plain and Tall (MacLachlan) '86
Summer of My German Soldier (Greene)
    '74
Tancy (Hurmence) '85
True Confessions of Charlotte Doyle (Avi)
    '91

Golden Kite Honor

Children of the River (Crew) '90
Everywhere (Brooks) '91
Franklin Delano Roosevelt (Freedman)
    '91

Greenaway

Kate Greenaway Medal
The Library Association, 7 Ridgemount
    St., London WS1E 7AE, England. 71-
    636-7543

This annual award honors the illustrator of an outstanding fiction or nonfiction children's book written in English and published during the previous year. Books published simultaneously in the UK and abroad are also eligible. The Kate Greenaway Medal was first awarded in 1955 to honor Kate Greenaway, a 19th century illustrator, and is sponsored by Peters Library Service, Ltd. The award is a medal.

Good Night, Mr. Tom (Magorian) '82
War Boy (Foreman) '90

IRA

IRA Children's Book Award
International Reading Association, 800
    Barksdale Rd., Box 8139, Newark,
    DE 19714-8139. 302-731-10057

This annual award is given to an author's first or second book, either fiction or nonfiction, to recognize unusual promise in the children's book field. Books from any country and in any language copyrighted during the calendar year are eligible. Awards are given in two categories: younger readers (four to ten years) and older readers (ten to sixteen years). The award consists of a $1,000 prize, and has been given since 1975.

Children of the River (Crew) '90
Good Night, Mr. Tom (Magorian) '82
Prairie Songs (Conrad) '86
Ratha's Creature (Bell) '84
String in the Harp (Bond) '77
Summer to Die (Lowry) '78
Third-Story Cat (Baker) '88
Words by Heart (Sebestyen) '80

King

Coretta Scott King Book Award
American Library Association/Social Responsibilities Round Table, 50 E Huron St., Chicago, IL 60611. 1-800-545-2433

This award was established in 1969 to recognize African American authors and illustrators for outstanding contributions to children's literature which promotes a better understanding and appreciation of the culture and contribution of all peoples to the realization of the American Dream. The award is given annually, and to be eligible, books must have been published in the calendar year preceding the year of the award. The award consists of $250, a plaque, and a set of Britannica or World Book Encyclopedias. The award was established by Glyndon Flynt Greer to commemorate the life and works of Dr. Martin Luther King, Jr., and to honor Mrs. Coretta Scott King for her courage and determination in continuing to work for peace and world brotherhood.

Fallen Angels (Myers) '89
Friendship (Taylor) '88
Justin and the Best Biscuits in the World
    (Walter) '87
Road to Memphis (Taylor) '91
Sweet Whispers, Brother Rush (Hamilton) '83
Young Landlords (Myers) '80

National Jewish

National Jewish Book Award for Children's Literature
Jewish Book Council/Jewish Welfare Board, 15 E 26th St., New York, NY 10010-1579. 212-532-4949

This annual award, established in 1952, honors the most distinguished children's book on a Jewish theme originally written and published in English in either the United States or Canada, or recognizes cumulative contributions to Jewish juvenile literature. The award consists of $750 to the author and a citation to the publisher and to the author.

Becoming Gershona (Semel) '91
Devil's Arithmetic (Yolen) '89
Monday in Odessa (Sherman) '87
My Grandmother's Stories (Geras) '91
Number the Stars (Lowry) '90
Return (Levitin) '88

Newbery

John Newbery Medal
Association of Librarians in Service to Children, American Library Association, 50 E. Heuron St., Chicago, IL 60611. 800-545-2433

This annual award recognizes the author of the most distinguished contribution to American literature for children each year. Authors must be United States citizens or residents. The award was established in 1921 by Frederic C. Melcher, publisher, who donated the first medal, and honors John Newbery, noted 18th century British Bookseller. The award winners and possible Honor Books are selected by a committee of ALSC, announced at the ALA Midwinter Conference and awarded at the following Annual Conference. The award consists of a bronze medal and citation.

Adam of the Road (Gray) '43
Bridge to Terabithia (Paterson) '78
Bronze Bow (Speare) '62
Caddie Woodlawn (Brink) '36
Call It Courage (Sperry) '41
Carry On, Mr. Bowditch (Latham) '56
Dear Mr. Henshaw (Cleary) '84

Dicey's Song (Voigt) '83
Door in the Wall (De Angeli) '50
From the Mixed-Up Files of Mrs. Basil E. Frankweiler (Konigsburg) '68
Gathering of Days (Blos) '80
Grey King (Cooper) '76
Hero and the Crown (McKinley) '85
High King (Alexander) '69
Invincible Louisa (Meigs) '34
Island of the Blue Dolphins (O'Dell) '61
Jacob Have I Loved (Paterson) '81
Johnny Tremain (Forbes) '44
Joyful Noise (Fleischman) '89
Julie of the Wolves (George) '73
King of the Wind (Henry) '49
Lincoln (Freedman) '88
M. C. Higgins, the Great (Hamilton) '75
Maniac Magee (Spinelli) '91
Mrs. Frisby and the Rats of NIMH (O'Brien) '72
Number the Stars (Lowry) '90
Onion John (Krumgold) '60
Rabbit Hill (Lawson) '45
Rifles for Watie (Keith) '58
Roll of Thunder, Hear My Cry (Taylor) '77
Sarah, Plain and Tall (MacLachlan) '86
Shiloh (Naylor) '92
Slave Dancer (Fox) '74
Summer of the Swans (Byars) '71
Up a Road Slowly (Hunt) '67
Visit to William Blake's Inn (Willard) '82
Westing Game (Raskin) '79
Whipping Boy (Fleischman) '87
Witch of Blackbird Pond (Speare) '59
Wrinkle in Time (L'Engle) '63

Newbery Honor

Across Five Aprils (Hunt) '65
Annie and the Old One (Miles) '72
Blue Sword (McKinley) '83
By the Shores of Silver Lake (Wilder) '40
Charlotte's Web (White) '53
Dark Is Rising (Cooper) '74
Dogsong (Paulsen) '86
Enchantress from the Stars (Engdahl) '71
Fledgling (Langton) '81
Great Gilly Hopkins (Paterson) '79
Headless Cupid (Snyder) '72
Incident at Hawk's Hill (Eckert) '72
Justin Morgan Had a Horse (Henry) '46

Like Jake and Me (Jukes) '85
Little Town on the Prairie (Wilder) '42
Moves Make the Man (Brooks) '85
Mr. *Popper's Penguins* (Atwater & Atwater) '39
My Brother Sam Is Dead (Collier & Collier) '75
My Side of the Mountain (George) '60
Nothing but the Truth (Avi) '91
Old Yeller (Gipson) '57
One-Eyed Cat (Fox) '83
Our Eddie (Ish-Kishor) '70
Philip Hall Likes Me, I Reckon Maybe (Greene) '75
Planet of Junior Brown (Hamilton) '72
Ramona and Her Father (Cleary) '78
Ramona Quimby, Age 8 (Cleary) '82
Ring of Endless Light (L'Engle) '81
Road from Home (Kherdian) '80
Sign of the Beaver (Speare) '84
Sing Down the Moon (O'Dell) '71
Solitary Blue (Voigt) '84
String in the Harp (Bond) '77
Sweet Whispers, Brother Rush (Hamilton) '83
Tombs of Atuan (Le Guin) '72
Upstairs Room (Reiss) '73
Wish Giver (Brittain) '84
Witches of Worm (Snyder) '73

Notables

Notable Children's Books
Association of Librarians in Service to Children, American Library Association, 50 E Huron St., Chicago, IL 60611. 800-545-2433

These outstanding fiction and nonfiction titles for children are selected annually by a committee of ALSC. The contents of the list are announced at the ALA Midwinter Conference. Books must have been published during the previous calendar year to be eligible.

Actor's Life for Me! (Gish) '87
After the Dancing Days (Rostkowski) '86
Afternoon of the Elves (Lisle) '89
Agony of Alice (Naylor) '85
Along the Tracks (Bergman) '91
Amy's Eyes (Kennedy) '85
Anastasia Again! (Lowry) '81

And One for All (Nelson) '89
As the Waltz Was Ending (Butterworth) '82
Battle Horse (Kullman) '81
Behind the Attic Wall (Cassedy) '83
Bells of Christmas (Hamilton) '89
Best Bad Thing (Uchida) '83
Big Book for Peace (Alexander et al.) '90
Bill Peet (Peet) '89
Bingo Brown, Gypsy Lover (Byars) '90
Black and White (Macaulay) '90
Blackberries in the Dark (Jukes) '85
Blossom Culp and the Sleep of Death (Peck) '86
Blue Sword (McKinley) '82
Blue-Eyed Daisy (Rylant) '85
Borning Room (Fleischman) '91
Borrowers Avenged (Norton) '82
Broccoli Tapes (Slepian) '89
Buffalo Brenda (Pinkwater) '89
Bully for You, Teddy Roosevelt! (Fritz) '91
Buster's World (Reuter) '89
Canada Geese Quilt (Kinsey-Warnock) '89
Castle in the Air (Jones) '91
Cat Poems (Livingston) '87
Chrysanthemum (Henkes) '91
Come Sing, Jimmy Jo (Paterson) '85
Cracker Jackson (Byars) '85
Crutches (Hartling) '89
Cuckoo Sister (Alcock) '86
Cybil War (Byars) '81
Dakota Dugout (Turner) '85
Dear Mr. Henshaw (Cleary) '83
Devil's Donkey (Brittain) '81
Diamond Tree (Schwartz) '91
Dicey's Song (Voigt) '82
Dinosaur Mountain (Arnold) '89
Dixie Storms (Hall) '90
Dogsong (Paulsen) '85
Dragon of the Lost Sea (Yep) '82
Duplicate (Sleator) '88
Eva (Dickinson) '89
Everywhere (Brooks) '90
Facts and Fictions of Minna Pratt (MacLachlan) '88
Family Project (Ellis) '88
Fighting Ground (Avi) '84
Fine White Dust (Rylant) '86
First Hard Times (Smith) '83
Formal Feeling (Oneal) '82
Fran Ellen's House (Sachs) '87
Franklin Delano Roosevelt (Freedman) '90

Friendship (Taylor) '87
Frog Prince, Continued (Scieszka) '91
Gathering (Hamilton) '81
Girl from Yamhill (Cleary) '88
Goats (Cole) '87
Good Night, Mr. Tom (Magorian) '82
Great American Gold Rush (Blumberg) '89
Great Little Madison (Fritz) '89
Hatchet (Paulsen) '87
Healer (Dickinson) '85
Hero and the Crown (McKinley) '84
Hey World, Here I Am! (Little) '89
Hide Crawford Quick! (Froehlich) '83
Hiroshima No Pika (Maruki) '82
Hit and Run (Phipson) '85
How It Feels to Be Adopted (Krementz) '82
How It Feels When a Parent Dies (Krementz) '81
How It Feels When Parents Divorce (Krementz) '84
How Many Spots Does a Leopard Have? (Lester) '89
Howl's Moving Castle (Jones) '86
In a Dark, Dark Room (Schwartz) '84
In Summer Light (Oneal) '85
Indian Chiefs (Freedman) '87
Interstellar Pig (Sleator) '84
Into a Strange Land (Ashabranner & Ashabranner) '87
Island on Bird Street (Orlev) '84
Jeremy Visick (Wiseman) '81
Josie Gambit (Shura) '86
Journey (Hamanaka) '90
Joyful Noise (Fleischman) '88
Keeper (Naylor) '86
Kestrel (Alexander) '82
Land I Lost (Huynh) '82
Lester's Turn (Slepian) '81
Let the Circle Be Unbroken (Taylor) '81
Light in the Attic (Silverstein) '81
Like Jake and Me (Jukes) '84
Lincoln (Freedman) '87
Little by Little (Little) '88
Lives of Christopher Chant (Jones) '88
Lon Po Po (Young) '89
Lyddie (Paterson) '91
Maggie by My Side (Butler) '87
Magical Adventures of Pretty Pearl (Hamilton) '83
Maniac Magee (Spinelli) '90
Martin's Mice (King-Smith) '89

Me, Mop, and the Moondance Kid (Myers) '88
Merlin Dreams (Dickinson) '88
Midnight Horse (Fleischman) '90
Monkey Island (Fox) '91
More Stories Julian Tells (Cameron) '86
Moves Make the Man (Brooks) '84
Mozart Season (Wolff) '91
My Prairie Year (Harvey) '86
My War with Goggle-Eyes (Fine) '89
Nekomah Creek (Crew) '91
New Kid on the Block (Prelutsky) '84
Nothing but the Truth (Avi) '91
Number the Stars (Lowry) '89
On My Honor (Bauer) '86
One Hundredth Thing about Caroline (Lowry) '83
One-Eyed Cat (Fox) '84
Outlaws of Sherwood (McKinley) '88
Outside Child (Bawden) '89
Pennywhistle Tree (Smith) '91
People Could Fly (Hamilton) '85
Place Where Nobody Stopped (Segal) '91
Playing Beatie Bow (Park) '82
Poems of A. Nonny Mouse (Prelutsky) '89
Quest for a Maid (Hendry) '90
Rabbi's Girls (Hurwitz) '82
Rachel Chance (Thesman) '90
Rats on the Roof (Marshall) '91
Remembering the Good Times (Peck) '85
Return (Levitin) '87
Return to Bitter Creek (Smith) '86
Rhythm Road (Morrison) '88
Ronia, the Robber's Daughter (Lindgren) '83
Root Cellar (Lunn) '83
Sarah, Plain and Tall (MacLachlan) '85
Saturnalia (Fleischman) '90
Save Queen of Sheba! (Moeri) '81
Secret World of Polly Flint (Cresswell) '84
Shabanu (Staples) '89
Shades of Gray (Reeder) '89
Shiloh (Naylor) '91
Shining Company (Sutcliff) '90
Sign of the Beaver (Speare) '83
Silent Voice (Cunningham) '81
Solitary Blue (Voigt) '83
Something Big Has Been Here (Prelutsky) '90
Stepping on the Cracks (Hahn) '91
Sweet Whispers, Brother Rush (Hamilton) '82

Sweetgrass (Hudson) '89
Tales of the Early World (Hughes) '91
Telling of the Tales (Brooke) '90
Time's Up (Heide) '82
Touch Wood (Roth-Hano) '88
*Traitor (Fritz) '81
Travelers by Night (Alcock) '85
*True Confessions of Charlotte Doyle (Avi) '90
True Story of the Three Little Pigs, by A. Wolf (Scieszka) '89
*Truth about Unicorns (Giblin) '91
Two Short and One Long (Aamundsen) '90
Two-Thousand-Pound Goldfish (Byars) '82
Unclaimed Treasures (MacLachlan) '84
Up from Jericho Tel (Konigsburg) '86
*Village by the Sea (Fox) '88
*Visit to William Blake's Inn (Willard) '81
*Voyage of the Frog (Paulsen) '89
Waiting for the Rain (Gordon) '87
Wave in Her Pocket (Joseph) '91
*Way Things Work (Macaulay) '88
*Way to Sattin Shore (Pearce) '84
*Weasel (DeFelice) '90
*Whipping Boy (Fleischman) '86
*White Peak Farm (Doherty) '90
Willie Bea and the Time the Martians Landed (Hamilton) '83
Window (Baker) '91
Winter Room (Paulsen) '89
*Wish Giver (Brittain) '83
Witches (Dahl) '83
*Woodsong (Paulsen) '90
Year of Impossible Goodbyes (Choi) '91
*Young Landlords (Myers) '79

O'Dell

Scott O'Dell Award for Historical Fiction
Bulletin of the Center for Children's Books, 1100 E 57th St., Chicago, IL 60637. 312-702-8293

This award, established in 1981 by Scott O'Dell, and awarded for the first time in 1984, encourages and recognizes the writing of good historical fiction, which provides young readers with books that interest them in the history that has helped shaped their country and their world. Titles written by a United States citizen, published by a US publisher for chil-

dren or young adults, and set in the US, Canada or South America are eligible. The award consists of $5,000, and is given only when merited.

Charley Skedaddle (Beatty) '88
*Sarah, Plain and Tall (MacLachlan) '86
*Shades of Gray (Reeder) '89

Poe

Edgar Allan Poe Award—Best Young Adult Novel
Mystery Writers of America, 236 W. 27th St., New York, NY 10001. 212-255-7005

This award recognizes an author for outstanding contribution in mystery, crime and suspense writing for young adults. Books published in the United States during the calendar year of the award are eligible. The award was established in 1945, and consists of a scroll and a ceramic bust of Edgar Allan Poe.

Are You in the House Alone? (Peck) '77
Callender Papers (Voigt) '84
Kidnapping of Christina Lattimore (Nixon) '80
Megan's Island (Roberts) '89
Night Cry (Naylor) '85
Other Side of Dark (Nixon) '87
Sandman's Eyes (Windsor) '86
Seance (Nixon) '81
*Stonewords (Conrad) '91
Taking Terri Mueller (Mazer) '82
Z for Zachariah (O'Brien) '76

SLJ/C

School Library Journal Best of the Year in Children's Books
School Library Journal, Cahners Publishing Co., 249 W. 17th St., New York, 10017. 212-463-6759

This list consists of the best titles written for children and reviewed in SLJ during the calendar year. Titles are selected by the editors of SLJ and appear in the December issue of the magazine.

Abduction (Newth) '89
After the Rain (Mazer) '87

Afternoon of the Elves (Lisle) '89
Agnes Cecilia (Gripe) '90
Alice in Rapture, Sort of (Naylor) '89
And One for All (Nelson) '89
Animal, the Vegetable, and John D. Jones (Byars) '82
Athletic Shorts (Crutcher) '91
Battle Horse (Kullman) '81
Behind the Attic Wall (Cassedy) '83
Best Bad Thing (Uchida) '83
Bill Peet (Peet) '89
Bingo Brown and the Language of Love (Byars) '89
Bingo Brown, Gypsy Lover (Byars) '90
Blackberries in the Dark (Jukes) '85
Borning Room (Fleischman) '91
Borrowed Children (Lyon) '88
Borrowers Avenged (Norton) '82
Boy Who Reversed Himself (Sleator) '86
Boys' War (Murphy) '91
Broccoli Tapes (Slepian) '89
Building Blocks (Voigt) '84
Bully for You, Teddy Roosevelt! (Fritz) '91
Burning Questions of Bingo Brown (Byars) '88
Chartbreaker (Cross) '87
Checking on the Moon (Davis) '91
Chrysanthemum (Henkes) '91
Class Dismissed II (Glenn) '86
Come Sing, Jimmy Jo (Paterson) '85
Cookcamp (Paulsen) '91
Cracker Jackson (Byars) '85
Cuckoo Sister (Alcock) '86
Daphne's Book (Hahn) '83
Day That Elvis Came to Town (Marino) '91
Dealing with Dragons (Wrede) '90
Dear Mr. Henshaw (Cleary) '83
December Rose (Garfield) '87
Deep Wizardry (Duane) '85
Devil's Donkey (Brittain) '81
Dixie Storms (Hall) '90
Dogsong (Paulsen) '85
Duplicate (Sleator) '88
Eva (Dickinson) '89
Everywhere (Brooks) '90
Exploring the Titanic (Ballard) '88
Fine White Dust (Rylant) '86
For Laughing Out Loud (Prelutsky) '91
Franklin Delano Roosevelt (Freedman) '90
Frog Prince (Berenzy) '89

Ghost Drum (Price) '87
Goats (Cole) '87
Good Courage (Tolan) '88
Great American Gold Rush (Blumberg) '89
Great Little Madison (Fritz) '89
Green Futures of Tycho (Sleator) '81
Haunting (Mahy) '82
Healer (Dickinson) '85
Heartbeats (Sieruta) '89
Hero and the Crown (McKinley) '84
Hey World, Here I Am! (Little) '89
How It Feels When a Parent Dies (Krementz) '81
In a Dark, Dark Room (Schwartz) '84
In Summer Light (Oneal) '85
In the Year of the Boar and Jackie Robinson (Lord) '84
Indian Chiefs (Freedman) '87
Interstellar Pig (Sleator) '84
Into a Strange Land (Ashabranner & Ashabranner) '87
Jeremy Visick (Wiseman) '81
Journey (Hamanaka) '90
Kid in the Red Jacket (Park) '87
Knights of the Kitchen Table (Scieszka) '91
Libby on Wednesday (Snyder) '90
Light in the Attic (Silverstein) '81
Like Jake and Me (Jukes) '84
Lincoln (Freedman) '87
Lon Po Po (Young) '89
Loving Ben (Laird) '89
Lyddie (Paterson) '91
Midnight Horse (Fleischman) '90
Midnight Hour Encores (Brooks) '86
More Stories Julian Tells (Cameron) '86
Moves Make the Man (Brooks) '84
Mummy, the Will, and the Crypt (Bellairs) '83
My Name Is Sus5an Smith. The 5 Is Silent (Plummer) '91
My War with Goggle-Eyes (Fine) '89
New Kid on the Block (Prelutsky) '84
Next-Door Neighbors (Ellis) '90
No Kidding (Brooks) '89
Nothing but the Truth (Avi) '91
Number the Stars (Lowry) '89
On My Honor (Bauer) '86
Our Sixth-Grade Sugar Babies (Bunting) '90
Paradise Cafe (Brooks) '90
Pennywhistle Tree (Smith) '91

*People Could Fly (Hamilton) '85
Phoenix Rising (Grant) '89
*Playing Beatie Bow (Park) '82
Poetspeak (Janeczko) '83
Princess Ashley (Peck) '87
*Ralph S. Mouse (Cleary) '82
Redwall (Jacques) '87
Reluctantly Alice (Naylor) '91
Remarkable Journey of Prince Jen (Alexander) '91
*Remembering the Good Times (Peck) '85
*Return (Levitin) '87
*Return to Bitter Creek (Smith) '86
*Root Cellar (Lunn) '83
Rosemary's Witch (Turner) '91
*Sarah, Plain and Tall (MacLachlan) '85
*Saturnalia (Fleischman) '90
Seventeen Against the Dealer (Voigt) '89
*Shining Company (Sutcliff) '90
Shoebag (James) '90
*Sign of the Beaver (Speare) '83
Sixteen (Gallo) '84
*Something Big Has Been Here (Prelutsky) '90
*Stepping on the Cracks (Hahn) '91
*Sweet Whispers, Brother Rush (Hamilton) '82
*Sweetgrass (Hudson) '89
Sydney, Herself (Rodowsky) '89
*Tancy (Hurmence) '84
Time Train (Fleischman) '91
*Traitor (Fritz) '81
Trial of Anna Cotman (Alcock) '90
Tricksters (Mahy) '87

*True Confessions of Charlotte Doyle (Avi) '90
*Truth about Unicorns (Giblin) '91
25¢ Miracle (Nelson) '86
*Village by the Sea (Fox) '88
Voices from the Civil War (Meltzer) '89
*Voyage of the Frog (Paulsen) '89
*Way Things Work (Macaulay) '88
*Way to Sattin Shore (Pearce) '84
*Weasel (DeFelice) '90
*Whipping Boy (Fleischman) '86
*White Peak Farm (Doherty) '90
Wise Child (Furlong) '87
*Wish Giver (Brittain) '83
Witch Baby (Block) '91
Witch Week (Jones) '82
Wolf of Shadows (Strieber) '85
*Woodsong (Paulsen) '90
Year without Michael (Pfeffer) '87

Taylor

Sydney Taylor Manuscript Award
Association of Jewish Libraries, c/o National Foundation for Jewish Culture, Room 1034, 15 East 26th St., New York, NY 10010. 212-678-8092

This annual award was established to encourage outstanding new books on Jewish themes that would be of interest to all children. The award consists of $1000.

*Never to Forget (Meltzer) '77

BIBLIOGRAPHY BY AUTHOR

Aamundsen, Nina Ring. *Two Short and One Long*. Translated from the Norwegian. Houghton Mifflin 1990. (MS)

Alcock, Vivien. *The Cuckoo Sister*. Delacorte 1985. (MS-JH)

Alcock, Vivien. *Travelers by Night*. Delacorte 1985, pb Dell 1990. (MS)

Alcock, Vivien. *The Trial of Anna Cotman*. Delacorte 1990, pb Dell 1992. (MS-JH)

Alexander, Lloyd. *The High King*. Holt 1968, pb Dell 1969. (MS-JH)

Alexander, Lloyd. *The Kestrel*. Book 3 of the Westmark Trilogy. Dutton 1982, pb Dell 1983. (MS-JH)

Alexander, Lloyd. *The Remarkable Journey of Prince Jen*. Dutton 1991, pb Dell 1993. (MS-JH)

Alexander, Lloyd et al. *The Big Book for Peace*. Dutton 1990. (EL-MS)

Arnold, Caroline. *Dinosaur Mountain: Graveyard of the Past*. Clarion 1989. (MS)

Ashabranner, Brent, and Ashabranner, Melissa. *Into a Strange Land: Unaccompanied Refugee Youth in America*. Dodd Mead 1987. (MS-JH)

Atwater, Richard, and Atwater, Florence. *Mr. Popper's Penguins*. Little Brown 1938, 1988, pb Dell 1978. (EL)

Avi. *The Fighting Ground*. HarperCollins 1984, pb Trophy 1987. (MS-JH)

Avi. *Nothing But the Truth: A Documentary Novel*. Orchard 1991, pb Avon 1991. (JH)

Avi. *The True Confessions of Charlotte Doyle*. Orchard 1990, pb Avon 1990. (MS-JH)

Babbitt, Natalie. *Tuck Everlasting*. Farrar Straus & Giroux 1975, pb 1985. (MS)

Baker, Jeannie. *Window*. Greenwillow 1991, pb Puffin 1993. (EL-MS)

Baker, Leslie. *The Third-Story Cat*. Little Brown 1987, pb 1990. (EL)

Ballard, Robert D. *Exploring the Titanic*. Scholastic 1988, pb 1991. (MS-JH)

Bauer, Marion Dane. *On My Honor*. Houghton Mifflin 1987, pb Dell 1987. (MS)

Bauer, Marion Dane. *Rain of Fire*. Houghton Mifflin 1983. (MS-JH)

Bawden, Nina. *The Outside Child*. Lothrop Lee & Shepard 1989, pb Puffin 1994. (MS-JH)

Beatty, Patricia. *Charley Skedaddle*. Morrow 1987, pb Troll 1988. (MS-JH)

Bell, Clare. *Ratha's Creature*. Atheneum 1983, pb Grafton 1988. (MS-JH)

Bellairs, John. *The Mummy, the Will, and the Crypt*. Dial 1983, pb Bantam 1985. (MS)

Berenzy, Alix. *A Frog Prince*. Holt 1989, pb Owlet 1991. (MS-JH)

Bergman, Tamar. *Along the Tracks*. Translated from the Hebrew by Michael Swirsky. Houghton Mifflin 1991, pb 1995. (MS)

Block, Francesca Lia. *Witch Baby*. HarperCollins 1991, pb Trophy 1992. (JH)

Blos, Joan W. *A Gathering of Days: A New England Girl's Journal, 1830-32*. Macmillan 1979, pb 1990. (MS)

Blumberg, Rhoda. *The Great American Gold Rush*. Bradbury 1989. (MS-JH)

Bond, Nancy. *A String in the Harp*. Macmillan 1976. (MS)

Bridgers, Sue Ellen. *All Together Now*. Knopf 1979, pb Bantam 1990. (MS)

Brink, Carol Ryrie. *Caddie Woodlawn*. Macmillan 1935, 1973, pb 1990. (MS)

Brittain, Bill. *Devil's Donkey.* HarperCollins 1981, pb 1982. (MS)

Brittain, Bill. *The Wish Giver: Three Tales of Coven Tree.* HarperColllins 1983, pb 1985. (MS)

Brooke, William. *A Telling of the Tales: Five Stories.* HarperCollins 1990, pb 1993. (MS)

Brooks, Bruce. *Everywhere.* Harper & Row 1990, pb Trophy 1992. (MS-JH)

Brooks, Bruce. *Midnight Hour Encores.* HarperCollins 1986, pb 1988. (JH)

Brooks, Bruce. *The Moves Make the Man.* HarperCollins 1984, pb 1987. (JH)

Brooks, Bruce. *No Kidding.* HarperCollins 1989, pb 1991. (JH)

Brooks, Martha. *Paradise Cafe, and Other Stories.* Joy Street 1990, pb Scholastic 1993. (JH)

Bunting, Eve. *One More Flight.* Warne 1976. (MS)

Bunting, Eve. *Our Sixth-Grade Sugar Babies.* HarperCollins 1990, pb 1992. (MS)

Butler, Beverly. *Maggie by My Side.* Dodd Mead 1987. (MS-JH)

Butterworth, Emma M. *As the Waltz Was Ending.* Four Winds 1982, pb Scholastic 1991. (JH)

Byars, Betsy. *The Animal, The Vegetable, and John D. Jones.* Delacorte 1982, 1992, pb 1983. (MS)

Byars, Betsy. *Bingo Brown and the Language of Love.* Viking 1989, pb Puffin 1991. (MS)

Byars, Betsy. *Bingo Brown, Gypsy Lover.* Viking 1990, pb Puffin 1992. (MS-JH)

Byars, Betsy. *The Burning Questions of Bingo Brown.* Viking 1988, pb Puffin 1990. (MS)

Byars, Betsy. *Cracker Jackson.* Viking 1985, pb Puffin 1986. (MS)

Byars, Betsy. *The Cybil War.* Viking 1981, pb Puffin 1990. (MS)

Byars, Betsy. *The Night Swimmers.* Delacorte 1980, pb Dell 1983. (MS)

Byars, Betsy. *Summer of the Swans.* Viking 1970, pb Puffin 1984. (MS)

Byars, Betsy. *The Two-Thousand-Pound Goldfish.* Harper & Row 1982, pb Scholastic 1991. (MS)

Cameron, Ann. *More Stories Julian Tells.* Knopf 1986, pb 1989. (EL-MS)

Cassedy, Sylvia. *Behind the Attic Wall.* Crowell 1983, pb Avon 1985. (MS)

Choi, Sook Nyul. *Year of Impossible Goodbyes.* Houghton Mifflin 1991, pb Dell 1993. (MS-JH)

Cleary, Beverly. *Dear Mr. Henshaw.* Morrow 1983, pb Dell 1984. (MS-JH)

Cleary, Beverly. *A Girl from Yamhill: A Memoir.* Morrow 1988, pb Dell 1989. (MS-JH)

Cleary, Beverly. *Ralph S. Mouse.* Morrow 1982, pb Dell 1983. (EL-MS)

Cleary, Beverly. *Ramona and Her Father.* Morrow 1977, pb Avon 1990. (EL-MS)

Cleary, Beverly. *Ramona and Her Mother.* Morrow 1979, pb Avon 1990. (EL-MS)

Cleary, Beverly. *Ramona Quimby, Age 8.* Morrow 1981, Dell 1982. (EL-MS)

Cole, Brock. *The Goats.* Farrar Straus & Giroux 1987, pb 1990. (MS-JH)

Collier, James Lincoln, and Collier, Christopher. *My Brother Sam Is Dead.* Four Winds 1974, Scholastic 1977, pb 1985. (MS-JH)

Conrad, Pam. *Prairie Songs.* Harper & Row 1985, pb 1987. (MS-JH)

Conrad, Pam. *Stonewords: A Ghost Story.* HarperCollins 1990, pb 1991. (MS-JH)

Cooper, Susan. *The Dark Is Rising.* Macmillan 1973, pb 1986. (MS-JH)

Cooper, Susan. *The Grey King.* Part of "The Dark Is Rising" sequence. Macmillan 1975, pb Collier Macmillan 1986. (MS-JH)

Cresswell, Helen. *The Secret World of Polly Flint.* Macmillan 1984, Aladdin 1991. (MS-JH)

Crew, Linda. *Children of the River.* Delacorte 1989, pb Dell 1991. (JH)

Crew, Linda. *Nekomah Creek.* Delacorte 1991, pb Dell 1993. (MS)

Cross, Gillian. *Chartbreaker.* Holiday 1987, pb Dell 1989. (JH)

Cross, Gillian. *Wolf.* Holiday 1991, pb Scholastic 1993. (JH)

Crutcher, Chris. *Athletic Shorts.* Greenwillow 1991, pb Dell 1992. (JH)

Cunningham, Julia. *Come to the Edge.* Pantheon 1977. (MS)

Cunningham, Julia. *The Silent Voice.* Dutton 1981. (MS-JH)

Dahl, Roald. *The Witches*. Farrar Straus & Giroux 1983, pb Puffin 1989. (EL–MS)

Davis, Jenny. *Checking on the Moon*. Orchard 1991, pb Dell 1993. (MS–JH)

De Angeli, Marguerite. *The Door in the Wall: A Story of Medieval London*. Doubleday 1949, 1968, Dell 1990. (MS)

DeFelice, Cynthia. *Weasel*. Macmillan 1990, pb Avon 1991. (MS–JH)

Dickinson, Peter. *Eva*. Delacorte 1989, pb Dell 1990. (JH)

Dickinson, Peter. *Healer*. Delacorte 1985, pb Dell 1987. (JH)

Dickinson, Peter. *Merlin Dreams*. Delacorte 1988. (MS–JH)

Doherty, Berlie. *White Peak Farm*. Orchard 1990. (MS–JH)

Duane, Diane. *Deep Wizardry*. Delacorte 1985, pb Dell 1992. (MS–JH)

Eckert, Allan W. *The Incident at Hawk's Hill*. Dell 1972, pb Bantam 1987, pb Little Brown 1995. (MS–JH)

Ellis, Sarah. *A Family Project*. Macmillan 1988, pb Dell 1991. (MS–JH)

Ellis, Sarah. *Next-Door Neighbors*. Macmillan 1990, Douglas & McIntyre 1990. (MS)

Ellis, Sarah. *Pick-up Sticks*. Douglas & McIntyre 1991, Macmillan 1992, pb Doublas & McIntyre 1992. (MS–JH)

Engdahl, Sylvia Louise. *Enchantress from the Stars*. Atheneum 1980, pb Collier Macmillan 1989. (JH)

Fine, Anne. *My War with Goggle-Eyes*. Little Brown 1989, pb 1990. (MS–JH)

Fleischman, Paul. *The Borning Room*. HarperCollins 1991, pb Trophy 1993. (MS–JH)

Fleischman, Paul. *Joyful Noise: Poems for Two Voices*. Harper & Row 1988. (MS–JH)

Fleischman, Paul. *Saturnalia*. Harper & Row 1990, pb 1992. (MS–JH)

Fleischman, Paul. *Time Train*. HarperCollins 1991. (EL)

Fleischman, Sid. *The Midnight Horse*. Greenwillow 1990, pb Dell 1992. (MS)

Fleischman, Sid. *The Whipping Boy*. Greenwillow 1986, pb Troll 1987. (MS)

Forbes, Esther. *Johnny Tremain: A Novel for Old and Young*. Houghton Mifflin 1943, pb Dell 1987. (MS–JH)

Foreman, Michael. *War Boy: A Country Childhood*. Arcade 1990. (MS–JH)

Fox, Paula. *Monkey Island*. Orchard 1991, pb Dell 1993. (MS–JH)

Fox, Paula. *One-Eyed Cat*. Bradbury 1984, pb Dell 1985. (MS–JH)

Fox, Paula. *A Place Apart*. Farrar Straus & Giroux 1980, pb NAL Dutton 1982. (MS–JH)

Fox, Paula. *The Slave Dancer*. Macmillan 1982, pb Dell 1975. (MS–JH)

Fox, Paula. *The Village by the Sea*. Franklin Watts 1988, pb Dell 1990. (MS–JH)

Freedman, Russell. *Franklin Delano Roosevelt*. Houghton Mifflin 1990, pb 1992. (MS–JH)

Freedman, Russell. *Indian Chiefs*. Holiday 1987. (MS–JH)

Freedman, Russell. *Lincoln: A Photobiography*. Clarion 1987. (MS–JH)

Fritz, Jean. *Bully for You, Teddy Roosevelt!* Putnam 1991. (MS–JH)

Fritz, Jean. *The Great Little Madison*. Putnam 1989. (MS–JH)

Fritz, Jean. *Traitor: The Case of Benedict Arnold*. Putnam 1981, pb Puffin 1989. (MS–JH)

Froehlich, Margaret Walden. *Hide Crawford Quick!* Houghton Mifflin 1983. (MS)

Furlong, Monica. *Wise Child*. Knopf 1987. (JH)

Gallo, Donald sel. *Sixteen: Short Stories by Outstanding Writers for Young Adults*. Delacorte 1984, pb Dell 1984. (JH)

Garfield, Leon. *The December Rose*. Viking 1986, pb Puffin 1988. (MS–JH)

George, Jean Craighead. *Julie of the Wolves*. Harper & Row 1972, pb HarperCollins 1974. (MS–JH)

George, Jean Craighead. *My Side of the Mountain*. Dutton 1988, pb Viking 1991. (MS–JH)

Geras, Adele. *My Grandmother's Stories: A Collection of Jewish Folk Tales*. Knopf 1990. (EL–MS)

Giblin, James Cross. *The Truth about Unicorns*. HarperCollins 1991. (MS–JH)

Gipson, Fred. *Old Yeller*. Harper & Row 1956, Buccaneer 1992, pb Trophy 1990. (MS)

Gish, Lillian. *An Actor's Life for Me!* Viking 1987. (MS–JH)

Glenn, Mel. *Class Dismissed II: More High School Poems.* Houghton Mifflin 1986. (JH)

Gordon, Sheila. *Waiting for the Rain: A Novel of South Africa.* Orchard 1987. (JH)

Grant, Cynthia. *Phoenix Rising; or, How to Survive Your Life.* Atheneum 1989, pb Trophy 1991. (JH)

Gray, Elizabeth Janet. *Adam of the Road.* Viking 1942, pb Puffin 1987. (MS)

Greene, Bette. *Philip Hall Likes Me, I Reckon Maybe.* Dial 1974, pb Dell 1975. (MS)

Greene, Bette. *Summer of My German Soldier.* Dial 1973, pb Bantam 1984. (MS–JH)

Gregory, Kristiana. *Jenny of the Tetons.* Harcourt Brace Jovanovich 1989, pb 1991. (MS–JH)

Gripe, Maria. *Agnes Cecilia.* Translated from the Swedish by Rika Lesser. Harper & Row 1990. (MS–JH)

Hahn, Mary Downing. *Daphne's Book.* Moughton Mifflin 1983, pb Bantam 1985. (MS–JH)

Hahn, Mary Downing. *Stepping on the Cracks.* Clarion 1991, Camelot 1992. (MS–JH)

Hall, Barbara. *Dixie Storms.* Harcourt Brace Jovanovich 1990. (JH)

Hamanaka, Sheila. *The Journey: Japanese Americans, Racism, and Renewal.* Orchard 1990. (MS–JH)

Hamilton, Virginia. *Anthony Burns: The Defeat and Triumph of a Fugitive Slave.* Knopf 1988, pb 1988. (JH)

Hamilton, Virginia. *The Bells of Christmas.* Harcourt Brace Jovanovich 1989. (MS)

Hamilton, Virginia. *The Gathering.* Book 3 of the Justice Trilogy. Greenwillow 1981, pb Harcourt 1989. (MS–JH)

Hamilton, Virginia. *M.C. Higgins, the Great.* Macmillan 1974, pb Collier 1987, pb Aladdin 1993. (MS–JH)

Hamilton, Virginia. *The Magical Adventures of Pretty Pearl.* Harper & Row 1983, pb 1986. (MS–JH)

Hamilton, Virginia. *The People Could Fly: American Black Folk Tales.* Knopf 1985, pb 1993. (EL–MS)

Hamilton, Virginia. *The Planet of Junior Brown.* Macmillan 1971, pb 1986. (MS–JH)

Hamilton, Virginia. *Sweet Whispers, Brother Rush.* Philomel 1982. (JH)

Hamilton, Virginia. *Willie Bea and the Time the Martians Landed.* Greenwillow 1983, pb Macmillan 1989. (MS–JH)

Hartling, Peter. *Crutches.* Translated from the German by Elizabeth D. Crawford. Lothrop, Lee & Shepard 1988. (MS–JH)

Harvey, Brett. *My Prairie Year: Based on the Diary of Elenore Plaisted.* Holiday 1986, pb 1993. (EL–MS)

Heide, Florence Parry. *Time's Up.* Holiday 1982. (EL–MS)

Hendry, Frances Mary. *Quest for a Maid.* Farrar Straus & Giroux 1990, pb 1992. (MS–JH)

Henkes, Kevin. *Chrysanthemum.* Greenwillow 1991. (EL)

Henry, Marguerite. *Justin Morgan Had a Horse.* Follet 1945, revised edition Rand McNally 1954, pb Macmillan 1989, pb Aladdin 1991. (MS–JH)

Henry, Marguerite. *King of the Wind.* Rand McNally 1948, pb Macmillan 1991. (MS)

Houston, James. *River Runners: A Tale of Hardship and Bravery.* Atheneum 1979, pb Puffin 1992. (MS–JH)

Hudson, Jan. *Sweetgrass.* Philmel 1989, pb Scholastic 1991. (MS–JH)

Hughes, Ted. *Tales of the Early World.* Faber & Faber 1988. (MS–JH)

Hunt, Irene. *Across Five Aprils.* Follett 1964, Silver Burdett 1993, pb Modern Curriculum 1991. (MS–JH)

Hunt, Irene. *Up a Road Slowly.* Follett 1966, pb Berkley 1987. (JH)

Hurmence, Belinda. *Tancy.* Clarion 1984. (JH)

Hurwitz, Johanna. *The Rabbi's Girls.* Morrow 1982, pb Puffin 1989. (MS)

Huynh, Quang Nhuong. *The Land I Lost: Adventures of a Boy in Vietnam.* Harper & Row 1982, 1990, pb 1986. (EL–MS)

Ish-Kishor, Sulamith. *Our Eddie.* Patheon 1969, reissue 1992. (JH)

Jacques, Brian. *Redwall.* Philomel 1987, pb Avon 1990. (MS–JH)

James, Mary. *Shoebag.* Scholastic 1990, pb 1990. (EL–MS)

Janeczko, Paul B., sel. *Poetspeak: In Their Work, About Their Work.* Bradbury 1983, pb Collier 1991. (JH)

Jones, Diana Wynne. *Castle in the Air.* Greenwillow 1991, (MS–JH)

Jones, Diana Wynne. *Howl's Moving Castle.* Greenwillow 1986. (MS–JH)

Jones, Diana Wynne. *The Lives of Christopher Chant.* Greenwillow 1988, pb McKay 1990. (MS)

Jones, Diana Wynne. *Witch Week.* Greenwillow 1982, 1993, pb Knopf 1988. (MS)

Joseph, Lynn. *A Wave in Her Pocket: Stories from Trinidad.* Clarion 1991. (MS)

Jukes, Mavis. *Blackberries in the Dark.* Knopf 1985, Knopf 1992, pb Dell 1987, pb Random 1994. (EL–MS)

Jukes, Mavis. *Like Jake and Me.* Knopf 1984, pb Knopf 1987. (EL–MS)

Keith, Harold. *Rifles for Watie.* Crowell 1957, Harper 1991, pb 1987. (MS–JH)

Kennedy, Richard. *Amy's Eyes.* HarperCollins 1985, pb 1988. (MS)

Kerr, M. E. *Gentlehands.* Harper & Row 1978. (JH)

Kherdian, David. *The Road from Home: The Story of an Armenian Girl.* Greenwillow 1979, pb Puffin 1988, pb Beech Tree 1995. (MS)

King-Smith, Dick. *Martin's Mice.* Crown 1988, pb Dell 1990. (EL–MS)

Kinsey-Warnock, Natalie. *The Canada Geese Quilt.* Cobblehill 1989, pb Dell 1992. (EL–MS)

Konigsburg, E. L. *From the Mixed-Up Files of Mrs. Basil E. Frankweiler.* Atheneum 1967, pb Dell 1977. (MS)

Konigsburg, E. L. *Up from Jericho Tel.* Atheneum 1986. (MS)

Krementz, Jill. *How It Feels to Be Adopted.* Knopf 1982. (MS–JH)

Krementz, Jill. *How It Feels When a Parent Dies.* Knopf 1981. (MS–JH)

Krementz, Jill. *How It Feels When Parents Divorce.* Knopf 1984. (MS–JH)

Krumgold, Joseph. *Onion John.* Harper & Row 1959, 1987. (MS)

Kullman, Harry. *The Battle Horse.* Macmillan 1982. (MS–JH)

Laird, Elizabeth. *Loving Ben.* Delacorte 1989. (MS–JH)

Langton, Jane. *The Fledgling.* Harper 1980, pb Harper 1981. (MS)

Latham, Jean Lee. *Carry On, Mr. Bowditch.* Houghton Mifflin 1955, pb 1973. (JH)

Lawson, Robert. *Rabbit Hill.* Viking 1944, pb Puffin 1987. (EL)

Lee, Dennis. *Garbage Delight.* Gage 1977. (EL–MS)

Le Guin, Ursula K. *The Tombs of Atuan.* Simon & Schuster 1971, pb Bantam 1984. (JH)

L'Engle, Madeleine. *A Ring of Endless Light.* Farrar Straus & Giroux 1980, pb Dell 1981. (JH)

L'Engle, Madeleine. *A Swiftly Tilting Planet.* Farrar Straus & Giroux 1978, pb Dell 1979. (JH)

L'Engle, Madeleine. *A Wrinkle in Time.* Book 1 of The Time Trilogy. Farrar Straus Giroux 1962, pb Dell 1962. (MS)

Lester, Julius. *How Many Spots Does a Leopard Have? and Other Tales.* Scholastic 1989. (EL–MS)

Levitin, Sonia. *The Return.* Atheneum 1987, pb Fawcett Juniper 1987. (MS–JH)

Lindgren, Astrid. *Ronia, the Robber's Daughter.* Translated from the Swedish by Patricia Crampton. Viking 1983, pb Puffin 1985. (MS–JH)

Lisle, Janet Taylor. *Afternoon of the Elves.* Orchard 1989, pb Apple 1991. (MS)

Little, Jean. *Hey World, Here I Am!* Harper & Row 1989, pb 1990. (MS–JH)

Little, Jean. *Little by Little: A Writer's Education.* Viking 1987, pb Puffin 1991. (MS–JH)

Livingston, Myra Cohn, sel. *Cat Poems.* Holiday 1987. (EL)

Lord, Bette Bao. *In the Year of the Boar and Jackie Robinson.* Harper & Row 1984, pb 1986. (EL–MS)

Lowry, Lois. *Anastasia Again!* Houghton Mifflin 1981, pb 1982. (MS)

Lowry, Lois. *Number the Stars.* Houghton Mifflin 1989, pb Dell 1990. (MS–JH)

Lowry, Lois. *The One Hundredth Thing about Caroline.* Houghton Mifflin 1983, pb Dell 1985. (MS)

Lowry, Lois. *Rabble Starkey.* Houghton Mifflin 1987, pb Dell 1988. (MS–JH)

Lowry, Lois. *A Summer to Die.* Houghton Mifflin 1977, pb Bantam 1984. (JH)

Lunn, Janet. *The Root Cellar.* Scribner's 1983 (c 1981), pb Lester & Orpen Dennys 1985, pb Puffin 1996. (MS–JH)

Lyon, George Ella. *Borrowed Children.* Franklin Watts 1988, pb Bantam 1990. (MS)

Macaulay, David. *Black and White.* Houghton Mifflin 1990. (EL–MS)

Macaulay, David. *Pyramid.* Houghton Mifflin 1975. (MS)

Macaulay, David. *The Way Things Work.* Houghton Mifflin 1988. (MS–JH)

MacLachlan, Patricia. *The Facts and Fictions of Minna Pratt.* Harper & Row 1988, pb HarperCollins 1990. (MS–JH)

MacLachlan, Patricia. *Sarah, Plain and Tall.* Harper & Row 1985, pb 1987. (EL–MS)

MacLachlan, Patricia. *Unclaimed Treasures.* HarperCollins 1984, pb 1987. (MS–JH)

Magorian, Michelle. *Good Night, Mr. Tom.* Harper & Row 1982. (MS–JH)

Mahy, Margaret. *The Haunting.* Atheneum 1983, pb Dell 1991. (MS)

Mahy, Margaret. *The Tricksters.* McElderry 1986, pb Scholastic 1988. (JH)

Major, Kevin. *Hold Fast.* Clarke Irwin 1978, Delacorte 1981, pb Dell 1981. (JH)

Marino, Jan. *The Day That Elvis Came to Town.* Little Brown 1991, pb Avon 1993. (JH)

Marsden, John. *So Much to Tell You.* Joy Street / Little Brown 1989, pb Fawcett Juniper 1990. (JH)

Marshall, James. *Rats on the Roof, and Other Stories.* Dial 1991. (EL–MS)

Maruki, Toshi. *Hiroshima No Pika.* Lothrop Lee & Shepard 1980, pb 1982. (EL–MS)

Mazer, Norma Fox. *After the Rain.* Morrow 1987, pb Avon 1987. (MS–JH)

Mazer, Norma Fox. *Dear Bill, Remember Me? and Other Stories.* Delacorte 1976, pb Dell 1989. (JH)

Mazer, Norma Fox. *Taking Terri Mueller.* Morrow 1983, pb Avon 1981. (MS–JH)

McKinley, Robin. *The Blue Sword.* Greenwillow 1982, pb Ace nd. (JH)

McKinley, Robin. *The Hero and the Crown.* Greenwillow 1984, pb Ace 1987. (JH)

McKinley, Robin. *Outlaws of Sherwood.* Greenwillow 1988, pb Ace 1989. (MS–JH)

Meigs, Cornelia. *Invincible Louisa: The Story of the Author of 'Little Women'.* Little Brown 1933, 1968, pb Scholastic 1988. (MS–JH)

Meltzer, Milton. *Never to Forget: The Jews of the Holocaust.* Harper & Row 1976, pb Dell 1977. (JH)

Meltzer, Milton, ed. *Voices from the Civil War: A Documentary History of the Great American Conflict.* Crowell 1989 pb Trophy 1992. (JH)

Miles, Miska. *Annie and the Old One.* Little 1972, pb 1985. (EL–MS)

Moeri, Louise. *Save Queen of Sheba!* Dutton 1981, pb Avon 1982, pb Puffin 1994. (MS)

Mohr, Nicholasa. *Nilda.* Harper & Row 1973, 2nd ed. Arte Publico 1986. (MS)

Morrison, Lillian, sel. *Rhythm Road: Poems to Move To.* Lothrop Lee & Shepard 1988. (MS–JH)

Murphy, Jim. *The Boys' War: Confederate and Union Soldiers Talk About the Civil War.* Clarion 1990, pb Clarion 1993. (MS–JH)

Myers, Walter Dean. *Fallen Angels.* Scholastic 1988, pb 1989. (JH)

Myers, Walter Dean. *Me, Mop, and the Moondance Kid.* Doubleday 1988, pb Dell 1991. (MS)

Myers, Walter Dean. *The Young Landlords.* Viking 1979, Peter Smith 1992, pb Puffin 1989. (MS–JH)

Naylor, Phyllis Reynolds. *The Agony of Alice.* Atheneum 1985. (MS)

Naylor, Phyllis Reynolds. *Alice in Rapture, Sort of.* Atheneum 1989, pb Dell 1991. (MS)
Naylor, Phyllis Reynolds. *The Keeper.* Atheneum 1986. (JH)
Naylor, Phyllis Reynolds. *Night Cry.* Atheneum 1985. (MS-JH)
Naylor, Phyllis Reynolds. *Reluctantly Alice.* Atheneum 1991, pb Dell 1992. (MS-JH)
Naylor, Phyllis Reynolds. *Shiloh.* Macmillan 1991, Dell Yearling 1992. (MS)
Nelson, Theresa. *And One for All.* Orchard 1989, pb Dell 1991. (MS-JH)
Nelson, Theresa. *The 25 Cent Miracle.* Macmillan 1986, pb 1987. (MS-JH)
Newth, Mette. *The Abduction.* Translated from the Norwegian by Tiina Nunnally and Steve Murray. Farrar, Straus, & Giroux 1989, pb 1993. (JH)
Nixon, Joan Lowery. *The Kidnapping of Christina Lattimore.* Harcourt Brace 1979, pb Dell 1980. (MS-JH)
Nixon, Joan Lowery. *The Other Side of Dark.* Delacorte 1986, pb 1992. (JH)
Nixon, Joan Lowery. *The Seance.* Harcourt Brace 1980, pb Dell 1981. (MS-JH)
Norton, Mary. *The Borrowers Avenged.* Harcourt Brace 1982, pb Odyssey 1990. (MS)
Nostlinger, Christine. *Konrad.* Translated from the German by Anthea Bell. Avon 1983. (EL-MS)
O'Brien, Robert C. *Mrs. Frisby and the Rats of NIMH.* Atheneum 1971, pb Macmillan 1986. (MS)
O'Brien, Robert C. *Z for Zachariah.* Macmillan 1975, pb 1987. (JH)
O'Dell, Scott. *Island of the Blue Dolphins.* Houghton Mifflin 1960, pb Dell 1978. (MS-JH)
O'Dell, Scott. *Sing Down the Moon.* Houghton Mifflin 1970, pb Dell 1976. (MS)
Oneal, Zibby. *A Formal Feeling.* Viking 1982, pb Puffin 1990. (JH)
Oneal, Zibby. *In Summer Light.* Viking 1985, pb Bantam 1986. (JH)
Orlev, Uri. *The Island on Bird Street.* Translated from the Hebrew by Hillel Halkin. Houghton Mifflin 1984. (MS-JH)
Park, Barbara. *The Kid in the Red Jacket.* Knopf 1987, pb 1988, pb Bullseye 1995. (EL-MS)
Park, Ruth. *Playing Beatie Bow.* Atheneum 1982, pb Puffin 1984. (MS-JH)
Paterson, Katherine. *Bridge to Terabithia.* Crowell 1977, pb Trophy 1987. (MS-JH)
Paterson, Katherine. *Come Sing, Jimmy Jo.* Dutton 1985, pb Avon 1986. (MS-JH)
Paterson, Katherine. *The Great Gilly Hopkins.* T. Y. Crowell 1978, pb HarperCollins 1987. (MS)
Paterson, Katherine. *Jacob Have I Loved.* Crowell 1980, pb Avon 1981, pb Harper 1990. (MS-JH)
Paterson, Katherine. *Lyddie.* Dutton 1991, pb Puffin 1992. (MS-JH)
Paulsen, Gary. *The Cookcamp.* Orchard 1991, pb Dell 1992. (MS-JH)
Paulsen, Gary. *Dogsong.* Bradbury 1985, pb Puffin 1987. (MS-JH)
Paulsen, Gary. *Hatchet.* Macmillan 1987, pb Puffin 1988. (MS-JH)
Paulsen, Gary. *The Voyage of the Frog.* Orchard 1989, pb Dell 1990. (MS-JH)
Paulsen, Gary. *The Winter Room.* Orchard 1989, pb Dell 1991. (MS-JH)
Paulsen, Gary. *Woodsong.* Bradbury 1990, pb Puffin 1991. (MS-JH)
Pearce, Philippa. *The Way to Sattin Shore.* Peter Smith nd, Greenwillow 1983, pb Puffin 1985. (MS-JH)
Pearson, Kit. *The Sky Is Falling.* Viking 1989, Viking 1990. (MS-JH)
Peck, Richard. *Are You in the House Alone?* Viking 1975, pb Dell 1976. (JH)
Peck, Richard. *Blossom Culp and the Sleep of Death.* Delacorte 1986, pb Dell 1994. (MS)
Peck, Richard. *Princess Ashley.* Delacorte 1987, pb Dell 1988. (JH)
Peck, Richard. *Remembering the Good Times.* Delacorte 1985, pb Dell 1986. (JH)
Peet, Bill. *Bill Peet: An Autobiography.* Houghton Mifflin 1989, pb 1994. (EL-MS)
Pfeffer, Susan Beth. *The Year without Michael.* Bantam 1987, pb 1988. (JH)
Phipson, Joan. *Hit and Run.* Atheneum 1985, pb Macmillan 1989. (JH)
Pinkwater, Jill. *Buffalo Brenda.* Macmillan 1989, pb Aladdin 1992. (MS-JH)

Plummer, Louise. *My Name Is Sus5an Smith. The 5 Is Silent.* Delacorte 1991. (JH)

Prelutsky, Jack, sel. *For Laughing Out Loud: Poems to Tickle Your Funnybone.* Knopf 1991. (EL–MS)

Prelutsky, Jack. *The New Kid on the Block.* Greenwillow 1984. (EL–MS)

Prelutsky, Jack, sel. *Poems of A. Nonny Mouse.* Knopf 1989, pb 1991. (EL–MS)

Prelutsky, Jack. *Something Big Has Been Here.* Greenwillow 1990. (EL–MS)

Price, Susan. *The Ghost Drum: A Cat's Tale.* Farrar Straus & Giroux 1987, pb 1989. (MS–JH)

Raskin, Ellen. *The Westing Game.* Dutton 1978, pb Avon 1984. (MS–JH)

Reeder, Carolyn. *Shades of Gray.* Macmillan 1989, pb Avon 1989. (MS–JH)

Reiss, Johanna. *The Upstairs Room.* Harper 1972, Crowell 1987, pb HarperCollins 1990. (MS–JH)

Reuter, Bjarne. *Buster's World.* Translated from the Danish by Anthea Bell. Dutton 1989, pb Puffin 1991. (MS)

Roberts, Willo Davis. *Megan's Island.* Atheneum 1988, pb Aladdin 1990. (MS–JH)

Rodowsky, Colby. *Sydney, Herself.* Farrar Straus & Giroux 1989, pb 1993. (MS–JH)

Rostkowski, Margaret I. *After the Dancing Days.* HarperCollins 1986, pb 1988. (MS–JH)

Roth-Hano, Renee. *Touch Wood: A Girlhood in Occupied France.* Macmillan 1988, pb Puffin 1989. (JH)

Rylant, Cynthia. *A Blue-Eyed Daisy.* Macmillan 1985, pb Dell 1987. (MS–JH)

Rylant, Cynthia. *A Fine White Dust.* Macmillan 1986, pb Dell 1987. (MS–JH)

Sachs, Marilyn. *Fran Ellen's House.* Dutton 1987, pb Avon 1989. (MS)

Schwartz, Alvin, sel. *In a Dark, Dark Room, and Other Scary Stories.* Harper & Row 1984, pb Trophy 1985. (MS)

Schwartz, Howard, and Rush, Barbara, sels. *The Diamond Tree: Jewish Tales from Around the World.* HarperCollins 1991 (EL–MS)

Scieszka, Jon. *The Frog Prince, Continued.* Viking 1991. (EL–MS)

Scieszka, Jon. *Knights of the Kitchen Table.* Viking 1991, pb Puffin 1993. (EL–MS)

Scieszka, Jon. *The True Story of the Three Little Pigs, by A. Wolf.* Viking 1989. (EL)

Sebestyen, Ouida. *Words by Heart.* Little Brown 1979, pb Bantam 1983. (MS–JH)

Segal, Jerry. *The Place Where Nobody Stopped.* Orchard 1991. (MS–JH)

Semel, Nava. *Becoming Gershona.* Translated from the Hebrew by Seymour Simkes. Viking 1990, pb Puffin 1992. (MS)

Sherman, Eileen Bluestone. *Monday in Odessa.* Jewish Publ. Soc. 1986. (MS–JH)

Shura, Mary Frances. *The Josie Gambit.* Dodd Mead 1986, pb Avon 1988. (MS–JH)

Sieruta, Peter. *Heartbeats, and Other Stories.* Harper & Row 1989, pb Trophy 1991. (JH)

Silverstein, Shel. *A Light in the Attic.* Harper & Row 1981. (EL–MS)

Sleator, William. *The Boy Who Reversed Himself.* Dutton 1986, pb Bantam 1990. (MS–JH)

Sleator, William. *The Duplicate.* Dutton 1988, pb Bantam 1990. (JH)

Sleator, William. *The Green Futures of Tycho.* Dutton 1981, pb Puffin 1991. (MS–JH)

Sleator, William. *Interstellar Pig.* Dutton 1984, pb Bantam 1986. (JH)

Slepian, Jan. *The Broccoli Tapes.* Putnam 1989, pb Scholastic 1990. (MS–JH)

Slepian, Jan. *Lester's Turn.* Macmillan 1981. (MS–JH)

Smith, Doris Buchanan. *The First Hard Times.* Viking 1983, pb Puffin 1990. (MS)

Smith, Doris Buchanan. *The Pennywhistle Tree.* Putnam 1991. (MS–JH)

Smith, Doris Buchanan. *Return to Bitter Creek.* Viking 1986, pb Puffin 1988. (MS–JH)

Smucker, Barbara Claassen. *Days of Terror.* Clarke Irwin 1979, pb Puffin 1981. (MS–JH)

Snyder, Zilpha Keatley. *The Headless Cupid.* Atheneum 1971, pb Dell 1985. (MS–JH)

Snyder, Zilpha Keatley. *Libby on Wednesday.* Delacorte 1990, pb Dell 1991. (MS–JH)

Snyder, Zilpha Keatley. *The Witches of Worm.* Atheneum 1972, pb Dell 1986. (MS–JH)

Speare, Elizabeth George. *The Bronze Bow.* Houghton Mifflin 1961, pb Houghton Mifflin 1973. (JH)

Speare, Elizabeth George. *The Sign of the Beaver*. Houghton Mifflin 1983, pb Dell 1993. (MS-JH)

Speare, Elizabeth George. *The Witch of Blackbird Pond*. Houghton Mifflin 1958, pb Dell 1972. (MS-JH)

Sperry, Armstrong. *Call It Courage*. Macmillan 1940, pb Aladdin 1990. (MS)

Spinelli, Jerry. *Maniac Magee*. Little Brown 1990, pb HarperCollins 1992. (MS-JH)

Staples, Suzanne Fisher. *Shabanu: Daughter of the Wind*. Knopf 1989. (JH)

Strieber, Whitley. *Wolf of Shadows*. Knopf 1985. (JH)

Sutcliff, Rosemary. *The Shining Company*. Farrar Straus & Giroux 1990, pb 1992. (JH)

Taylor, Mildred D. *The Friendship*. Dial 1987, pb Bantam 1989 (with *The Gold Cadillac*). (MS-JH)

Taylor, Mildred D. *The Gold Cadillac*. Dial 1987, pb Bantam 1989 (with *The Friendship*). (MS-JH)

Taylor, Mildred D. *Let the Circle Be Unbroken*. Dial 1981, Bantam 1983. (MS-JH)

Taylor, Mildred D. *Mississippi Bridge*. Dial 1990, pb Bantam 1992. (MS-JH)

Taylor, Mildred D. *The Road to Memphis*. Dial 1990. (JH)

Taylor, Mildred D. *Roll of Thunder, Hear My Cry*. (MS-JH)

Thesman, Jean. *Rachel Chance*. Houghton Mifflin 1990, pb Avon 1990. (MS-JH)

Tolan, Stephanie. *A Good Courage*. Morrow 1988. (JH)

Turner, Ann. *Dakota Dugout*. Macmillan 1985, pb 1989. (EL)

Turner, Ann. *Rosemary's Witch*. HarperCollins 1991, pb 1994. (MS-JH)

Uchida, Yoshiko. *The Best Bad Thing*. Atheneum 1983, pb Macmillan 1986. (MS)

Van Allsburg, Chris. *Jumanji*. Houghton Mifflin 1981. (MS)

Van Allsburg, Chris. *Polar Express*. Houghton Mifflin 1985. (EL)

Voigt, Cynthia. *Building Blocks*. Macmillan 1984, pb Fawcett 1985. (MS-JH)

Voigt, Cynthia. *The Callender Papers*. Macmillan 1983, pb Ballantine 1984. (MS-JH)

Voigt, Cynthia. *Dicey's Song*. Macmillan 1982, Fawcett 1984. (MS-JH)

Voigt, Cynthia. *Seventeen Against the Dealer*. Macmillan 1989, pb Fawcett 1990. (JH)

Voigt, Cynthia. *A Solitary Blue*. Atheneum / McClelland & Stewart 1983, pb Fawcett 1987. (MS-JH)

Walter, Mildred Pitts. *Justin and the Best Biscuits in the World*. Lothrop Lee and Shepard 1986. (EL-MS)

Westall, Robert. *The Machine Gunners*. Greenwillow 1976, pb Knopf 1990. (MS-JH)

White, E. B. *Charlotte's Web*. Harper & Row 1952, pb Trophy 1974. (EL-MS)

Wieler, Diana. *Bad Boy*. Douglas & McIntyre 1989, pb Delacorte 1992. (JH)

Wilder, Laura Ingalls. *By the Shores of Silver Lake*. Harper 1939, HarperCollins 1961, pb HarperCollins 1971. (MS)

Wilder, Laura Ingalls. *Little Town on the Prairie*. Harper 1941, HarperCollins 1961. (MS)

Willard, Nancy. *A Visit to William Blake's Inn: Poems for Innocent and Experienced Travelers*. Harcourt Brace 1981, pb Voyager/Harcourt 1982. (EL-MS)

Windsor, Patricia. *The Sandman's Eyes*. Delacorte 1985, pb Dell 1992. (JH)

Wiseman, David. *Jeremy Visick*. Houghton Mifflin 1981, pb 1990. (MS)

Wolff, Virginia Euwer. *The Mozart Season*. Holt 1991, pb Scholastic 1993. (MS-JH)

Wrede, Patricia. *Dealing with Dragons*. Harcourt 1990, pb Scholastic 1992. (MS-JH)

Yep, Laurence. *Dragon of the Lost Sea*. Harper 1982, pb 1988. (MS-JH)

Yolen, Jane. *The Devil's Arithmetic*. Viking 1988, pb Puffin 1990. (MS-JH)

Yolen, Jane. *The Girl Who Cried Flowers, and Other Tales*. HarperCollins 1974. (EL-MS)

Young, Ed. trans. *Lon Po Po: A Red-Riding-Hood Story from China*. Philomel 1989. (EL-MS)

BIBLIOGRAPHY BY AGE LEVEL

Elementary

Annie and the Old One (Miles)
Big Book for Peace (Alexander et al.)
Bill Peet (Peet)
Black and White (Macaulay)
Blackberries in the Dark (Jukes)
Canada Geese Quilt (Kinsey-Warnock)
Cat Poems (Livingston)
Charlotte's Web (White)
Chrysanthemum (Henkes)
Dakota Dugout (Turner)
Diamond Tree (Schwartz & Rush)
For Laughing Out Loud (Prelutsky)
Frog Prince, Continued (Scieszka)
Garbage Delight (Lee)
Girl Who Cried Flowers (Yolen)
Hiroshima No Pika (Maruki)
How Many Spots Does a Leopard Have? (Lester)
In the Year of the Boar and Jackie Robinson (Lord)
Justin and the Best Biscuits in the World (Walter)
Kid in the Red Jacket (Park)
Knights of the Kitchen Table (Scieszka)
Konrad (Nostlinger)
Land I Lost (Huynh)
Light in the Attic (Silverstein)
Like Jake and Me (Jukes)
Lon Po Po (Young)
Martin's Mice (King-Smith)
More Stories Julian Tells (Cameron)
Mr. Popper's Penguins (Atwater and Atwater)
My Grandmother's Stories (Geras)
My Prairie Year (Harvey)
New Kid on the Block (Prelutsky)
People Could Fly (Hamilton)
Poems of A. Nonny Mouse (Prelutsky)
Polar Express (Van Allsburg)
Rabbit Hill (Lawson)
Ralph S. Mouse (Cleary)
Ramona and Her Father (Cleary)
Ramona and Her Mother (Cleary)
Ramona Quimby, Age 8 (Cleary)
Rats on the Roof (Marshall)
Rhythm Road (Morrison)
Sarah, Plain and Tall (MacLachlan)
Shoebag (James)
Something Big Has Been Here (Prelutsky)
Third-Story Cat (Baker)
Time Train (Fleischman)
Time's Up (Heide)
True Story of the Three Little Pigs, by A. Wolf (Scieszka)
Visit to William Blake's Inn (Willard)
Window (Baker)
Witches (Dahl)

Middle School

Across Five Aprils (Hunt)
Actor's Life for Me! (Gish)
Adam of the Road (Gray)
After the Dancing Days (Rostowski)
After the Rain (Mazer)
Afternoon of the Elves (Lisle)
Agnes Cecilia (Gripe)
Agony of Alice (Naylor)
Alice in Rapture, Sort Of (Naylor)
All Together Now (Bridgers)
Along the Tracks (Bergman)
Amy's Eyes (Kennedy)
Anastasia Again! (Lowry)
And One for All (Nelson)
Animal, the Vegetable, and John D. Jones (Byars)
Annie and the Old One (Miles)
Battle Horse (Kullman)
Becoming Gershona (Semel)
Behind the Attic Wall (Cassedy)
Bells of Christmas (Hamilton)
Best Bad Thing (Uchida)
Big Book for Peace (Alexander et al.)
Bill Peet (Peet)
Bingo Brown and the Language of Love (Byars)
Bingo Brown, Gypsy Lover (Byars)
Black and White (Macaulay)
Blackberries in the Dark (Jukes)
Blossom Culp and the Sleep of Death (Peck)
Blue-Eyed Daisy (Rylant)
Borning Room (Fleischman)

Borrowed Children (Lyon)
Borrowers Avenged (Norton)
Boy Who Reversed Himself (Sleator)
Boys' War (Murphy)
Bridge to Terabithia (Paterson)
Broccoli Tapes (Slepian)
Buffalo Brenda (Pinkwater)
Building Blocks (Voigt)
Bully for You, Teddy Roosevelt! (Fritz)
Burning Questions of Bingo Brown
  (Byars)
Buster's World (Reuter)
By the Shores of Silver Lake (Wilder)
Caddie Woodlawn (Brink)
Call It Courage (Sperry)
Callender Papers (Voigt)
Canada Geese Quilt (Kinsey-Warnock)
Carry On, Mr. Bowditch (Latham)
Castle in the Air (Jones)
Cat Poems (Livingston)
Charley Skedaddle (Beatty)
Charlotte's Web (White)
Checking on the Moon (Davis)
Come Sing, Jimmy Jo (Paterson)
Come to the Edge (Cunningham)
Cookcamp (Paulsen)
Cracker Jackson (Byars)
Crutches (Hartling)
Cuckoo Sister (Alcock)
Cybil War (Byars)
Daphne's Book (Hahn)
Dark Is Rising (Cooper)
Days of Terror (Smucker)
Dealing with Dragons (Wrede)
Dear Bill, Remember Me? (Mazer)
Dear Mr. Henshaw (Cleary)
December Rose (Garfield)
Deep Wizardry (Duane)
Devil's Arithmetic (Yolen)
Devil's Donkey (Brittain)
Diamond Tree (Schwartz & Rush)
Dicey's Song (Voigt)
Dinosaur Mountain (Arnold)
Dogsong (Paulsen)
Door in the Wall (De Angeli)
Dragon of the Lost Sea (Yep)
Everywhere (Brooks)
Exploring the Titanic (Ballard)
Facts and Fictions of Minna Pratt (Ma-
  cLachlan)
Family Project (Ellis)
Fighting Ground (Avi)
Fine White Dust (Rylant)
First Hard Times (Smith)
Fledgling (Langton)
For Laughing Out Loud (Prelutsky)

Fran Ellen's House (Sachs)
Franklin Delano Roosevelt (Freedman)
Friendship (Taylor)
Frog Prince (Berenzy)
Frog Prince, Continued (Scieszka)
From the Mixed-Up Files of Mrs. Basil
  E. Frankweiler (Konigsburg)
Garbage Delight (Lee)
Gathering (Hamilton)
Gathering of Days (Blos)
Ghost Drum (Price)
Girl from Yamhill (Cleary)
Girl Who Cried Flowers (Yolen)
Goats (Cole)
Gold Cadillac (Taylor)
Good Night, Mr. Tom (Magorian)
Great American Gold Rush (Blumberg)
Great Gilly Hopkins (Paterson)
Great Little Madison (Fritz)
Green Futures of Tycho (Sleator)
Grey King (Cooper)
Hatchet (Paulsen)
Haunting (Mahy)
Headless Cupid (Snyder)
Hey World, Here I Am! (Little)
Hide Crawford Quick! (Froehlich)
High King (Alexander)
Hiroshima No Pika (Maruki)
How It Feels to Be Adopted (Krementz)
How It Feels When a Parent Dies (Kre-
  mentz)
How It Feels When Parents Divorce (Kre-
  mentz)
How Many Spots Does a Leopard Have?
  (Lester)
Howl's Moving Castle (Jones)
In a Dark, Dark Room (Schwartz)
In the Year of the Boar and Jackie
  Robinson (Lord)
Incident at Hawk's Hill (Eckert)
Indian Chiefs (Freedman)
Into a Strange Land (Ashabranner & As-
  habranner)
Invincible Louisa (Meigs)
Island of the Blue Dolphins (O'Dell)
Island on Bird Street (Orlev)
Jacob Have I Loved (Paterson)
Jenny of the Tetons (Gregory)
Jeremy Visick (Wiseman)
Johnny Tremain (Forbes)
Josie Gambit (Shura)
Journey (Hamanaka)
Joyful Noise (Fleischman)
Julie of the Wolves (George)
Jumanji (Van Allsburg)
Justin and the Best Biscuits in the

Silent Voice (Cunningham)
Sing Down the Moon (O'Dell)
Sky Is Falling (Pearson)
Slave Dancer (Fox)
Solitary Blue (Voigt)
Something Big Has Been Here (Prelutsky)
Stepping on the Cracks (Hahn)
Stonewords (Conrad)
String in the Harp (Bond)
Summer of My German Soldier (Greene)
Summer of the Swans (Byars)
Sweetgrass (Hudson)
Sydney, Herself (Rodowsky)
Taking Terri Mueller (Mazer)
Tales of the Early World (Hughes)
Telling of the Tales (Brooke)
Time's Up (Heide)
Traitor (Fritz)
Travelers by Night (Alcock)
Trial of Anna Cotman (Alcock)
True Confessions of Charlotte Doyle (Avi)
Truth about Unicorns (Giblin)
Tuck Everlasting (Babbitt)
25¢ Miracle (Nelson)
Two Short and One Long (Aamundsen)
Two-Thousand-Pound Goldfish (Byars)
Unclaimed Treasures (MacLachlan)
Up from Jericho Tel (Konigsburg)
Upstairs Room (Reiss)
Village by the Sea (Fox)
Visit to William Blake's Inn (Willard)
Voyage of the Frog (Paulsen)
War Boy (Foreman)
Wave in Her Pocket (Joseph)
Way Things Work (Macaulay)
Way to Sattin Shore (Pearce)
Weasel (DeFelice)
Westing Game (Raskin)
Whipping Boy (Fleischman)
White Peak Farm (Doherty)
Willie Bea and the Time the Martians Landed (Hamilton)
Window (Baker)
Winter Room (Paulsen)
Wish Giver (Brittain)
Witch of Blackbird Pond (Speare)
Witch Week (Jones)
Witches (Dahl)
Witches of Worm (Snyder)
Woodsong (Paulsen)
Words by Heart (Sebestyen)
Wrinkle in Time (L'Engle)
Year of Impossible Goodbyes (Choi)
Young Landlords (Myers)

Junior High

Abduction (Newth)
Across Five Aprils (Hunt)
Actor's Life for Me! (Gish)
After the Dancing Days (Rostowski)
After the Rain (Mazer)
Agnes Cecilia (Gripe)
And One for All (Nelson)
Anthony Burns (Hamilton)
Are You in the House Alone? (Peck)
As the Waltz Was Ending (Butterworth)
Athletic Shorts (Crutcher)
Bad Boy (Wieler)
Battle Horse (Kullman)
Bingo Brown, Gypsy Lover (Byars)
Blue Sword (McKinley)
Blue-Eyed Daisy (Rylant)
Borning Room (Fleischman)
Boy Who Reversed Himself (Sleator)
Boys' War (Murphy)
Bridge to Terabithia (Paterson)
Broccoli Tapes (Slepian)
Bronze Bow (Speare)
Buffalo Brenda (Pinkwater)
Building Blocks (Voigt)
Bully for You, Teddy Roosevelt! (Fritz)
Callender Papers (Voigt)
Carry On, Mr. Bowditch (Latham)
Castle in the Air (Jones)
Charley Skedaddle (Beatty)
Chartbreaker (Cross)
Checking on the Moon (Davis)
Children of the River (Crew)
Class Dismissed II (Glenn)
Come Sing, Jimmy Jo (Paterson)
Cookcamp (Paulsen)
Crutches (Hartling)
Cuckoo Sister (Alcock)
Daphne's Book (Hahn)
Dark Is Rising (Cooper)
Day That Elvis Came to Town (Marino)
Days of Terror (Smucker)
Dealing with Dragons (Wrede)
Dear Bill, Remember Me? (Mazer)
Dear Mr. Henshaw (Cleary)
December Rose (Garfield)
Deep Wizardry (Duane)
Devil's Arithmetic (Yolen)
Dicey's Song (Voigt)
Dixie Storms (Hall)
Dogsong (Paulsen)
Dragon of the Lost Sea (Yep)
Duplicate (Sleator)
Enchantress from the Stars (Engdahl)
Eva (Dickinson)

Everywhere (Brooks)
Exploring the Titanic (Ballard)
Facts and Fictions of Minna Pratt (Ma-
cLachlan)
Fallen Angels (Myers)
Family Project (Ellis)
Fighting Ground (Avi)
Fine White Dust (Rylant)
Formal Feeling (Oneal)
Franklin Delano Roosevelt (Freedman)
Friendship (Taylor)
Frog Prince (Berenzy)
Gathering (Hamilton)
Gentlehands (Kerr)
Ghost Drum (Price)
Girl from Yamhill (Cleary)
Goats (Cole)
Gold Cadillac (Taylor)
Good Courage (Tolan)
Good Night, Mr. Tom (Magorian)
Great American Gold Rush (Blumberg)
Great Little Madison (Fritz)
Green Futures of Tycho (Sleator)
Grey King (Cooper)
Hatchet (Paulsen)
Headless Cupid (Snyder)
Healer (Dickinson)
Heartbeats (Sieruta)
Hero and the Crown (McKinley)
Hey World, Here I Am! (Little)
Hide Crawford Quick (Froehlich)
High King (Alexander)
Hit and Run (Phipson)
Hold Fast (Major)
How It Feels to Be Adopted (Krementz)
How It Feels When a Parent Dies (Kre-
mentz)
How It Feels When Parents Divorce (Kre-
mentz)
Howl's Moving Castle (Jones)
In Summer Light (Oneal)
Incident at Hawk's Hill (Eckert)
Indian Chiefs (Freedman)
Interstellar Pig (Sleator)
Into a Strange Land (Ashabranner)
Invincible Louisa (Meigs)
Island of the Blue Dolphins (O'Dell)
Island on Bird Street (Orlev)
Jacob Have I Loved (Paterson)
Jenny of the Tetons (Gregory)
Johnny Tremain (Forbes)
Josie Gambit (Shura)
Journey (Hamanaka)
Joyful Noise (Fleischman)
Julie of the Wolves (George)
Justin Morgan Had a Horse (Henry)

Keeper (Naylor)
Kestrel (Alexander)
Kidnapping of Christina Lattimore
(Nixon)
Lester's Turn (Slepian)
Let the Circle Be Unbroken (Taylor)
Libby on Wednesday (Snyder)
Lincoln (Freedman)
Little by Little (Little)
Loving Ben (Laird)
Lyddie (Paterson)
M.C. Higgins, the Great (Hamilton)
Machine Gunners (Westall)
Maggie by My Side (Butler)
Magical Adventures of Pretty Pearl
(Hamilton)
Maniac Magee (Spinelli)
Megan's Island (Roberts)
Merlin Dreams (Dickinson)
Midnight Hour Encores (Brooks)
Mississippi Bridge (Taylor)
Monday in Odessa (Sherman)
Monkey Island (Fox)
Moves Make the Man (Brooks)
Mozart Season (Wolff)
My Brother Sam Is Dead (Collier & Col-
lier)
My Name Is SusSan Smith (Plummer)
My Side of the Mountain (George)
My War with Goggle-Eyes (Fine)
Never to Forget (Meltzer)
Night Cry (Naylor)
No Kidding (Brooks)
Nothing but the Truth (Avi)
Number the Stars (Lowry)
One-Eyed Cat (Fox)
Other Side of Dark (Nixon)
Our Eddie (Ish-Kishor)
Outlaws of Sherwood (McKinley)
Outside Child (Bawden)
Paradise Cafe (Brooks)
Pennywhistle Tree (Smith)
Phoenix Rising (Grant)
Pick-Up Sticks (Ellis)
Place Apart (Fox)
Place Where Nobody Stopped (Segal)
Planet of Junior Brown (Hamilton)
Playing Beatie Bow (Park)
Poetspeak (Janeczko)
Prairie Songs (Conrad)
Princess Ashley (Peck)
Quest for a Maid (Hendry)
Rabble Starkey (Lowry)
Rachel Chance (Thesman)
Rain of Fire (Bauer)
Ratha's Creature (Bell)

Redwall (Jacques)
Reluctantly Alice (Naylor)
Remarkable Journey of Prince Jen (Alexander)
Remembering the Good Times (Peck)
Return (Levitin)
Return to Bitter Creek (Smith)
Rhythm Road (Morrison)
Rifles for Watie (Keith)
Ring of Endless Light (L'Engle)
River Runners (Houston)
Road to Memphis (Taylor)
Roll of Thunder, Hear My Cry (Taylor)
Ronia, the Robber's Daughter (Lindgren)
Root Cellar (Lunn)
Rosemary's Witch (Turner)
Sandman's Eyes (Windsor)
Saturnalia (Fleischman)
Save Queen of Sheba! (Moeri)
Seance (Nixon)
Secret World of Polly Flint (Cresswell)
Seventeen Against the Dealer (Voigt)
Shabanu (Staples)
Shades of Gray (Reeder)
Shining Company (Sutcliff)
Sign of the Beaver (Speare)
Silent Voice (Cunningham)
Sixteen (Gallo)
Sky Is Falling (Pearson)
Slave Dancer (Fox)
So Much to Tell You (Marsden)
Solitary Blue (Voigt)
Stepping on the Cracks (Hahn)
Stonewords (Conrad)
Summer of My German Soldier (Greene)
Summer to Die (Lowry)
Sweet Whispers, Brother Rush (Hamilton)
Sweetgrass (Hudson)
Swiftly Tilting Planet (L'Engle)
Sydney, Herself (Rodowsky)

Taking Terri Mueller (Mazer)
Tales of the Early World (Hughes)
Tancy (Hurmence)
Tombs of Atuan (Le Guin)
Touch Wood (Roth-Hano)
Traitor (Fritz)
Trial of Anna Cotman (Alcock)
Tricksters (Mahy)
True Confessions of Charlotte Doyle (Avi)
Truth about Unicorns (Giblin)
25 Miracle (Nelson)
Unclaimed Treasures (MacLachlan)
Up a Road Slowly (Hunt)
Upstairs Room (Reiss)
Village by the Sea (Fox)
Voices from the Civil War (Meltzer)
Voyage of the Frog (Paulsen)
Waiting for the Rain (Gordon)
War Boy (Foreman)
Way Things Work (Macaulay)
Way to Sattin Shore (Pearce)
Weasel (DeFelice)
Westing Game (Raskin)
White Peak Farm (Doherty)
Willie Bea and the Time the Martians Landed (Hamilton)
Winter Room (Paulsen)
Wise Child (Furlong)
Witch Baby (Block)
Witch of Blackbird Pond (Speare)
Witches of Worm (Snyder)
Wolf (Cross)
Wolf of Shadows (Strieber)
Woodsong (Paulsen)
Words by Heart (Sebestyen)
Year of Impossible Goodbyes (Choi)
Year without Michael (Pfeffer)
Young Landlords (Myers)
Z for Zachariah (O'Brien)

SELECTIVE BIBLIOGRAPHY
BY THEME AND GENRE

Activism

And One for All (Nelson) MS–JH
Checking on the Moon (Davis) MS–JH
Waiting for the Rain (Gordon) JH
Young Landlords (Myers) MS–JH

Adventure (see also Fantasy; Survival; Science Fiction)

Adam of the Road (Gray) MS
Bronze Bow (Speare) JH
Call It Courage (Sperry) MS
Fighting Ground (Avi) MS–JH
From the Mixed-Up Files of Mrs. Basil E. Frankweiler (Konigsburg) MS
Healer (Dickinson) JH
Machine Gunners (Westall) MS–JH
Outlaws of Sherwood (McKinley) MS–JH
River Runners (Houston) MS–JH
Third-Story Cat (Baker) EL
Time Train (Fleischman) EL
Travelers by Night (Alcock) MS
True Confessions of Charlotte Doyle (Avi) MS–JH
Whipping Boy (Fleischman) MS
Wolf (Cross) JH

Aged

After the Rain (Mazer) MS–JH
Annie and the Old One (Miles) EL–MS
Blackberries in the Dark (Jukes) EL–MS
Borning Room (Fleischman) MS–JH
Canada Geese Quilt (Kinsey-Warnock) EL–MS
Checking on the Moon (Davis) MS–JH
Cookcamp (Paulsen) MS–JH
Dicey's Song (Voigt) MS–JH
Everywhere (Brooks) MS–JH
Justin and the Best Biscuits in the World (Walter) EL–MS
Seventeen Against the Dealer (Voigt) JH
Wave in Her Pocket (Joseph) MS
Winter Room (Paulsen) MS–JH

Animals

Adam of the Road (Gray) MS
Blue-Eyed Daisy (Rylant) MS–JH
Broccoli Tapes (Slepian) MS–JH
Cat Poems (Livingston) EL
Charlotte's Web (White) EL–MS
Deep Wizardry (Duane) MS–JH
Dogsong (Paulsen) MS–JH
Eva (Dickinson) JH
Fledgling (Langton) MS
Frog Prince (Berenzy) MS–JH
Frog Prince, Continued (Scieszka) EL–MS
Hero and the Crown (McKinley) JH
How Many Spots Does a Leopard Have? (Lester) EL–MS
Incident at Hawk's Hill (Eckert) MS–JH
Joyful Noise (Fleischman) MS–JH
Julie of the Wolves (George) MS–JH
Justin Morgan Had a Horse (Henry) MS–JH
King of the Wind (Henry) MS
Maggie by My Side (Butler) MS–JH
Martin's Mice (King-Smith) EL–MS
Mr. Popper's Penguins (Atwater & Atwater) EL
Mrs. Frisby and the Rats of NIMH (O'Brien) MS
My Side of the Mountain (George) MS–JH
Old Yeller (Gipson) MS
One More Flight (Bunting) MS
One-Eyed Cat (Fox) MS–JH
Rabbit Hill (Lawson) EL
Ralph S. Mouse (Cleary) EL–MS
Rats on the Roof (Marshall) EL–MS
Redwall (Jacques) MS–JH
Shiloh (Naylor) MS
Shoebag (James) EL–MS
Tales of the Early World (Hughes) MS–JH
Third-Story Cat (Baker) EL
Time Train (Fleischman) EL

Travelers by Night (Alcock) MS
True Story of the Three Little Pigs
    (Scieszka) EL
Truth about Unicorns (Giblin) MS-JH
Visit to William Blake's Inn (Willard)
    EL-MS
Witches of Worm (Snyder) MS-JH
Wolf (Cross) JH
Wolf of Shadows (Strieber) JH
Woodsong (Paulsen) MS-JH

Art

Bill Peet (Peet) EL-MS
In Summer Light (Oneal) JH
My Name Is Sus5an Smith (Plummer)
    MS-JH
Truth about Unicorns (Giblin) MS-JH

Biography and Autobiography

Actor's Life for Me! (Gish) MS-JH
Anthony Burns (Hamilton) JH
As the Waltz Was Ending (Butterworth)
    JH
Carry On, Mr. Bowditch (Latham) JH
Bill Peet (Peet) EL-MS
Bully for You, Teddy Roosevelt! (Fritz)
    MS-JH
Franklin Delano Roosevelt (Freedman)
    MS-JH
Girl from Yamhill (Cleary) MS-JH
Great Little Madison (Fritz) MS-JH
Indian Chiefs (Freedman) MS-JH
Invincible Louisa (Meigs) MS-JH
Land I Lost (Huynh) EL-MS
Lincoln (Freedman) MS-JH
Little by Little (Little) MS-JH
Road from Home (Kherdian) MS
Traitor (Fritz) MS-JH
Upstairs Room (Reiss) MS-JH
War Boy (Foreman) MS-JH
Woodsong (Paulsen) MS-JH

Child Abuse

Cracker Jackson (Byars) MS
Daphne's Book (Hahn) MS-JH
Ghost Drum (Price) MS-JH
Good Night, Mr. Tom (Magorian)
    MS-JH
Healer (Dickinson) JH
Hold Fast (Major) JH
Our Eddie (Ish-Kishor) JH
Summer of My German Soldier (Greene)
    MS-JH

Crime and Delinquency (see also Mystery and Suspense)

Are You in the House Alone? (Peck) JH
Bad Boy (Wieler) JH
Checking on the Moon (Davis) MS-JH
Cracker Jackson (Byars) MS
Great Gilly Hopkins (Paterson) MS
Hit and Run (Phipson) JH
Outlaws of Sherwood (McKinley) MS-JH
Rain of Fire (Bauer) MS-JH
Ronia, the Robber's Daughter (Lindgren)
    MS-JH
Stepping on the Cracks (Hahn) MS-JH
Traitor (Fritz) MS-JH
Trial of Anna Cotman (Alcock) MS-JH
True Confessions of Charlotte Doyle
    (Avi) MS-JH
Year without Michael (Pfeffer) JH

Dance

As the Waltz Was Ending (Butterworth)
    JH

Death and Mourning

After the Rain (Mazer) MS-JH
Blackberries in the Dark (Jukes) EL-MS
Bridge to Terabithia (Paterson) MS-JH
Broccoli Tapes (Slepian) MS-JH
Charlotte's Web (White) EL-MS
Dicey's Song (Voigt) MS-JH
Everywhere (Brooks) MS-JH
Family Project (Ellis) MS-JH
Formal Feeling (Oneal) JH
Hiroshima No Pika (Maruki) EL-MS
Hold Fast (Major) JH
How It Feels When a Parent Dies (Kre-
    mentz) MS-JH
Lester's Turn (Slepian) MS-JH
Night Swimmers (Byars) MS
On My Honor (Bauer) MS
Phoenix Rising (Grant) JH
Place Apart (Fox) MS-JH
Rabbi's Girls (Hurwitz) MS
Return to Bitter Creek (Smith) MS-JH
Ring of Endless Light (L'Engle) JH
String in the Harp (Bond) MS
Summer to Die (Lowry) JH
Voyage of the Frog (Paulsen) MS-JH

Environmental Issues

Deep Wizardry (Duane) MS-JH
Eva (Dickinson) JH
M.C. Higgins, the Great (Hamilton)
   MS-JH
Window (Baker) EL-MS

Ethical Issues

Across Five Aprils (Hunt) MS-JH
Afternoon of the Elves (Lisle) MS
And One for All (Nelson) MS-JH
Anthony Burns (Hamilton) JH
Battle Horse (Kullman) MS-JH
Bronze Bow (Speare) JH
Eva (Dickinson) JH
Friendship (Taylor) MS-JH
Lester's Turn (Slepian) MS-JH
Martin's Mice (King-Smith) EL-MS
Moves Make the Man (Brooks) JH
My Brother Sam Is Dead (Collier)
   MS-JH
Nothing but the Truth (Avi) JH
On My Honor (Bauer) MS
One-Eyed Cat (Fox) MS-JH
Our Sixth-Grade Sugar Babies (Bunting)
   MS
Saturnalia (Fleischman) MS-JH
Shades of Gray (Reeder) MS-JH
Shiloh (Naylor) MS
Slave Dancer (Fox) MS-JH
Stepping on the Cracks (Hahn) MS-JH
Traitor (Fritz) MS-JH
True Confessions of Charlotte Doyle
   (Avi) MS-JH
Weasel (DeFelice) MS-JH

Ethnic Groups: African-American

Anthony Burns (Hamilton) JH
Bells of Christmas (Hamilton) MS
Fallen Angels (Myers) JH
Friendship (Taylor) MS-JH
Gold Cadillac (Taylor) MS-JH
How Many Spots Does a Leopard Have?
   (Lester) EL-MS
Justin and the Best Biscuits in the World
   (Walter) EL-MS
Let the Circle Be Unbroken (Taylor)
   MS-JH
M.C. Higgins, the Great (Hamilton)
   MS-JH
Me, Mop, and the Moondance Kid (My-
   ers) MS
Mississippi Bridge (Taylor) MS-JH

More Stories Julian Tells (Cameron)
   EL-MS
Moves Make the Man (Brooks) JH
People Could Fly (Hamilton) EL-MS
Philip Hall Likes Me, I Reckon Maybe
   (Greene) MS
Planet of Junior Brown (Hamilton)
   MS-JH
Road to Memphis (Taylor) JH
Roll of Thunder, Hear My Cry (Taylor)
   MS-JH
Slave Dancer (Fox) MS-JH
Sweet Whispers, Brother Rush (Hamil-
   ton) JH
Tancy (Hurmence) JH
Waiting for the Rain (Gordon) JH
*Willie Bea and the Time the Martians
   Landed* (Hamilton) MS-JH
Words by Heart (Sebestyen) MS-JH
Young Landlords (Myers) MS-JH

Ethnic Groups: Asian

Best Bad Thing (Uchida) MS
Children of the River (Crew) JH
*In the Year of the Boar and Jackie
   Robinson* (Lord) EL-MS
Into a Strange Land (Ashabranner & As-
   habranner) MS-JH
Journey (Hamanaka) MS-JH
Land I Lost (Huynh) EL-MS
Shabanu (Staples) JH
Year of Impossible Goodbyes (Choi)
   MS-JH

Ethnic Groups: Hispanic

Into a Strange Land (Ashabranner & Ashabranner) MS-JH
Nilda (Mohr) MS

Ethnic Groups: Jewish

Along the Tracks (Bergman) MS
Devil's Arithmetic (Yolen) MS-JH
Diamond Tree (Schwartz) EL-MS
Island on Bird Street (Orlev) MS-JH
Monday in Odessa (Sherman) MS-JH
My Grandmother's Stories (Geras)
   EL-MS
Number the Stars (Lowry) MS-JH
Our Eddie (Ish-Kishor) JH
Rabbi's Girls (Hurwitz) MS
Return (Levitin) MS-JH
Upstairs Room (Reiss) MS-JH

Ethnic Groups: Native American

Abduction (Newth) JH
Annie and the Old One (Miles) EL–MS
Dogsong (Paulsen) MS–JH
Indian Chiefs (Freedman) MS–JH
Island of the Blue Dolphins (O'Dell)
　MS–JH
Jenny of the Tetons (Gregory) MS–JH
Julie of the Wolves (George) MS–JH
Saturnalia (Fleischman) MS–JH
Sign of the Beaver (Speare) MS–JH
Sing Down the Moon (O'Dell) MS
Sweetgrass (Hudson) MS–JH
Weasel (DeFelice) MS–JH

Ethnic Groups: Polynesian

Call It Courage (Sperry) MS

Family Relationships

Across Five Aprils (Hunt) MS–JH
After the Rain (Mazer) MS–JH
Agnes Cecilia (Gripe) MS–JH
Agony of Alice (Naylor) MS
Alice in Rapture, Sort Of (Naylor) MS
All Together Now (Bridgers) MS
Anastasia Again! (Lowry) MS
*Animal, the Vegetable, and John D.
　Jones* (Byars) MS
Annie and the Old One (Miles) EL–MS
Becoming Gershona (Semel) MS
Bells of Christmas (Hamilton) MS
Best Bad Thing (Uchida) MS
Bingo Brown and the Language of Love
　(Byars) MS
Blackberries in the Dark (Jukes) EL–MS
Blue-Eyed Daisy (Rylant) MS–JH
Borning Room (Fleischman) MS–JH
Borrowed Chldren (Lyon) MS
Bridge to Terabithia (Paterson) MS–JH
Building Blocks (Voigt) MS–JH
Buster's World (Reuter) MS
By the Shores of Silver Lake (Wilder) MS
Caddie Woodlawn (Brink) MS
Callender Papers (Voigt) MS–JH
Canada Geese Quilt (Kinsey-Warnock)
　EL–MS
Checking on the Moon (Davis) MS–JH
Come Sing, Jimmy Jo (Paterson) MS–JH
Cookcamp (Paulsen) MS–JH
Cracker Jackson (Byars) MS
Cuckoo Sister (Alcock) MS–JH
Daphne's Book (Hahn) MS–JH
Day That Elvis Came to Town (Marino)
　JH

Days of Terror (Smucker) MS–JH
Dear Mr. Henshaw (Cleary) MS–JH
Dicey's Song (Voigt) MS–JH
Dixie Storms (Hall) JH
Everywhere (Brooks) MS–JH
Facts and Fictions of Minna Pratt
　(MacLachlan) MS–JH
Family Project (Ellis) MS–JH
First Hard Times (Smith) MS
Formal Feeling (Oneal) JH
Fran Ellen's House (Sachs) MS
Gold Cadillac (Taylor) MS–JH
Great Gilly Hopkins (Paterson) MS
Hatchet (Paulsen) MS–JH
Haunting (Mahy) MS
Headless Cupid (Snyder) MS–JH
Healer (Dickinson) JH
Hero and the Crown (McKinley) JH
Hit and Run (Phipson) JH
Hold Fast (Major) JH
How It Feels to be Adopted (Krementz)
　MS–JH
How It Feels When a Parent Dies (Kre-
　mentz) MS–JH
How It Feels When Parents Divorce (Kre-
　mentz) MS–JH
In Summer Light (Oneal) JH
Jacob Have I Loved (Paterson) MS–JH
Jenny of the Tetons (Gregory) MS–JH
Julie of the Wolves (George) MS–JH
Justin and the Best Biscuits in the World
　(Walter) EL–MS
Kidnapping of Christina Lattimore
　(Nixon) MS–JH
Let the Circle Be Unbroken (Taylor)
　MS–JH
Like Jake and Me (Jukes) EL–MS
Little Town on the Prairie (Wilder) MS
Loving Ben (Laird) MS–JH
Lyddie (Paterson) MS–JH
Megan's Island (Roberts) MS–JH
Midnight Hour Encores (Brooks) JH
Monday in Odessa (Sherman) MS–JH
More Stories Julian Tells (Cameron)
　EL–MS
Mozart Season (Wolff) MS–JH
My Name Is Sus5an Smith (Plummer)
　MS–JH
My War with Goggle-Eyes (Fine) MS–JH
Nekomah Creek (Crew) MS
Night Swimmers (Byars) MS
Nilda (Mohr) MS
No Kidding (Brooks) JH
Old Yeller (Gipson) MS
On My Honor (Bauer) MS
One Hundredth Thing about

Caroline (Lowry) MS
One-Eyed Cat (Fox) MS–JH
Onion John (Krumgold) MS
Other Side of Dark (Nixon) JH
Our Eddie (Ish-Kishor) JH
Outside Child (Bawden) MS–JH
Phoenix Rising (Grant) JH
Pick-Up Sticks (Ellis) MS–JH
Place Apart (Fox) MS–JH
Princess Ashley (Peck) JH
Rabbi's Girls (Hurwitz) MS
Rabble Starkey (Lowry) MS–JH
Rachel Chance (Thesman) MS–JH
Rain of Fire (Bauer) MS–JH
Ramona and Her Father (Cleary) EL–MS
Ramona and Her Mother (Cleary)
    EL–MS
Ramona Quimby, Age 8 (Cleary) EL–MS
Reluctantly Alice (Naylor) MS–JH
Return to Bitter Creek (Smith) MS–JH
Ring of Endless Light (L'Engle) JH
Road to Memphis (Taylor) JH
Roll of Thunder, Hear My Cry (Taylor)
    MS–JH
Root Cellar (Lunn) MS–JH
Rosemary's Witch (Turner) MS–JH
Secret World of Polly Flint (Cresswell)
    MS–JH
Seventeen Against the Dealer (Voigt) JH
Shabanu (Staples) JH
Shades of Gray (Reeder) MS–JH
Shoebag (James) EL–MS
Sky Is Falling (Pearson) MS–JH
So Much to Tell You (Marsden) JH
Solitary Blue (Voigt) MS–JH
Stonewords (Conrad) MS–JH
String in the Harp (Bond) MS
Summer of My German Soldier (Greene)
    MS–JH
Summer to Die (Lowry) JH
Sweet Whispers, Brother Rush (Hamilton) JH
Sweetgrass (Hudson) MS–JH
Sydney, Herself (Rodowsky) MS–JH
Taking Terri Mueller (Mazer) MS–JH
Time's Up (Heide) EL–MS
25¢ Miracle (Nelson) MS–JH
Two-Thousand-Pound Goldfish (Byars)
    MS
Unclaimed Treasures (MacLachlan)
    MS–JH
Up a Road Slowly (Hunt) JH
Village by the Sea (Fox) MS–JH
Voyage of the Frog (Paulsen) MS–JH
Way to Sattin Shore (Pearce) MS–JH
White Peak Farm (Doherty) MS–JH

*Willie Bea and the Time the Martians
    Landed* (Hamilton) MS–JH
Winter Room (Paulsen) MS–JH
Witch Baby (Block) JH
Wolf (Cross) JH
Wrinkle in Time (L'Engle) MS
Year of Impossible Goodbyes (Choi)
    MS–JH
Year Without Michael (Pfeffer) JH

Fantasy

Amy's Eyes (Kennedy) MS
Behind the Attic Wall (Cassedy) MS
Blue Sword (McKinley) JH
Borrowers Avenged (Norton) MS
Castle in the Air (Jones) MS–JH
Dark Is Rising (Cooper) MS–JH
Dealing with Dragons (Wrede) MS–JH
Deep Wizardry (Duane) MS–JH
Dragon of the Lost Sea (Yep) MS–JH
Fledgling (Langton) MS
Frog Prince (Berenzy) MS–JH
Gathering (Hamilton) MS–JH
Ghost Drum (Price) MS–JH
Grey King (Cooper) MS–JH
Hero and the Crown (McKinley) JH
High King (Alexander) MS–JH
Howl's Moving Castle (Jones) MS–JH
Jumanji (Van Allsburg) MS
Kestrel (Alexander) MS–JH
Knights of the Kitchen Table (Scieszka)
    EL–MS
Lives of Christopher Chant (Jones) MS
Merlin Dreams (Dickinson) MS–JH
Mrs. Frisby and the Rats of NIMH
    (O'Brien) MS
Polar Express (Van Allsburg) EL
Redwall (Jacques) MS–JH
Remarkable Journey of Prince Jen (Alexander) MS–JH
Secret World of Polly Flint (Cresswell)
    MS–JH
String in the Harp (Bond) MS
Swiftly Tilting Planet (L'Engle) JH
Tombs of Atuan (Le Guin) JH
Truth about Unicorns (Giblin) MS–JH
Tuck Everlasting (Babbitt) MS
Visit to William Blake's Inn (Willard)
    EL–MS
Wise Child (Furlong) JH
Wish Giver (Brittain) MS
Witches (Dahl) EL–MS
Wrinkle in Time (L'Engle) MS

Folklore and Myth

Diamond Tree (Schwartz) EL–MS
Frog Prince (Berenzy) MS–JH
Frog Prince, Continued (Scieszka)
   EL–MS
Ghost Drum (Price) MS–JH
Girl Who Cried Flowers (Yolen) EL–MS
*How Many Spots Does the Leopard
   Have?* (Lester) EL–MS
My Grandmother's Stories (Geras)
   EL–MS
Outlaws of Sherwood (McKinley) MS–JH
People Could Fly (Hamilton) EL–MS
Tales of the Early World (Hughes)
   MS–JH
Telling of the Tales (Brooke) MS
True Story of the Three Little Pigs
   (Scieszka) EL
Wave in Her Pocket (Joseph) MS

Friendship

Abduction (Newth) JH
Adam of the Road (Gray) MS
After the Dancing Days (Rostowski)
   MS–JH
Afternoon of the Elves (Lisle) MS
All Together Now (Bridgers) MS
Anastasia Again! (Lowry) MS
And One for All (Nelson) MS–JH
Bad Boy (Wieler) JH
Battle Horse (Kullman) MS–JH
Becoming Gershona (Semel) MS
Best Bad Thing (Uchida) MS
Bridge to Terabithia (Paterson) MS–JH
Broccoli Tapes (Slepian) MS–JH
Bronze Bow (Speare) JH
Buffalo Brenda (Pinkwater) JH
Charlotte's Web (White) EL–MS
Chrysanthemum (Henkes) EL
Cracker Jackson (Byars) MS
Crutches (Hartling) MS–JH
Cybil War (Byars) MS
Daphne's Book (Hahn) MS–JH
Day That Elvis Came to Town (Marino)
   JH
Dear Mr. Henshaw (Cleary) MS–JH
Deep Wizardry (Duane) MS–JH
Enchantress from the Stars (Engdahl) JH
Friendship (Taylor) MS–JH
Good Night, Mr. Tom (Magorian) MS–JH
Grey King (Cooper) MS–JH
In Summer Light (Oneal) JH
*In the Year of the Boar and Jackie
   Robinson* (Lord) EL–MS

Josie Gambit (Shura) MS–JH
Kestrel (Alexander) MS–JH
Kid in the Red Jacket (Park) EL–MS
Lester's Turn (Slepian) MS–JH
Me, Mop, and the Moondance Kid (My-
   ers) MS
Monkey Island (Fox) MS–JH
Moves Make the Man (Brooks) JH
Next-Door Neighbors (Ellis) MS
Number the Stars (Lowry) MS–JH
One More Flight (Bunting) MS
Onion John (Krumgold) MS
Outlaws of Sherwood (McKinley) MS–JH
Pennywhistle Tree (Smith) MS–JH
Philip Hall Likes Me, I Reckon Maybe
   (Greene) MS
Pick-Up Sticks (Ellis) MS–JH
Place Apart (Fox) MS–JH
Planet of Junior Brown (Hamilton)
   MS–JH
Princess Ashley (Peck) JH
Rain of Fire (Bauer) MS–JH
Reluctantly Alice (Naylor) MS–JH
Remembering the Good Times (Peck) JH
Rifles for Watie (Keith) MS–JH
River Runners (Houston) MS–JH
Ronia, the Robber's Daughter (Lindgren)
   MS–JH
Root Cellar (Lunn) MS–JH
Shining Company (Sutcliff) JH
Shoebag (James) EL–MS
Sign of the Beaver (Speare) MS–JH
Sky Is Falling (Pearson) MS–JH
Stepping on the Cracks (Hahn) MS–JH
Stonewords (Conrad) MS–JH
Summer of My German Soldier (Greene)
   MS–JH
Third-Story Cat (Baker) EL
Trial of Anna Cotman (Alcock) MS–JH
25¢ Miracle (Nelson) MS–JH
Two Short and One Long (Aamundsen)
   MS
Up from Jericho Tel (Konigsburg) MS
Village by the Sea (Fox) MS–JH
Waiting for the Rain (Gordon) JH
Whippng Boy (Fleischman) MS
Witch of Blackbird Pond (Speare) MS–JH
Witches of Worm (Snyder) MS–JH
Young Landlords (Myers) MS–JH

Games, Jokes, Riddles

Black and White (Macaulay) EL–MS
Interstellar Pig (Sleator) JH
Josie Gambit (Shura) MS–JH
Jumanji (Van Allsburg) MS

Handicaps

After the Dancing Days (Rostowkski) MS–JH
All Together Now (Bridgers) MS
Crutches (Hartling) MS–JH
Door in the Wall (De Angeli) MS
Franklin Delano Roosevelt (Freedman) MS–JH
Hide Crawford Quick! (Froehlich) MS
Johnny Tremain (Forbes) MS–JH
Lester's Turn (Slepian) MS–JH
Little by Little (Little) MS–JH
Little Town on the Prairie (Wilder) MS
Loving Ben (Laird) MS–JH
Maggie by My Side (Butler) MS–JH
Pick-Up Sticks (Ellis) MS–JH
Summer of the Swans (Byars) MS
Sweet Whispers, Brother Rush (Hamilton) JH

Health and Illness

After the Rain (Mazer) MS
Borrowed Children (Lyon) MS
Canada Geese Quilt (Kinsey-Warnock) EL–MS
Door in the Wall (De Angeli) MS
Everywhere (Brooks) MS–JH
Healer (Dickinson) JH
Keeper (Naylor) JH
Phoenix Rising (Grant) JH
Rabble Starkey (Lowry) MS–JH
Sandman's Eyes (Windsor) JH
Summer to Die (Lowry) JH
Sweet Whispers, Brother Rush (Hamilton) JH
Sweetgrass (Hudson) MS–JH
Village by the Sea (Fox) MS–JH

Historical Fiction

Abduction (Newth) JH
Across Five Aprils (Hunt) MS–JH
Adam of the Road (Gray) MS
After the Dancing Days (Rostowski) MS–JH
All Together Now (Bridgers) MS
Along the Tracks (Bergman) MS
And One for All (Nelson) MS–JH
Bells of Christmas (Hamilton) MS
Best Bad Thing (Uchida) MS
Blossom Culp and the Sleep of Death (Peck) MS
Borning Room (Fleischman) MS–JH
Bronze Bow (Speare) JH
By the Shores of Silver Lake (Wilder) MS

Caddie Woodlawn (Brink) MS
Callender Papers (Voigt) MS–JH
Charley Skedaddle (Beatty) MS–JH
Crutches (Hartling) MS–JH
Dakota Dugout (Turner) EL
Day That Elvis Came to Town (Marino) JH
Days of Terror (Smucker) MS–JH
December Rose (Garfield) MS–JH
Door in the Wall (De Angeli) MS
Fallen Angels (Myers) JH
Fighting Ground (Avi) MS–JH
Friendship (Taylor) MS–JH
Gathering of Days (Blos) MS
Gold Cadillac (Taylor) MS–JH
Island of the Blue Dolphins (O'Dell) MS–JH
Island on Bird Street (Orlev) MS–JH
Jenny of the Tetons (Gregory) MS–JH
Jeremy Visick (Wiseman) MS
Johnny Tremain (Forbes) MS–JH
Justin Morgan Had a Horse (Henry) MS–JH
King of the Wind (Henry) MS
Let the Circle Be Unbroken (Taylor) MS–JH
Little Town on the Prairie (Wilder) MS
Lyddie (Paterson) MS–JH
Machine Gunners (Westall) MS–JH
Mississippi Bridge (Taylor) MS–JH
Monday in Odessa (Sherman) MS
My Brother Sam Is Dead (Collier) MS–JH
My Prairie Year (Harvey) EL–MS
Number the Stars (Lowry) MS–JH
Outlaws of Sherwood (McKinley) MS–JH
Prairie Songs (Conrad) MS–JH
Quest for a Maid (Hendry) MS–JH
Rabbi's Girls (Hurwitz) MS
Rain of Fire (Bauer) MS–JH
Rifles for Watie (Keith) MS–JH
Road to Memphis (Taylor) JH
Roll of Thunder, Hear My Cry (Taylor) MS–JH
Saturnalia (Fleischman) MS–JH
Save Queen of Sheba! (Moeri) MS–JH
Shades of Gray (Reeder) MS–JH
Shining Company (Sutcliff) JH
Sign of the Beaver (Speare) MS–JH
Silent Voice (Cunningham) MS–JH
Sing Down the Moon (O'Dell) MS
Sky Is Falling (Pearson) MS–JH
Slave Dancer (Fox) MS–JH
Stepping on the Cracks (Hahn) MS–JH
Summer of My German Soldier (Greene) MS–JH

Tancy (Hurmence) MS–JH
Touch Wood (Roth-Hano) JH
True Confessions of Charlotte Doyle (Avi) MS–JH
Weasel (DeFelice) MS–JH
Whipping Boy (Fleischman) MS
Willie Bea and the Time the Martians Landed (Hamilton) MS–JH
Wise Child (Fulong) JH
Witch of Blackbird Pond (Speare) MS–JH
Year of Impossible Goodbyes (Choi) MS–JH

History (see also Biography; Historical Fiction)

Boys' War (Murphy) MS–JH
Dinosaur Mountain (Arnold) MS–JH
Exploring the Titanic (Ballard) MS–JH
Great American Gold Rush (Blumberg) MS–JH
Hiroshima No Pika (Maruki) EL–MS
Journey (Hamanaka) MS–JH
Justin and the Best Biscuits in the World (Walter) EL–MS
Pyramid (Macaulay) MS
Truth about Unicorns (Giblin) MS–JH
Voices from the Civil War (Meltzer) JH

Holidays

Bells of Christmas (Hamilton) MS
Polar Express (Van Allsburg) EL
Willie Bea and the Time the Martians Landed (Hamilton) MS–JH

Homeless (see also Runaways)

Along the Tracks (Bergman) MS
Crutches (Hartling) MS–JH
Island on Bird Street (Orlev) MS–JH
Monkey Island (Fox) MS–JH
Planet of Junior Brown (Hamilton) MS–JH
Silent Voice (Cunningham) MS–JH

Homosexuality

Bad Boy (Wieler) JH
Witch Baby (Block) JH

Horror

In a Dark, Dark Room (Schwartz) MS

Humor

Agony of Alice (Naylor) MS
Animal, the Vegetable, and John D. Jones (Byars) MS
Bingo Brown and the Language of Love (Byars) MS
Bingo Brown, Gypsy Lover (Byars) MS–JH
Black and White (Macaulay) EL–MS
Blossom Culp and the Sleep of Death (Peck) MS
Borrowers Avenged (Norton) MS
Buffalo Brenda (Pinkwater) JH
Burning Questions of Bingo Brown (Byars) MS
Buster's World (Reuter) MS
Castle in the Air (Jones) MS–JH
Dealing with Dragons (Wrede) MS–JH
For Laughing Out Loud (Prelutsky) EL–MS
Frog Prince, Continued (Scieszka) EL–MS
From the Mixed-Up Files of Mrs. Basil E. Frankweiler (Konigsburg) MS
Garbage Delight (Lee) EL–MS
Howl's Moving Castle (Jones) MS–JH
Jumanji (Van Allsburg) MS
Knights of the Kitchen Table (Scieszka) EL–MS
Konrad (Nostlinger) EL–MS
Light in the Attic (Silverstein) EL–MS
Mr. Popper's Penguins (Atwater & Atwater) EL
New Kid on the Block (Prelutsky) EL–MS
Our Sixth-Grade Sugar Babies (Bunting) MS
Poems of A. Nonny Mouse (Prelutsky) EL–MS
Ralph S. Mouse (Cleary) EL–MS
Ramona Quimby, Age 8 (Cleary) EL–MS
Rats on the Roof (Marshall) EL–MS
Shoebag (James) EL–MS
Something Big Has Been Here (Prelutsky) EL–MS
Time's Up (Heide) EL–MS
True Story of the Three Little Pigs (Scieszka) EL
Two-Thousand-Pound Goldfish (Byars) MS

Immigrants

Becoming Gershona (Semel) MS
Best Bad Thing (Uchida) MS
Children of the River (Crew) JH
Days of Terror (Smucker) MS–JH

In the Year of the Boar and Jackie Robinson (Lord) EL–MS
Into a Strange Land (Ashabranner & Ashabranner) MS–JH
Road from Home (Kherdian) MS
Two Short and One Long (Aamundsen) MS
Winter Room (Paulsen) MS–JH

Interviews

How It Feels to Be Adopted (Krementz) MS–JH
How It Feels When a Parent Dies (Krementz) MS–JH
How It Feels When Parents Divorce (Krementz) MS–JH
Into a Strange Land (Ashabranner & Ashabranner) MS–JH

Minorities: See Ethnic Groups

Moving

Agony of Alice (Naylor) MS
Anastasia Again! (Lowry) MS
Broccoli Tapes (Slepian) MS–JH
Checking on the Moon (Davis) MS–JH
Come Sing, Jimmy Jo (Paterson) MS–JH
Cookcamp (Paulsen) MS–JH
Dear Mr. Henshaw (Cleary) MS–JH
First Hard Times (Smith) MS
Fran Ellen's House (Sachs) MS
Kid in the Red Jacket (Park) EL–MS
Pick-Up Sticks (Ellis) MS–JH
Shades of Gray (Reeder) MS–JH
Sky Is Falling (Pearson) MS–JH

Music

Adam of the Road (Gray) MS
Chartbreaker (Cross) JH
Come Sing, Jimmy Jo (Paterson) MS–JH
Facts and Fictions of Minna Pratt (MacLachlan) MS–JH
Midnight Hour Encores (Brooks) JH
Mozart Season (Wolff) MS–JH
Pennywhistle Tree (Smith) MS–JH
Slave Dancer (Fox) MS–JH

Mystery and Suspense

Are You in the House Alone? (Peck) JH
Callender Papers (Voigt) MS–JH

Cuckoo Sister (Alcock) MS–JH
December Rose (Garfield) MS–JH
Duplicate (Sleator) JH
Headless Cupid (Snyder) MS–JH
Jeremy Visick (Wiseman) MS
Kidnapping of Christina Lattimore (Nixon) MS–JH
Megan's Island (Roberts) MS–JH
Midnight Horse (Fleischman) MS
Mummy, the Will, and the Crypt (Bellairs) MS
Night Cry (Naylor) MS–JH
One Hundredth Thing about Caroline (Lowry) MS
Other Side of Dark (Nixon) JH
Sandman's Eyes (Windsor) JH
Seance (Nixon) MS–JH
Silent Voice (Cunningham) MS–JH
Taking Terri Mueller (Mazer) MS–JH
Up from Jericho Tel (Konigsburg) MS
Way to Sattin Shore (Pearce) MS–JH
Westing Game (Raskin) MS–JH
Witch Week (Jones) MS
Wolf (Cross) JH

Nature

Incident at Hawk's Hill (Eckert) MS–JH
Joyful Noise (Fleischman) MS–JH
My Prairie Year (Harvey) EL–MS
My Side of the Mountain (George) MS–JH
Woodsong (Paulsen) MS–JH

Nonfiction (see also Biography; Poetry)

Big Book for Peace (Alexander et al) EL–MS
Boys' War (Murphy) MS–JH
Dinosaur Mountain (Arnold) MS–JH
Exploring the Titanic (Ballard) MS–JH
Hiroshima No Pika (Maruki) EL–MS
Into a Strange Land (Ashabranner & Ashabranner) MS–JH
Journey (Hamanaka) MS–JH
Maggie by My Side (Butler) MS–JH
Pyramid (Macaulay) MS
Truth about Unicorns (Giblin) MS–JH
Voices from the Civil War (Meltzer) JH
Way Things Work (Macaulay) MS–JH

Occult and Paranormal

Afternoon of the Elves (Lisle) MS
Agnes Cecilia (Gripe) MS–JH
Behind the Attic Wall (Cassedy) MS
Blossom Culp and the Sleep of Death (Peck) MS
Blue Sword (McKinley) JH
Dark Is Rising (Cooper) MS–JH
Devil's Donkey (Brittain) MS
Enchantress from the Stars (Engdahl) JH
Everywhere (Brooks) MS–JH
Gathering (Hamilton) MS–JH
Haunting (Mahy) MS
Headless Cupid (Snyder) MS–JH
Healer (Dickinson) JH
Midnight Horse (Fleischman) MS
Mummy, the Will, and the Crypt (Bellairs) MS
Quest for a Maid (Hendry) MS–JH
Rosemary's Witch (Turner) MS–JH
Seance (Nixon) MS–JH
Secret World of Polly Flint (Cresswell) MS–JH
Stonewords (Conrad) MS–JH
Sweet Whispers (Hamilton) JH
Up from Jericho Tel (Konigsburg) MS
Witch Week (Jones) MS
Wise Child (Furlong) JH
Wish Giver (Brittain) MS
Witches (Dahl) EL–MS
Witches of Worm (Snyder) MS–JH

Other Countries / Other Cultures

Abduction (Newth) JH
Adam of the Road (Gray) MS
Agnes Cecilia (Gripe) MS–JH
As the Waltz Was Ending (Butterworth) JH
Bad Boy (Wieler) JH
Battle Horse (Kullman) JH
Becoming Gershona (Semel) MS
Buster's World (Reuter) MS
Call It Courage (Sperry) MS
Chartbreaker (Cross) JH
Children of the River (Crew) JH
Crutches (Hartling) MS–JH
Cuckoo Sister (Alcock) MS–JH
Days of Terror (Smucker) MS–JH
Good Night, Mr. Tom (Magorian) MS–JH
Hey World, Here I Am! (Little) MS–JH
Hiroshima No Pika (Maruki) EL–MS
How Many Spots Does a Leopard Have? (Lester) EL–MS

Island of the Blue Dolphins (O'Dell) MS–JH
Island on Bird Street (Orlev) MS–JH
Jeremy Visick (Wiseman) MS
King of the Wind (Henry) MS–JH
Land I Lost (Huynh) EL–MS
Monday in Odessa (Sherman) MS–JH
Number the Stars (Lowry) MS–JH
Pyramid (Macaulay) MS
Quest for a Maid (Hendry) MS–JH
Return (Levitin) MS–JH
River Runners (Houston) MS–JH
Road from Home (Kherdian) MS
Secret World of Polly Flint (Cresswell) MS–JH
Shabanu (Staples) JH
Silent Voice (Cunningham) MS–JH
Sky Is Falling (Pearson) MS–JH
So Much to Tell You (Marsden) JH
String in the Harp (Bond) MS
Touch Wood (Roth-Hano) JH
Two Short and One Long (Aamundsen) MS
War Boy (Foreman) MS–JH
Wave in Her Pocket (Joseph) MS
Way to Sattin Shore (Pearce) MS–JH
Waiting for the Rain (Gordon) JH
White Peak Farm (Doherty) MS–JH
Wise Child (Furlong) JH
Wolf (Cross) JH
Year of Impossible Goodbyes (Choi) MS–JH

Peer Pressure

Agony of Alice (Naylor) MS
Alice in Rapture, Sort Of (Naylor) MS
Bad Boy (Wieler) JH
Battle Horse (Kullman) JH
Chrysanthemum (Henkes) EL
Daphne's Book (Hahn) MS–JH
Loving Ben (Laird) MS–JH
On My Honor (Bauer) MS
Pennywhistle Tree (Smith) MS–JH
Princess Ashley (Peck) JH
Rain of Fire (Bauer) MS–JH
Reluctantly Alice (Naylor) MS–JH
Trial of Anna Cotman (Alcock) MS–JH
Witch of Blackbird Pond (Speare) MS–JH

Photography

Lincoln (Freedman) MS–JH

Poetry

Big Book for Peace (Alexander et al.)
    EL–MS
Cat Poems (Livingston) EL
Class Dismissed II (Glenn) JH
For Laughing Out Loud (Prelutsky)
    EL–MS
Garbage Delight (Lee) EL–MS
Joyful Noise (Fleischman) MS–JH
Light in the Attic (Silverstein) EL–MS
New Kid on the Block (Prelutsky) EL–MS
Poems of A. Nonny Mouse (Prelutsky)
    EL–MS
Poetspeak (Janeczko) JH
Rhythm Road (Morrison) MS–JH
Something Big Has Been Here (Pre-
    lutsky) EL–MS
Visit to William Blake's Inn (Willard)
    EL–MS

Politics

Anthony Burns (Hamilton) JH
Bully for You, Teddy Roosevelt! (Fritz)
    MS–JH
Franklin Delano Roosevelt (Freedman)
    MS–JH
Great Little Madison (Fritz) MS–JH
Kestrel (Alexander) MS–JH
Lincoln (Freedman) MS–JH
Traitor (Fritz) MS–JH

Prejudice

Bad Boy (Wieler) JH
Battle Horse (Kullman) JH
Day That Elvis Came to Town (Marino)
    JH
Days of Terror (Smucker) MS–JH
Devil's Arithmetic (Yolen) MS–JH
Friendship (Taylor) MS–JH
Gold Cadillac (Taylor) MS–JH
*In the Year of the Boar and Jackie
    Robinson* (Lord) EL–MS
Island on Bird Street (Orlev) MS–JH
Jenny of the Tetons (Gregory) MS–JH
Journey (Hamanaka) MS–JH
Let the Circle Be Unbroken (Taylor)
    MS–JH
Little by Little (Little) MS–JH
Mississippi Bridge (Taylor) MS–JH
Monday in Odessa (Sherman) MS–JH
Nekomah Creek (Crew) MS
Next-Door Neighbors (Ellis) MS
Number the Stars (Lowry) MS–JH
Rabbi's Girls (Hurwitz) MS

Rachel Chance (Thesman) MS–JH
Return (Levitin) MS–JH
Rifles for Watie (Keith) MS–JH
Road from Home (Kherdian) MS
Road to Memphis (Taylor) JH
Roll of Thunder, Hear My Cry (Taylor)
    MS–JH
Sing Down the Moon (O'Dell) MS
Summer of My German Soldier (Greene)
    MS–JH
Touch Wood (Roth-Hano) JH
Two Short and One Long (Aamundsen)
    MS
Waiting for the Rain (Gordon) JH
Witch of Blackbird Pond (Speare) MS–JH

Problem Parents

Afternoon of the Elves (Lisle) MS
Blue-Eyed Daisy (Rylant) MS–JH
Building Blocks (Voigt) MS–JH
Come to the Edge (Cunningham) MS
Cookcamp (Paulsen) MS–JH
Cuckoo Sister (Alcock) MS–JH
Daphne's Book (Hahn) MS–JH
Dicey's Song (Voigt) MS–JH
Fran Ellen's House (Sachs) MS
In Summer Light (Oneal) JH
Monkey Island (Fox) MS–JH
Our Eddie (Ish-Kishor) JH
Outside Child (Bawden) MS–JH
So Much to Tell You (Marsden) JH
Solitary Blue (Voigt) MS–JH
Time's Up (Heide) El–MS
25¢ Miracle (Nelson) MS–JH
Witches of Worm (Snyder) MS–JH
Wolf (Cross) JH

Psychology

Afternoon of the Elves (Lisle) MS
Bad Boy (Wieler) JH
Formal Feeling (Oneal) JH
Fran Ellen's House (Sachs) MS
Keeper (Naylor) JH
Prairie Songs (Conrad) MS–JH
So Much to Tell You (Marsden) JH
Witches of Worm (Snyder) MS–JH

Religion

Bronze Bow (Speare) JH
Days of Terror (Smucker) MS–JH
Devil's Arithmetic (Yolen) MS–JH
Fine White Dust (Rylant) MS–JH

Gathering of Days (Blos) MS–JH
Healer (Dickinson) JH
Nilda (Mohr) MS
Rabbi's Girls (Hurwitz) MS
Return (Levitin) MS
Tales of the Early World (Hughes)
   MS–JH

Rites of Passage

Blue-Eyed Daisy (Rylant) MS–JH
Borning Room (Fleischman) MS–JH
Call It Courage (Sperry) MS
Dogsong (Paulsen) MS–JH
Fallen Angels (Myers) JH
Fighting Ground (Avi) MS–JH
Hatchet (Paulsen) MS–JH
Julie of the Wolves (George) MS–JH
Midnight Hour Encores (Brooks) JH
Night Cry (Naylor) MS–JH
Rifles for Watie (Keith) MS–JH
River Runners (Houston) MS–JH
Road to Memphis (Taylor) JH
Shabanu (Staples) JH
Solitary Blue (Voigt) MS–JH
Tancy (Hurmence) MS–JH

Romance

Alice in Rapture, Sort of (Naylor) MS
Amy's Eyes (Kennedy) MS
Bingo Brown and the Language of Love
   (Byars) MS
Bingo Brown, Gypsy Lover (Byars)
   MS–JH
Castle in the Air (Jones) MS–JH
Chartbreaker (Cross) JH
Children of the River (Crew) JH
Cybil War (Byars) MS
Facts and Fictions of Minna Pratt
   (MacLachlan) MS–JH
Frog Prince (Berenzy) MS–JH
Ghost Drum (Price) MS–JH
Heartbeats (Sieruta) JH
High King (Alexander) MS–JH
In Summer Light (Oneal) JH
Kestrel (Alexander) MS–JH
Our Sixth-Grade Sugar Babies (Bunting)
   MS
Paradise Cafe (Brooks) JH
Ring of Endless Light (L'Engle) JH
Ronia, the Robber's Daughter (Lindgren)
   MS–JH
Sweetgrass (Hudson) MS–JH
Unclaimed Treasures (MacLachlan)
   MS–JH
Witch Baby (Block) JH

Runaways

Chartbreaker (Cross) JH
Come to the Edge (Cunningham) MS
*From the Mixed-Up Files of Mrs. Basil
   E. Frankweiler* (Konigsburg) MS
Hold Fast (Major) JH
Julie of the Wolves (George) MS–JH
My Side of the Mountain (George)
   MS–JH
One More Flight (Bunting) MS
25¢ Miracle (Nelson) MS–JH
Year without Michael (Pfeffer) JH

School

Agony of Alice (Naylor) MS
Behind the Attic Wall (Cassedy) MS
Burning Questions of Bingo Brown
   (Byars) MS
Buster's World (Reuter) MS
Chrysanthemum (Henkes) EL
Class Dismissed II (Glenn) JH
Daphne's Book (Hahn) MS–JH
Dear Mr. Henshaw (Cleary) MS–JH
Hey World, Here I Am! (Little) MS–JH
Kid in the Red Jacket (Park) EL–MS
Moves Make the Man (Brooks) JH
Nekomah Creek (Crew) MS
Nothing but the Truth (Avi) JH
Our Sixth-Grade Sugar Babies (Bunting)
   MS
Princess Ashley (Peck) JH
Ralph S. Mouse (Cleary) EL–MS
Ramona Quimby, Age 8 (Cleary) EL–MS
Reluctantly Alice (Naylor) MS–JH
So Much to Tell You (Marsden) JH
Witch Week (Jones) MS

Science and Technology

Carry On, Mr. Bowditch (Latham) JH
Dinosaur Mountain (Arnold) MS–JH
Exploring the Titanic (Ballard) MS–JH
Pyramid (Macaulay) MS
Way Things Work (Macaulay) MS–JH

Science Fiction

Boy Who Reversed Himself (Sleator)
   MS–JH
Duplicate (Sleator) JH
Enchantress from the Stars (Engdahl) JH
Eva (Dickinson) JH

Gathering (Hamilton) MS–JH
Green Futures of Tycho (Sleator) MS–JH
Interstellar Pig (Sleator) JH
Konrad (Nostlinger) EL–MS
Mrs. Frisby and the Rats of NIMH
    (O'Brien) MS
Time Train (Fleischman) EL
Wolf of Shadows (Strieber) JH
Wrinkle in Time (L'Engle) MS
Z for Zachariah (O'Brien) JH

Secrets

Afternoon of the Elves (Lisle) MS
Becoming Gershona (Semel) MS
Bridge to Terabithia (Paterson) MS–JH
Callender Papers (Voigt) MS–JH
Cracker Jackson (Byars) MS
Cuckoo Sister (Alcock) MS–JH
Daphne's Book (Hahn) MS–JH
Day That Elvis Came to Town (Marino)
    JH
Dixie Storms (Hall) JH
On My Honor (Bauer) MS
One-Eyed Cat (Fox) MS–JH
Outside Child (Bawden) MS–JH
Pennywhistle Tree (Smith) MS–JH
Shiloh (Naylor) MS
So Much to Tell You (Marsden) JH
Summer of My German Soldier (Greene)
    MS–JH
Taking Terri Mueller (Mazer) MS–JH
Tombs of Atuan (Le Guin) JH
Two Short and One Long (Aamundsen)
    MS
Way to Sattin Shore (Pearce) MS–JH
Wolf (Cross) JH

Self-Knowledge

After the Dancing Days (Rostowski)
    MS–JH
Agony of Alice (Naylor) MS
Alice in Rapture, Sort Of (Naylor) MS
Athletic Shorts (Crutcher) JH
Becoming Gershona (Semel) MS
Borrowed Children (Lyon) MS
Bronze Bow (Speare) JH
Charley Skedaddle (Beatty) MS–JH
Charlotte's Web (White) EL–MS
Chartbreaker (Cross) JH
Children of the River (Davis) JH
Come to the Edge (Cunningham) MS
Cybil War (Byars) MS
Dealing with Dragons (Wrede) MS–JH

Dear Bill, Remember Me? (Mazer) JH
December Rose (Garfield) MS–JH
Devil's Arithmetic (Yolen) MS–JH
Dicey's Song (Voigt) MS–JH
Eva (Dickinson) JH
Facts and Fictions of Minna Pratt
    (MacLachlan) MS–JH
Fine White Dust (Rylant) MS–JH
Fran Ellen's House (Sachs) MS
Great Gilly Hopkins (Paterson) MS
Green Futures of Tycho (Sleator) MS–JH
Hey World, Here I Am! (Litttle) MS–JH
*In the Year of the Boar and Jackie
    Robinson* (Lord) EL–MS
Jacob Have I Loved (Paterson) MS–JH
Justin and the Best Biscuits in the World
    (Walter) EL–MS
Midnight Hour Encores (Brooks) JH
Mozart Season (Wolff) MS–JH
My Name Is Sus5an Smith (Plummer)
    MS–JH
Nilda (Mohr) MS
Old Yeller (Gipson) MS
On My Honor (Bauer) MS
Outside Child (Bawden) MS–JH
Philip Hall Likes Me, I Reckon Maybe
    (Greene) MS
Place Apart (Fox) MS–JH
Rabble Starkey (Lowry) MS–JH
Rachel Chance (Thesman) MS–JH
Reluctantly Alice (Naylor) MS–JH
Remarkable Journey of Prince Jen (Alex-
    ander) MS–JH
Road to Memphis (Taylor) JH
Slave Dancer (Fox) MS–JH
Solitary Blue (Voigt) MS–JH
Summer to Die (Lowry) JH
Sydney, Herself (Rodowsky) MS–JH
Tancy (Hurmence) JH
Time's Up (Heide) EL–MS
Tombs of Atuan (Le Guin) JH
Two-Thousand-Pound Goldfish (Byars)
    MS
Up a Road Slowly (Hunt) JH
Village by the Sea (Fox) MS–JH
Witch Baby (Block) JH

Sex and Sexuality

Bad Boy (Wieler) JH
Heartbeats (Sieruta) JH
Witch Baby (Block) JH

Short Stories

Athletic Shorts (Crutcher) JH
Big Book for Peace (Alexander et al.)
   EL–MS
Dear Bill, Remember Me? (Mazer) JH
Girl Who Cried Flowers (Yolen) EL–MS
Heartbeats (Sieruta) JH
How Many Spots Does a Leopard Have?
   (Lester) EL–MS
In a Dark, Dark Room (Schwartz) MS
Merlin Dreams (Dickinson) MS–JH
My Grandmother's Stories (Geras)
   EL–MS
Paradise Cafe (Brooks) JH
People Could Fly (Hamilton) EL–MS
Rats on the Roof (Marshall) EL–MS
Sixteen (Gallo) JH
Tales of the Early World (Hughes)
   MS–JH
Telling of the Tales (Brooke) MS
Wave in Her Pocket (Joseph) MS

Sports and Contests

Athletic Shorts (Crutcher) JH
Bad Boy (Wieler) JH
Battle Horse (Kullman) JH
King of the Wind (Henry) MS
Me, Mop, and the Moondance Kid
   (Myers) MS
Moves Make the Man (Brooks) JH
Mozart Season (Wolff) MS–JH
Woodsong (Paulsen) MS–JH

Substance Abuse

Blue-Eyed Daisy (Rylant) MS–JH
Borrowed Children (Lyon) MS
Day That Elvis Came to Town (Marino)
   JH
No Kidding (Brooks) JH
Village by the Sea (Fox) MS–JH

Suicide

Remembering the Good Times (Peck) JH

Survival

Along the Tracks (Bergman) MS
As the Waltz Was Ending (Butterworth)
   JH
Call It Courage (Sperry) MS
Crutches (Hartling) MS–JH

Days of Terror (Smucker) MS–JH
Dogsong (Paulsen) MS–JH
Hatchet (Paulsen) MS–JH
Incident at Hawk's Hill (Eckert) MS–JH
Island of the Blue Dolphins (O'Dell)
   MS–JH
Island on Bond Street (Orlev) MS–JH
Julie of the Wolves (George) MS–JH
King of the Wind (Henry) MS
Monkey Island (Fox) MS–JH
My Side of the Mountain (George)
   MS–JH
Save Queen of Sheba! (Moeri) MS–JH
True Confessions of Charlotte Doyle
   (Avi) MS–JH
Voyage of the Frog (Paulsen) MS–JH
Wolf of Shadows (Strieber) JH
Z for Zachariah (O'Brien) JH

Teen Pregnancy, Parenting

Our Sixth-Grade Sugar Babies (Bunting)
   MS

Theater

Actor's Life for Me! (Gish) MS–JH
Adam of the Road (Gray) MS
Up from Jericho Tel (Konigsburg) MS
Wolf (Cross) JH

Time Travel

Building Blocks (Voigt) MS–JH
Devil's Arithmetic (Yolen) MS–JH
Green Futures of Tycho (Sleator) MS–JH
Jeremy Visick (Wiseman) MS
Knights of the Kitchen Table (Scieszka)
   EL–MS
Root Cellar (Lunn) MS–JH
Secret Wold of Polly Flint (Cresswell)
   MS–JH
Stonewords (Conrad) MS–JH
String in the Harp (Bond) MS
Swiftly Tilting Planet (L'Engle) JH
Time Train (Fleischman) EL
Wrinkle in Time (L'Engle) MS

War

Across Five Aprils (Hunt) MS–JH
After the Dancing Days (Rostowski)
   MS–JH
Along the Tracks (Bergman) MS
And One for All (Nelson) MS–JH

As the Waltz Was Ending (Butterworth)
  JH
Big Book for Peace (Alexander et al.)
  EL–MS
Boys' War (Murphy) MS–JH
Charley Skedaddle (Beatty) MS–JH
Crutches (Hartling) MS–JH
Fallen Angels (Myers) JH
Fighting Ground (Avi) MS–JH
Hiroshima No Pika (Maruki) EL–MS
Island on Bird Street (Orlev) MS–JH
Johnny Tremain (Forbes) MS–JH
Machine Gunners (Westall) MS–JH
My Brother Sam Is Dead (Collier)
  MS–JH
Rain of Fire (Bauer) MS–JH
Shades of Gray (Reeder) MS–JH
Shining Company (Sutcliff) JH
Sky Is Falling (Pearson) MS–JH
Stepping on the Cracks (Hahn) MS–JH
Summer of My German Soldier (Greene)
  MS–JH
Upstairs Room (Reiss) MS–JH
Voices from the Civil War (Meltzer) JH
War Boy (Foreman) MS–JH
Year of Impossible Goodbyes (Choi)
  MS–JH

Women's Issues

Are You in the House Alone? (Peck) JH
Caddie Woodlawn (Brink) MS

Dealing with Dragons (Wrede) MS–JH
Howl's Moving Castle (Jones) MS–JH
Nekomah Creek (Crew) MS
Philip Hall Likes Me, I Reckon Maybe
  (Greene) MS
Shabanu (Staples) JH

Working

Carry On, Mr. Bowditch (Latham) JH
Come Sing, Jimmy Jo (Paterson) MS–JH
Cookcamp (Paulsen) MS–JH
Jacob Have I Loved (Paterson) MS–JH
Johnny Tremain (Forbes) MS–JH
Little Town on the Prairie (Wilder) MS
Lyddie (Paterson) MS–JH
River Runners (Houston) MS–JH
Seventeen Against the Dealer (Voigt) JH
White Peak Farm (Doherty) MS–JH
Winter Room (Paulsen) MS–JH
Young Landlords (Myers) MS–JH

Writing

Bill Peet (Peet) EL–MS
Dear Mr. Henshaw (Cleary) MS–JH
Girl from Yamhill (Cleary) MS–JH
Hey World, Here I Am! (Little) MS–JH
Invincible Louisa (Meigs) MS–JH
Little by Little (Little) MS–JH
Place Apart (Fox) MS–JH
Poetspeak (Janeczko) JH

INDEX TO BOOKTALKS AND BOOKTALKERS